# AUSTRIA BEHIND THE MASK

PAUL LENDVAI

# Austria Behind the Mask

*Politics of a Nation since 1945*

HURST & COMPANY, LONDON

First published in the United Kingdom in 2023 by
C. Hurst & Co. (Publishers) Ltd.,
New Wing, Somerset House, Strand, London WC2R 1LA
© Paul Lendvai, 2023
All rights reserved.

Distributed in the United States, Canada and Latin America by
Oxford University Press, 198 Madison Avenue, New York, NY 10016,
United States of America.

The right of Paul Lendvai to be identified as the author of
this publication is asserted by him in accordance with the
Copyright, Designs and Patents Act, 1988.

A Cataloguing-in-Publication data record for this book
is available from the British Library.

ISBN: 9781805260592

This book is printed using paper from registered sustainable
and managed sources.

Printed and bound in Great Britain by Bell and Bain Ltd, Glasgow.

www.hurstpublishers.com

# CONTENTS

*Preface*   vii

1. The Burden of the Past   1
2. Myth and Reality: The Legacy of the Habsburgs   23
3. Hitler's Shadow, Yesterday and Today   37
4. The Rollercoaster Ride of the FPÖ: From Friedrich Peter to Jörg Haider   53
5. Schüssel's Dangerous Experiment   69
6. Karl Renner and Bruno Kreisky: Two Great Personalities of Social Democracy   83
7. Greed instead of Principles: The Decline of Social Democracy   101
8. The ÖVP, the Most Unusual Conservative Party in Europe   125
9. From Wolfgang Schüssel to Sebastian Kurz: From Triumph to Crash   143
10. The "Real" Austrians and the Greens   177
11. A Deplorable Moral Picture   191

*Notes*   211
*Select Bibliography*   221
*Index of Names*   229
*Index*   235

# PREFACE

I belong to a minority with a hyphenated identity in Austria: as a native Hungarian with a foreign accent in a German-speaking country, as a Jew among Catholics and Protestants, without relatives in the country, since my late wife Margaret was English and my beloved wife Zsóka is, like me, a true Budapest-born.

And in spite of everything, I say, as does Joseph Roth in *The Emperor's Tomb*, that Austria is "not a state, not a homeland, not a nation" but "an Übernation", the only country, at least for me, where I, like Roth in his time, can be "at the same time patriot and citizen of the world". The present book is much more than a critical or chronological sequel to my work *Inside Austria: New Challenges, Old Demons*, written 15 years ago. Each chapter in this book deals with the main political forces—Christian Democrats, Social Democrats, right wing populists and the Greens, which have shaped the character of Austria since the end of the war. Beyond the different approach and new material, this book is harsher in its judgment of political personnel, but, I hope, not unfair.

This writing is a product of critical love and deep-rooted gratitude, but at the same time it is about concern for the future of Austria, which admitted me, like so many before me, as a political refugee on 4 February 1957, and naturalised me on 29 September

# PREFACE

1959. That is why I have conducted interviews with fifty-five politicians and public figures (their names are in the acknowledgements at the end of this book), processed the contemporary historical analyses and documents, and summarised my personal experiences.

I am not concerned with the question "What is going to happen?" but with the lessons of the past in relation to what we should avoid and what we should do. In this sense, then, the book is a wake-up call.

*Vienna, March 2023*

1

# THE BURDEN OF THE PAST

The early 1960s saw the first negotiations on the inclusion of neutral Austria in European integration, despite the Soviet Union's watchful suspicion as the signatory power of the Austrian State Treaty. At a press conference held by the President of the Federation of Austrian Industries, Franz Josef Mayer-Gunthof, the Vienna correspondent of the *New York Times*, Mike Handler, asked, with slight irritation, "Why does the President, like some other public personalities, always talk about the 'special position' of this country?"

Mayer-Gunthof, who had studied at Oxford, answered him in fluent English with an impromptu short lecture about the winding road from the collapse of the dual monarchy, through the Nazi era and the Second World War, to the Second Republic and the attainment of full independence through the State Treaty. He belonged to the founding generation and was proud to have successfully negotiated the first post-war loan for Austria with the London Hambros Bank. As a young Viennese correspondent of the *Financial Times*, and probably also as a newly minted Austrian citizen (since September 1959), I was deeply impressed by his elegant and convincing defence of the victim myth and Austria's special path between the blocs.

Only in retrospect, after more than 60 years of experiencing and studying the "Austria complex", could I understand how deeply the memory of this scene and of many similar conversations with the then Foreign Minister Bruno Kreisky and with historian friends, had shaped me in my study of Austrian history. But there is no doubt that the unshakeable foundation of my attitude towards Austria, especially in crisis situations, is the infinite gratitude for what this country and its people have offered me, the immigrant, like hundreds of thousands of others, providing not only a passport but also a new home in "dark times" (Bertolt Brecht).[1]

Despite this solidarity, it would be foolish to overlook the unmistakable deterioration of the country's domestic political situation and international position in recent decades, especially since the end of the Kreisky era (1970–83). As a foreign correspondent, later as editor-in-chief of the ORF (the Austrian Broadcasting Corporation) and as director of Radio Austria International, I have experienced not only the upswing of our country but also the upheavals and crises, not least in the mirror of my relations with authoritative politicians. In the next chapters, these personal impressions and experiences also determine my analysis of the twists and turns in contemporary history and the role of the legacy of the past.

*The question of identity*

Everything that is said about Austria today must be based on the fundamental thesis: "There is no historical entity in Europe whose existence is so bound up with the identity problems of its members as Austria". This statement comes from Friedrich Heer, the most important thinker of the Second Republic.[2] The fact that this prolific, independent scholar who was also called "a backward-looking prophet", did not get a professorship at Vienna University despite repeated attempts, recalls the case of Sigmund Freud. The epochal founder of psychoanalysis was kept out of the university because of his Jewishness; Heer was kept out because of his open mind. I remember our last meeting, shortly before his death. He had written a text about the provincialisation of Austria for the *Europäische Rundschau*, the quarterly that I edited, and invited me for a discussion in his tiny dramaturge's office in the Burgtheater. The gap between his international reputation and his shabby treatment by official Austria both provoked and confirmed his bitter diagnosis: "An inner history of the Second Republic had to deal primarily with the prevention of the formation of Austria's cultural functions by bearers of our two primary national vices, envy and disinterested meanness".[3]

The love-hate relationship of so many Austrian writers to their homeland is related to the "special case of Austria", to the tightrope walk between demonisation abroad and belittlement at home, marked by the country's involvement in National Socialism. Austria, as an artificial relic from the bankrupt Danube monarchy shattered by the victorious states, was called "a republic without republicans", "a country without a right to exist", "a country without a name" and "a body politic without a heart".

The Dual Monarchy was the second largest state in Europe in terms of area and the third largest in terms of population. This dialectic between the Austrians' external image and their self-image, which has engendered so many clichés and prejudices, can only be understood against the background of the disintegration of Austria-Hungary, the shrinking of a state entity from around 680,000 to just under 84,000 square kilometres and from 51 to 6.5 million inhabitants, the transformation of a great European power with the "most colourful mixture of peoples in Europe"

(Friedrich Umlauft) into a mutilated small state. The path to the Anschluss, the jubilation after the invasion of the German troops and the mass frenzy on Heldenplatz cannot be explained or understood without the shock associated with the collapse of the Austro-Hungarian monarchy.

This "state that nobody wanted" (Hellmut Andics) was about "the Austrian identity problem in the 20th century", namely that citizens "first had to learn to be Austrians, especially since in the monarchy the German-speaking inhabitants were simply called Germans".[4] They saw themselves as the actual *Staatsnation* (political nation) not only of the German-speaking half of the empire but of the entire Habsburg monarchy. This state against its will called itself "German Austria", a republic that was "part of the German Empire". As a result of the ban on annexation by the victorious powers, Austria soon had to change its name from "German Austria" to "Republic of Austria".

In his literary testament, *The World of Yesterday*, Stefan Zweig wrote: "For the first time in the course of history, to my knowledge, the paradoxical case arose that a country was forced to become independent which it itself bitterly rejected". The political elites, above all the Social Democrats, but also the German Nationalists and less so the Christian Social Conservatives, rejected the rump state. They were all, including Karl Renner (State Chancellor of the First Republic and Federal President of the Second Republic) and Otto Bauer (his rival and outstanding head of the social democracy party who went into exile), in favour of annexation to Germany.

A story from the memoirs of Adolf Schärf, the Federal President (1957–65) and first chairman of the Social Democrats (SPÖ) after the Second World War, provides the most convincing proof of how deeply rooted the idea of the Anschluss was. In the early summer of 1943, Schärf contradicted a German Social Democrat in Vienna who had come to ask him and his Austrian comrades to support the planned uprising against Hitler and raved that the Anschluss would be maintained even after Hitler's defeat: "The Anschluss is dead. The love of the German Reich has been exorcised from the Austrians". However, the British historian, Gordon Brook-Shepherd, pointed out that in Austria "the famous Schärf statement was often quoted, but none of the Austrians paused for a moment to marvel that a respectable and intelligent man like Schärf had to live for five years under the Nazis and Piefkes[5] to give up his old socialist dream—and even then only because a German tried to keep it alive".[6]

In his magnificent work, *The Struggle for Austrian Identity*, Friedrich Heer pointed out that the "permanent civil war" in the First Republic (1918–38) had been the result of the deeply rooted, conflicting identity crises of Austrians. Beyond the number of around 540,000 National Socialists registered in 1947, Brook-Shepherd estimated that before the 1948 amnesty, a quarter of the population was affected by the deprivation of voting rights. The Aryanisation of 70,000 homes, shops and businesses occupied by Jews contributed to the "start of a unique exercise in mass amnesia", Brook-Shepherd noted sarcastically: "Ten years after the Anschluss and less than three after the end of the Hitler terror, the Austrians had already begun to wipe their memories clean, and with them their consciences".

Friedrich Heer also stated in his above-mentioned work that the "hot potatoes" of the Austrians' identity crises were covered up by the leading politicians and the media in the shadow of the occupying powers. Only after the State Treaty of 1955 did people ask themselves—very late and very hesitantly: "What is Austria? Who is the Austrian? What is the meaning of life in being an Austrian? Is there an Austrian nation?" Heer also describes the passionate discussion on the existence of an Austrian nation, triggered by historian Ernst Hoor's warning against invoking Austria's character as a "second German state" and its "German mission". He had attacked the "anti-Austrian falsification of history", which undermined "the still weak foundation of our national and state community".

*The commitment to the Austrian nation*

At that time and even decades later, debates about the Austrian nation were by no means abstract disputes. In 1956, one in two respondents of an opinion poll claimed that Austria was not a nation, and as late as 1964, only 47 per cent professed to feel part of an Austrian nation; however, as many as 23 per cent said that "Austrians are beginning to feel like a nation". Although by the end of the 1970s the proportion of those who professed to be part of an Austrian nation had risen to two-thirds and the proportion of those who did not had fallen to 16 per cent, Heer remained very pessimistic in an article published after many discussions with schoolchildren, secondary school pupils and students:

> Our pupils still know next to nothing about the new history (...) Why are burning events wiped away, glossed over or played down, which lead to 13 March 1938? The reasons are simple: because history hurts. Almost all older Austrians, and here already also younger cohorts, but who are burdened by their fathers and mothers who came to success or failure in the First Austrian Republic and in the Third Reich—family history is one of the most sensitive areas of history—are afflicted with scars. With scars they don't like to talk about (...) The tragedy of Austria consists of the tragedies of people who have not been able to come to terms with their personal pasts, even today, if you scratch them or even just touch them, have not come to terms with them and therefore don't want to talk about them. And they certainly don't want 'their' children, who don't belong to them at all, but to the body of the people, to Austrian society, to learn about it at school.

That the German-Austrian problem also had cross-border aspects was confirmed by the lively discussion that the controversial essay by the Kiel historian Karl Dietrich Erdmann, "Three States, Two Nations, One People?", sparked off in 1986. At the time, Erdmann referred to the Federal Republic of Germany, the GDR and, as the third state and second nation, Austria. He even spoke of the "three-state nature of the German centre of Europe" or of "three-part Germany". The vast majority of Austrian historians vehemently rejected Erdmann's theses as "inadmissible" and "absurd". Gerald Stourzh, the respected historian, warned of a "tendency towards reunification" and of a revival of Greater German thought, of a possible not only museum-like "bringing home to the Reich". The cross-border debate was ignited above all with regard to the inclusion of Austria in the concept for the planned German Historical Museum in West Berlin, especially since Erdmann was also a member of the expert commission for the museum.[7]

The most media-effective political controversy, in the context of the commemorative year 1988 for the 50th anniversary of the "Anschluss", was triggered by Jörg Haider, then governor of Carinthia. In a television interview on 18 August 1988, Haider described the Austrian nation as an "ideological freak. Because ethnicity is one thing, and nationality is another thing". This statement was in the tradition of the Freedom Party of Austria's (FPÖ) relationship to German nationalism and National Socialism. Later, still under Haider, the FPÖ, which even today under Herbert Kickl is regarded as the "Heimatpartei", took a patriotic line, albeit mixed with unchanged xenophobia.

Since the State Treaty and the Neutrality Act of 1955 as identity-forming events, the "state that nobody wanted" gradually became "one that everybody wants" (Rudolf Burger). Despite the criticism of neutrality as a formula devoid of content, 79 per cent of respondents still wanted to hold on to neutrality in 2019. The explicit affirmation of the Austrian nation had also reached a peak of 82 per cent by 2007, with 8 per cent seeing Austria on the way to becoming a nation. Only 7 per cent answered that they did not feel it was becoming a nation.

*The new patriotism*

Such rapid birth of identity, probably also linked to the economic success story after two world wars, after the loss first of great power status and then of independence, might also be described as almost unprecedented in historical retrospect. Bruno Kreisky, perhaps Austria's most important statesman in the twentieth century, found once again the most fitting words in this respect. In a long conversation on the twenty-fifth anniversary of the State Treaty in the spring of 1980, he told me, among other things:

> Austrian patriotism is in any case so convincing because it is so self-evident, so natural and so little striking. The formula of 'Germany all', which has always been understood to mean that it should be above all, and that Austrian formula that all the Earth is subject to Austria, all these formulas are no longer valid for genuine patriotism. A true patriotism is relatively silent, wants its own country and does not even want a discussion of the subject. There are no discussions at all among young people, as there were in my time, about whether Austria should be there or stay there or not. It has disappeared. Today everyone takes it for granted that Austria is like Switzerland and that Austria is doing as well as Holland does.

There has been no talk of nostalgia for Germany, the Habsburgs or the monarchy for many years. In contrast to the "quiet patriotism" praised by Kreisky in his parliamentary farewell speech (28 September 1983), however, is the sometimes embarrassing national pride of the Austrians, for example during sporting events, which is also record-breaking in international comparison. In his fundamental work *The Paradoxical Republic*, the historian Oliver Rathkolb offers an explanation for the extremely exaggerated national pride with the key term "Austrosolipsism", the permanent, pathological self-centredness whose continuing roots he sees in the national conflicts of the last decades of the monarchy and in the dominant position of the German-speaking minority over the other minorities (with the exception of the Hungarians after the Compromise of 1867). He also summarises the theoretical discussions on the definitions of nation and identity with an emphasis on the trend towards general acceptance of the Austrian nation as a state nation, as a "political community of wills".

I shall come back to examples of permanent self-reflection between a deep-seated feeling of inferiority and immoderate overconfidence. One can see the extent of the sense of achievement and also the transformation of the Second Republic in contrast to the First Republic in the case of the emigration of Germans to Austria. Today, Germans are by far the largest group among foreign nationals living in Austria. On 1 January 2021, 208,732 German nationals lived in Austria, compared with 144,102 at the beginning of 2011. Who would have thought that the small neighbouring country would be the preferred EU destination of German emigrants? Do we need better proof that the "German complex" has been overcome in the name of political and economic viability?

Nevertheless, it would be unwise to take the results of the various opinion polls on the rapid nation-building process at face value. An empirical online survey on Austrian national consciousness conducted in June 2019, for example, found only 73 per cent in favour of affirming an Austrian nation, instead of 82 per cent in 2007. Seven per cent saw Austria on the way there, and 8 per cent denied it. Whether this surprising decline is only due to methodological process remains to be seen. The rejection is particularly clear among FPÖ sympathisers: only 69 per cent see Austria as an independent nation, while 14 per cent deny this. This, by far highest negative value, probably reflects the strong German-national roots among the FPÖ's supporters, despite the party leadership's emphasis on the party's character as a "homeland party".

*The great silence*

I do not dispute the success of identity promotion here, but I do want to warn against disregarding the Greater German tendencies and the effect of family traditions, especially the silence about the involvement of ancestors or friends in the Nazi era. I only recall three personal experiences that I myself also repressed until now.

One of my oldest friends was Prof. Adam Wandruszka (1914–97), the outstanding historian I met in Warsaw on my way to Austria in January 1957. At that time, he was the foreign editor of the Vienna daily, *Die Presse*. He helped me in making valuable contacts, as he also did for our mutual friend, the American contemporary historian Dennison Rusinow. With his help, I found my way to *Die Presse* as a commentator on developments in Eastern Europe and also met him in Cologne, where he was a professor at the university between 1959 and 1969. When I once asked him why he was in Cologne and not at the University of Vienna, he openly explained to me that he had been a Nazi student leader and that was why his appointment had been rejected. After he became a professor of Austrian history at Vienna University in 1969, I met him and his Italian wife from time to time, also together with the respected American historian Robert A. Kann, who emigrated after the Anschluss. At the time, I heard from Wandruszka that he had distanced himself from his past during his American captivity in the Concordia camp in the state of Kansas from 1943–6. In any case, he was one of the few Austrians who did not gloss over or conceal their past. As in so

# THE BURDEN OF THE PAST

many similar cases, I did not ask him what he did back then. Nor did he ever ask me how I survived the persecution of the Jews in Budapest. This mutual reticence was the rule rather than the exception in those days. It was only during the research for this work that I even learned from an interview that Wandruszka had been an illegal Nazi and had already joined the Sturmabteilung (SA) in 1933. Why did I never ask him about his past? Probably for the same reason that I avoided sensitive topics in two other cases, with even closer friends.

Prof. Franz Gerstenbrand (1924–2017) was an internationally renowned neurologist and founder of coma research in Vienna, who not only treated me and my late wife for many years but we also became close friends. The fact that he also maintained friendly relations with Federal Chancellor Bruno Kreisky beyond medical care contributed to our harmony. He had grown up in Moravia in Czechoslovakia, was a fighter pilot in the German air force during the Second World War, and studied and graduated at the University of Vienna. He stood by me emotionally in difficult personal situations. Nevertheless, I never spoke to him about his past. Not even when his wife told me that after reading my memoirs about the Hungarian Holocaust, he told her that he was ashamed of being German. Thus, even after many years and successes in Vienna, he did not call himself an Austrian. This time, too, I kept silent and did not broach the subject. Probably because I was afraid of his past during the Nazi era.

In the third personal case, it is somehow the other way round. A very close friend of mine is a former top conservative politician and successful entrepreneur, a few years younger than me, who helped me professionally a great deal. We met often and always talked openly about politics and business. I told my wife that if anything happened to me, she must immediately contact this friend first. Of course, I also gave him all my books as soon as they were published. During this half century of personal friendship, I only learned that he had been selected for the Nazi elite school Napola as a young boy. He never asked me about my experiences during the War, although all this is described in detail in several of my books. To this day, I suspect that he has not read them.

Undoubtedly the most positive example in this respect in my circle of acquaintances was my best friend and "Austria teacher", the great Catholic journalist Kurt Vorhofer (1929–95), with whom I had countless conversations about the present and the past over the years. "Now comes another gruesome story...", he sighed when I recalled the persecution in Hungary in 1944–5. It must be added, however, that his deep, sincere understanding was also helped by the life story of his wife Lydia. She had a Jewish father who, like numerous relatives, was killed by the Nazis. She was born in 1931, lived with her mother, had to change schools almost every year, and her childhood friends were without exception also "half-Jews". She became a devout Catholic, but the scars remained. This exceptional story in my circle of friends shows me in retrospect that the full truth about the Nazi reign of terror could only be grasped, and probably also wanted to be grasped, by those people whose families had always been anti-Nazi for whatever reason and who educated future generations in this regard. On a different note, are those young Austrians who, as early as 1968 and even more so after 1986, demanded their parents and grandparents, without letting up, to reveal their past during the Nazi era.

*Never forget!*

These case studies can be seen as isolated personal experiences. But I suspect that the silence criticised by Friedrich Heer has left its mark not only on teachers but also on a generation of grandparents and parents, especially in the families of the beneficiaries of the large-scale expropriation of tens of thousands of Jewish

# THE BURDEN OF THE PAST

flats, shops and businesses, especially in Vienna. As French historian Jacques Le Goff put it: "The Jews have become the memory people par excellence". Elie Wiesel, the writer, Holocaust survivor and Nobel Peace Prize laureate, stated in an interview that for every single Jew, the maxim has always applied: "To be a Jew means to remember".[8]

Of course, Nietzsche's maxim also applies to Austrian history after 1945, when he recommends to his readers "the art and power of being able to forget", because, Nietzsche continues "to all action belongs forgetting" and "blessed are the forgetful".[9] But for me, as probably for most people directly affected by the Shoah, many things cannot simply be "forgiven and forgotten". Time and again—for example in 1973 after the closure of the Schönau transit camp for Russian Jews, in 1986 at the time of the Waldheim affair and in 2000 after the formation of the Austrian People's Party (ÖVP)/FPÖ government—I have defended our country against blanket suspicions with full conviction in speeches and articles. I also acknowledge the undisputed change and achievements in coming to terms with the past. Despite this, or precisely because of it, I was deeply affected by the scandal surrounding the indescribable songbooks of the beating fraternities and the casual way in which they were justified by leading FPÖ officials ("we didn't know", "after all, it wasn't sung"). The rapid resurgence of the FPÖ from 2008 onwards also confirmed my concerns about the still large reservoir of potential FPÖ voters. Both the previously mentioned examples from my circle of friends and the events at the demonstrations during the pandemic raise justified doubts about the validity of some nice-sounding survey results about the past.

## *The long tradition of xenophobia*

In order to better understand the temporary success of the political instrumentalisation of migration movements, one should take a look at the true facts behind the romanticised portrayal of the Dual Monarchy that is so important for our tourism advertising. Even at the turn of the century in 1900, the influx of migrants, the defence mechanisms and the linguistic integration problems were not exceptions, but, according to historian Moritz Csáky, "belonged as a central category of this region to an important part of the everyday experience of life".[10] He points out that central Europe is a laboratory in which xenophobia or similar processes can be traced into the past. Around 1900, 62 per cent of Vienna's 1.7 million inhabitants were considered "foreigners", as only 38 per cent had been born there and had the right of domicile. In 1910, 467,158 inhabitants of Vienna were born in Bohemia and Moravia. Vienna was the city with the second largest Czech population at that time. Around 70 per cent of the representatives of Viennese modernism were migrants not born in Vienna, mostly of the first or second generation. Immigration from Bohemia, Moravia and Slovakia in particular left lasting traces in Vienna. As late as the second half of the twentieth century, 27.5 per cent of the main tenants in Vienna (i.e. 201,880 full-time registered persons) had a Czech surname. It is not generally known that two federal presidents, Franz Jonas and Kurt Waldheim, were of Czech origin. Csáky also points out that the half-million Czech migrants were met with similar antipathies and defence mechanisms and were expected to integrate perfectly in terms of language, as is expected of the much smaller number of immigrants from Africa today.

In his autobiography, the political scientist Anton Pelinka drew attention to a hidden consequence of the repressed pressure to Germanise—the supra-effort to prove oneself to the "German" environment, to show that one was at least as "German" as they were. Pelinka emphasises that the pan-German nationalism of Austrian origin was also to be understood from this pressure to adapt a non-German-speaking population, and he also mentions the high percentage of non-German names of Slavic origin under the Nazis. After the Second World War and under "normal", that is, peaceful conditions, the Freedom Party had two highly symbolic examples: on the one hand, the defence mechanism of the descendants of migrant families and on the other, of selective xenophobia. The example of the Germanisation of a Slavic name is represented by the change of name from Hojac to Westenthaler in the case of the politician Peter Westenthaler, who was promoted by Haider to become chairman of the FPÖ parliamentary group (2000–2). The case of Johann Gudenus, FPÖ parliamentary chairman, who resigned after the scandal over the "Ibiza" video with H.-C. Strache, shows how fickle attitudes towards foreigners can be. The FPÖ politician, notorious for his extremely xenophobic slogans, had already demanded in 2004 to "put an immediate end to systematic *Umvolkung*". This term, meaning forced massive assimilation borrowed from Nazi language, triggered general indignation. At an election rally in 2013, Gudenus went even further: "Now it's a case of taking the cudgels out of the bag for all asylum tricksters, criminals, illegal aliens, criminal Islamists and left-wing screamers".[11]

All this did not bother the politician in his private life in the slightest. In 2017, for example, he married a woman of Serbian origin in a civil ceremony, and a few weeks later he married her in a Serbian Orthodox church in Banja Luka in Republika Srpska, the Serb-ruled state of the Federation of Bosnia and Herzegovina. He and Vice-Chancellor Strache paid an official visit to President Aleksandar Vučić in Belgrade in February 2018. Strache reportedly referred to Kosovo as "part of Serbia" in an interview with the Belgrade newspaper *Politika*. The FPÖ won around half the votes of the 75,000 Viennese with Serbian roots in the 2015 Vienna city council elections, according to pollsters' estimates. The Freedom Party's repeated campaigns against Turks, Bosnians and Muslims in general have increased tensions between minority groups with different ethnic backgrounds and have exacerbated xenophobic prejudices in the Austrian capital.

The Yugoslav wars unleashed by the Greater Serb nationalists and the flight of Bosnians and Kosovo Albanians have not remained without consequences either. I have personally experienced time and again the power of traditional resentments but also the tendencies to "over-adapt". In the late 1980s, a US professor with Croatian roots called me on a visit to Vienna. He was very disappointed. By chance, he had discovered several Croatian names identical to his family name in the Viennese telephone book and called several numbers to ask if there might be any relatives among them. Without exception, the people he called were outraged, saying they had nothing to do with Croatia. It may have been an exaggerated or ill-considered spontaneous action on his part, but such an unfriendly response was undoubtedly also the expression of a pressure to conform that was still effective.

When during the Yugoslav wars I analysed the excesses of the Serbian army against the Kosovo Albanians on Austrian television, I was often reproached for this by Viennese of Serbian roots, ranging from the cleaners working at the TV-centre to taxi drivers. In case of Croatia, the response was different. For example, decades later a complete stranger was waiting for me after a visit to the cinema: "I'm a doctor from Croatia and wanted to thank you belatedly for your fair reporting on the war". Of course, there were also gruff reactions after critical remarks about Croatia. After a lecture on nationalist tendencies in Croatian politics, especially regarding the lack of facing up to the heritage of the fascist Ustasha regime, the Croatian ambassador present at the event turned to his Polish colleague and remarked, "No wonder—let's see, Lendvai is a Jew". The Polish colleague happened to be the Catholic resistance fighter, Jew rescuer and Auschwitz prisoner Władysław Bartoszewszki, a personal friend at that, who immediately told me about this remark. I decided to ignore this and to avoid any further contact with this Croatian ambassador. This is probably why I was particularly pleased that I could recount my relationship with Croatia in detail in the preface to the Croatian edition of my Orbán biography. The same consideration guided me in the introductory notes to the Slovenian edition of this book, where I was able to describe my changed personal relationship with Slovenia's "strong man", the Prime Minister at that time, Janez Janša. I have had friends in all ethnic groups of the disintegrated Yugoslavia and have always tried to inform my readers and viewers in balanced commentaries also about the human rights violations and outrages committed by Albanian, Croatian and Bosnian Muslim nationalists. In view of these experiences, I therefore strongly condemn the attempts to import the suicidal passions from the sunken multi-ethnic state into our country for the sake of supposed electoral advantages.

*Austria, the immigration country*

At the same time, however, I also reject the efforts that repeatedly seek to deny the fact that Austria has long since become a country of immigration. Here, too, a brief review helps to recall the beginning of this development. The figures on Austria as a destination for migration from the East after the Second World War confirm the diagnosis of the Prague poet Rainer Maria Rilke: "Austria has always remained under construction, it is a provisionality that has become chronic".[12] Let us first look at the balance of immigration between the end of the Second World War and the upheaval in the East in 1989–90: "Altogether, about 2.6 million people have come to Austria as settlers, refugees or trans-migrants since 1945. About 680,000 have settled here permanently, including 350,000 people with non-German mother tongues. Of 1.1 million immigrant or transmigrant guest workers and family members, about 500,000 have also remained in the country", wrote demographers Heinz Faßmann and Rainer Münz in mid-1991. At that time, about 12 per cent of the resident population was born outside what is now Austria and 7 per cent of the population were considered "foreigners" according to citizenship.[13] The two authors of this critical study (former Minister of Education Faßmann is currently President of the Austrian Academy of Sciences) stated that the Republic did not have a clearly recognisable, nationally coordinated migration policy, although in the longer term 25,000 immigrants per year would have been needed. A quarter of a century later, University Professor Faßmann co-authored a study for the report of the Migration Council for Austria, which I chaired. The ten panels of top scientists and experts, appointed by the then Federal Minister of the Interior, Johanna Mikl-Leitner, in 2014, proposed an annual net immigration of 50,000 persons in its comprehensive final report at the end of 2016. However, it is just as difficult to speak of a conceptual migration policy today as it was three decades ago!

In the meantime, however, the figures show a rapid increase in the number of people with a foreign place of birth. At the beginning of 2021, every fifth inhabitant of Austria (20.1 per cent) was born abroad, and in Vienna 37.1 per cent of people had a foreign place of birth. If people who were born abroad themselves or who had both parents born abroad are classified as migrants, then almost every second Viennese (46 per cent) is considered a migrant; every third resident has a foreign passport. In total, 1,587,251 people with foreign citizenship lived in Austria as of the cut-off date of January 2022.[14]

These overall statistics mask significant shifts in the composition of immigrants. Who would have thought that in this country that still contains deep-seated feelings of inferiority that Austria would be the preferred EU destination of German emigrants. According to the Austrian Integration Fund's (ÖIF) annual brochure, 244,927 people born in Germany were living in Austria at the beginning of 2021, three times as many as in 2000. They form by far the largest migrant group in our country, followed by Bosnians (172,373), Turks (159,068), Serbs (144,416), Romanians (134,206) and Hungarians (83,914).

The percentages of foreigners in general, of course, mask the wide range of reactions to them, from friendly acceptance of Germans to merely grudging toleration of Arabs, Black Africans or Afghans. There are surveys on how "rather helpful" or "rather harmful" immigrant groups are perceived for Austria's development. Migrants from the former Yugoslavia are seen as helpful by 53 to 57 per cent. Jewish returnees, Sudeten Germans and refugees from neighbouring communist countries are also seen as far more helpful than harmful. The ratio is already different for Turkish guest workers—37 versus 29 per cent. Refugees from the Middle East (Syrians) and Africa are seen as "rather helpful" by only 10 and 7 per cent, respectively.

The answers to the assessment of the respective integration, broken down by nationality, are interesting. "Very good" or "rather good" is the opinion of 51 and 37 per cent of the respondents, respectively, on the integration of German migrants; this is 28 and 49 per cent for Hungarians, 26 and 49 per cent for Croats, 16 and 48 per cent for Poles, 13 and 46 per cent for Bosnians, and 9 and 40 per cent for Serbs. Regarding Syrians and Iraqis, the percentages for "very good" and "rather good" are 17 and 14 per cent, respectively. Bringing up the rear are the Somalis with 2 and 12 per cent and the Afghans with 2 and 8 per cent. There is no reason to doubt the two surveys cited. A Statista poll from August 2021 showed that 53 per cent of the participants considered the coexistence of Austrians and foreigners to be bad and only 39 per cent considered it to be good.

The massive and economically beneficial immigration has undoubtedly increased the diversity of society, but at the same time it has weakened cohesion and increased division. Almost two-thirds of the 1,000 respondents (62 per cent) considered migration the greatest threat to Austrian identity in a representative survey conducted by the well-known social scientist Rudolf Bretschneider on behalf of the ÖIF and carried out in September 2020. The data on the areas of conflict are remarkable. At 55 per cent, a majority find that cohesion in Austria has deteriorated over the duration of their lives; only 9 per cent see an improvement. Some 95 per cent of the respondents see the admission of more refugees, 83 per cent see immigration to Austria and 80 per cent see the measures taken in September 2020 during the Covid pandemic as particularly divisive issues.[15]

It has already been noted in the above-mentioned essay by Faßmann and Münz (i.e. 30 years ago) that the willingness of the native population to accept refugees was "the most difficult to influence" and that, in contrast to 1956, for example, it was not likely to be very high. It was also stressed that the economic advantages and fiscal benefits of immigrants are considerably greater than the short-term burdens on the public budget and social security. Faßmann and Münz already pointed out at the time that so-called "foreigner problems" were often not caused by immigrants: "Unemployment, petty crime, undeclared work, housing shortages as well as xenophobia would exist in our country even without immigrants".

In my eyes, a key question beyond professional integration remains the emotional relationship to Austria. As a political refugee in 1956, I consider citizenship, as do six out of ten respondents in the Bretschneider study, to be significant for my identity as an Austrian. I will never forget how suspiciously my alien's passport was inspected during border crossings, despite my visa, and how proud I was to show my first Austrian passport. This feeling is memorably expressed in this poem by Bertolt Brecht:

# THE BURDEN OF THE PAST

> The passport is the noblest part
> of a human being.
> It does not come
> In such a simple way
> Like a human being.
> A human being can
> Anywhere be born,
> in the most careless way
> and for no good reason,
> but a passport never does.
> That's what it's recognised for,
> if it is good,
> while a man
> can be as good as he is
> and still not be recognised.[16]

In any case, it is gratifying that in the cited study only 40 per cent consider place of birth to be significant for the definition of being an Austrian. It is more important to speak the German language (74 per cent), to feel Austria is a home (69 per cent) or to appreciate the way of life, values and customs in Austria (61 per cent). As someone who was not born in Austria, I agree with the 41 per cent who consider it an important characteristic of Austrians to have local friends. I consider small or larger groupings of migrants with conscious or unconscious exclusion of "real Austrians" to be an insurmountable obstacle to full integration in the medium or long term. No wonder that in the survey 96 per cent said that immigrants had to adapt to the values and customs of Austria.

It is a truism that naturalisation does not mean integration. Hardly anyone has formulated this as memorably as the successful German-language writer Ilija Trojanow, who fled Bulgaria with his family as a child: "The refugee is a separate category of human being (...) No matter how many years have passed since his flight, the locals mark him as someone who does not share something essential with them. Even the shortest biography has room for his hyphenated identity".[17]

I am not one of those futurologists found everywhere these days, speculating and presenting conclusions about the consequences of the global turn of the times, marked by the Covid pandemic, climate change and Russia's war against Ukraine. I only hope that the willingness to help the refugees from Ukraine, reminiscent of the Hungarian uprising of 1956–7, will continue and that the renewed success of integration will make people understand Ilija Trojanow's warning: "The danger is not that we will become over-alienated, but that we will run out of foreigners".[18]

2

# MYTH AND REALITY

## THE LEGACY OF THE HABSBURGS

It was a brilliant summer day when a private plane from Switzerland landed in Hohenems in the province of Vorarlberg on 30 July 1996. The pilot was Karl Thomas Robert Maria Franziskus Georg Bahnam Habsburg-Lothringen, the 36-year-old grandson of the last Austrian Emperor, Charles I, and the eldest son of Otto Habsburg, the head of the House of Habsburg-Lothringen. When asked if he had anything to declare, he is said to have replied no. In his luggage, however, he was carrying a tiara worth, according to varying estimates, between 50,000 and 105,000 euros. The customs officers claimed that he had mentioned the tiara only when they had begun to examine the plane. In the criminal financial proceedings, Habsburg insisted that he had mentioned the tiara of his own accord. After his appeal against a fine, the case ended up 3 years later at the Appeals Senate of the Financial Directorate for Vorarlberg. The latter confirmed the verdict of the first instance and sentenced Karl Habsburg to a fine of 13,081 euros for attempted smuggling of a tiara. In his statement, Habsburg conceded that he had "perhaps made a mistake" but had never wanted to smuggle anything. According to the chairman of the senate, however, the defendant was by no means acting out of ignorance, but with intent.[1]

Despite this incident, Karl Habsburg was elected in the same year as a member of the European Parliament for the Austrian People's Party (ÖVP) after a successful preferential vote campaign. His short political career ended with the so-called World Vision donation scandal. This international charity arranged sponsorships for needy children around the world. An audit report confirmed transfers of considerable donations (around 46,500 euros) to Habsburg's Paneuropa movement. Part of this went to finance his election campaign in 1996. Paneuropa Austria Secretary General Wolfgang Krones and his wife, who was managing director of World Vision Austria, were later convicted. Karl Habsburg only paid back around 37,000 euros to the association in 2004, which was the sum that, according to Habsburg, had been used without his knowledge to finance his election campaign. Despite public pressure, he not only did not resign as an MEP but wanted to run again in June 1999. After the ÖVP failed to nominate him again for the EU elections, he entered the race with his own list as part of the Christian Social Alliance (CSA) (List Karl Habsburg), but could only win 1.5 per cent of the votes.

The fact that the then 86-year-old Otto Habsburg (himself a Christlich-Soziale Union MEP from 1979–99) backed his son and compared the attacks against Karl with the persecution of Jews caused general indignation. "The head of the House of Habsburg had lost all measure, all sense of proportion, and demolished himself after a long European career", wrote Austrian commentator Anneliese Rohrer, adding that this "could only be the tragic conclusion to a series of misconduct by his son; a series that was explained over and over again by 'blue-eyedness', naiveté and intrigues of others".[2]

## MYTH AND REALITY

Karl Habsburg (head of the House of Habsburg since 2007), again attracted attention in 2018–19 with a complaint against punishment for the use of the word "von" as proof of belonging to the nobility on his personal website. In the end, he failed at the Constitutional Court: the ban of using "von" does not violate the Constitution. The penalty for using nobility names is still stated in crowns in the old law (of 3 April 1919, on the abolition of nobility). Therefore, there was no penalty payment for Karl Habsburg, even though there was a guilty verdict. Apart from these court cases, as of recent years he is no longer an issue. Only the name of his younger brother, Georg Habsburg, recently appeared in the media when, after a checkered career in Hungary, he was appointed by the Orbán government as Hungarian ambassador in Paris at the end of 2020.

After this flashback to the minor compromising incidents in the life of the bearer of a great historical name, one might ask the question: Why is all this still interesting today? Why should one bother with it?

There is no confirmation in the political culture of the Second Republic for the claim that Austria has not overcome its fall from a world empire to a small state, even after a century. There is not the slightest sign of a longing for a monarchical movement, let alone for a restoration. At the same time, however, the traces of the Habsburg era, which ruled the country for 640 years, are still omnipresent in the tourist industry and in the cultural understanding of Austrians today. There are hardly any democracies in Europe that are built as strongly as Austria on monarchical foundations.[3]

Even now, not a year goes by without the publication of books on the historical long-term impact of the multiethnic state or on outstanding personalities in that period. The US political scientist A. Wess Mitchel underlined in the conclusion of his study *On the Grand Strategy of the Habsburg Empire* (2018),[4] the degree of "geopolitical stability and relative prosperity" in the heart of Europe, which has never been achieved since then. In a similar vein, the German-Bohemian-American writer Johannes Urzidil (1896–1970) once stated: "The Danube Monarchy resembled an anachronism and was at the same time a promise". In his work *The Habsburgs: Rise and Fall of a World Power* (2020), British historian Martyn Rady undertakes a reassessment of the ruling family ("the first global enterprise") and concludes with a detailed tribute to Otto Habsburg's personality: "He was probably the best emperor the Habsburgs never had". A judgment hardly shared in Austria itself.

*Otto Habsburg: an eventful history*

Viewed against the background of the sometimes important, albeit rather negative, role that Otto Habsburg played in the fate of Austria, the tragicomic adventures of the completely insignificant present head of the family reflect the irony of history in the mirror of the final decline of the former ruling family of a great European power. That is why I began the chapter on the traces of aristocracy in Austrian society and politics with the description of the pitiful end of the Habsburgs.

As for the "outstanding achievement" of Otto Habsburg noted by the British historian Martyn Rady, the positive sides in his long life (1912–2011) are undeniable, such as the consistent struggle for Austrian independence and against Hitler's Germany, albeit in the context of close contacts with the authoritarian Schuschnigg regime between 1935 and 1938. Schuschnigg, however, rejected Otto's demand to assume the chancellorship with special powers. Otto Habsburg and his family were sought by the Nazi regime after the Anschluss, and many monarchists were arrested. Rady also highlights the rescue of several thousand Jews in France through Otto's personal efforts and his commitment as an EU parliamentarian to the European unification process and to the admission of Eastern European post-communist states into the EU.

It is interesting that the British author ignored the darker side of Otto Habsburg's long life. The strong distrust of Austrian socialists and republicans towards members of the House of Habsburg stemmed from Otto's activity against Karl Renner's provisional state government in 1945 and his later declarations of political intent. Thus, in a letter to US President Harry Truman on 2 July 1945, he demanded that the Provisional Government not be recognised because it was a Trojan horse of the communists. Eventually, the Habsburg family settled in Pöcking, Bavaria, from where Otto Habsburg pursued his return to Austria. Some hints of his possible role as "state notary" or "chancellor of justice" provided his opponents with convenient arguments, in the conflict in the ÖVP/Social Democrats (SPÖ) coalition over Otto Habsburg's entry permit, which flared up in full in 1961–3.

The fuse of the Habsburg crisis, which from today's perspective seems bizarre and incomprehensible, was lit in June 1961, when the SPÖ in the coalition government refused to agree to a motion by Chancellor Gorbach to accept Otto's renunciation of a claim to rule as sufficient. Briefly, the background: after the founding of the Republic, parliament passed a law according to which all Habsburgs who did not expressly renounce their claims to rule were expelled from the country. They were not allowed to return to Austria unless they made such a declaration of renunciation. When the Administrative Court ruled in 1963 that Habsburgs' declaration of renunciation was sufficient for entry, there was serious turmoil in parliament. The SPÖ tried to depict a possible return of Otto as a great danger for the Republic. In parliament, the SPÖ joined forces with the Freedom Party of Austria (FPÖ) for the first time against the coalition partner ÖVP on a central issue to prevent his return despite the decision of a supreme court.

Under the single-party ÖVP government, Otto Habsburg then entered Austria legally for the first time on 31 October 1966, and there were no mass demonstrations.

The famous photo of Chancellor Kreisky's "historic handshake" at a reception in the Federal Chancellery with Otto Habsburg on 4 May 1972 at the fiftieth anniversary meeting of the Habsburg-led Pan-European Movement symbolises in the history books the Austrian Social Democracy's relaxed relationship with the Habsburgs. The eldest son of the last reigning emperor was even invited by Federal President Heinz Fischer to visit the Hofburg on his ninety-fifth birthday. "You have it nice here", the guest said, and Fischer spoke of "a long and useful" conversation.

As a postscript to Otto's eventful career, his special relationship with Hungary must be briefly mentioned. His role as patron at the legendary "Pan-European Picnic" on the border strip near Sopron went down in history because it was here in August 1989 that 640 citizens of Communist East Germany fled across the Austro-Hungarian border. This became the prelude to the end of the Iron Curtain.

Otto Habsburg had been raised by his mother Zita to be the future king of Hungary and therefore had to learn Hungarian. Immediately after the fall of communism, he paid a visit to Hungary, delivering his first public speech in Hungary, perhaps symbolically, to the Jewish community in Budapest. When I heard him speak at a conference of expatriate Hungarians in Budapest in the summer of 1996, I, like so many other participants, was amazed at his perfect Hungarian. A few years later, at an international conference in Prague, where we had both given presentations, he had me call him and held a lengthy conversation with me in Hungarian. The last time I met him was in Innsbruck at a conference where I moderated, and Otto Habsburg, already aged over 85 at that time, gave a brilliant speech on the situation in Europe completely without notes.

## MYTH AND REALITY

Otto Habsburg died at the age of 98; he left behind 7 children, 22 grandchildren and two great-grandchildren. He was buried after a mass in St. Stephen's Cathedral in the Capuchin crypt and his heart was buried separately in the Benedictine Abbey of Pannonhalma in Hungary, as a sign of his commitment to both halves of the Dual Monarchy.

It is estimated that there are more than 400 Habsburgs worldwide, and about two-thirds probably reside in Austria. The assets of the Habsburgs have been put at around 100 million euros. Estimates about indirect profit of the Austrian tourist industry from the Habsburg brand vary between 10 to 30 million euros.[5]

*Nobles as top officials*

Like so much of Austrian history after 1945, the promotion of the role of aristocrats in officialdom can also be traced back to Bruno Kreisky's tenure as foreign minister and then as chancellor. Otto Schulmeister, the conservative editor of the Viennese daily, *Die Presse*, once characterised Kreisky in a conversation with me: "What remains unforgettable about this man is that he wanted more than was available for him and the resources of his country. He was a kind of a 'great Austrian,' that is, one who did not understand Austria as merely the sum of its square kilometers".[6] This attitude of Kreisky's, which Schulmeister calls "Great Austrian" or "Austrian-patriotic", was something I had already experienced as a journalistic companion during his travels in communist Eastern Europe. He had a positive attitude to the Austro-Hungarian monarchy as a cultural and economic entity and to the people in the successor states. Even against opposition in his own party and to the chagrin of the catholic Cartellverband and the Masonic lodges, during his tenure as foreign minister (1959–66) and as Federal Chancellor (1970–83) he promoted quite a few officials from the ranks of the nobility. Some inner-party critics even sneered behind closed doors about a "renaissance of the aristocracy". His open-minded attitude towards artists and the aristocracy was an important factor in his appeal, both at home and also abroad.

When I interviewed him several times in his office at the Foreign Ministry in the early 1960s as a correspondent for the *Financial Times*, I dealt with his secretary Eva Chiari who had been a member of an Italian-Austrian noble family. His head of cabinet, Ambassador (Count) Olivier Rességuier, belonged to a family of French nobility. As his successor as head of cabinet, I got to know Rudolf Kirchschläger, a practicing Catholic without party affiliation (he was also a member of the Austrian People's Party for a time). In the first Kreisky government, Kirchschläger was appointed foreign minister despite opposition from within the party, and in 1974 he became a candidate (twice successfully) for the election of the Federal President. He was followed as foreign minister by the professional diplomat Erich Bielka (Ritter von Karltreu). It was probably a late legacy of the Kreisky era that (Count) Wolfgang Schallenberg and (Prince) Albert Rohan were able to serve as long-standing secretary generals (i.e. highest-ranking officials in the Foreign Ministry) in the 1990s. Aristocratic cabinet members under Kreisky also included Defence Minister Karl (Baron von) Lütgendorf (he later committed suicide as a result of a corruption scandal) and also Army Commander General Emil (Count) Spannocchi.

The high point of an aristocrat's political career since the collapse of the Dual Monarchy has undoubtedly been (Count) Alexander (full name: Alexander Georg Nicolas Christoph Wolfgang Tassilo) Schallenberg, first as foreign minister (from June 2019) and then as chancellor (October to December 2021). His aristocratic roots have nothing to do with political realities today or with his career. Schallenberg owed his rise exclusively to his patron and predecessor in both positions, Sebastian Kurz.

After his brief and uneventful tenure as chancellor he resumed his former position as foreign minister.

*Karel Schwarzenberg: a passionate European*

Nothing, however, can change the fact that the outstanding role in international politics in recent decades has been played by a descendant of the most famous Austrian-Central European noble family that is second only to the Habsburgs, Prince Karel Schwarzenberg.[7] I have had the good fortune to meet him repeatedly, both privately as well as for interviews and at international conferences, at almost every stage of his career in Vienna and Prague. His sparkling bon mots and brilliant speeches have deeply impressed both the audiences and the media. Long underestimated in the Viennese political milieu, this Catholic aristocrat, liberal intellectual, passionate European and uncompromising fighter against nationalism and anti-Semitism has emerged as a renaissance personality with many facets.

Even before I had met him personally, I first heard the name of his great-uncle, Prince Johannes Schwarzenberg, who was then Austrian ambassador (1955–66) in London, during a conversation with Foreign Minister Bruno Kreisky sometime in the early 1960s. Kreisky showed me (the young correspondent of the London *Financial Times*) the first page of a confidential report by the ambassador on the state of European integration negotiations with unmistakable pride. It read, verbatim, "The day before yesterday, while hunting, the Prime Minister told me in confidence that ...". The British head of government and former foreign minister was then Lord Home, friends with the Austrian aristocrat. "See what exclusive contacts little Austria can maintain with a great power!" boasted Kreisky, not hiding his weakness for the aristocracy. He even praised the ambassador's handwritten political reports in an unusual personal letter to him: "For some time now I have been reading your reports with real pleasure. One of the few pleasant interruptions of the daily routine".[8]

Some 20 years later, Kreisky gave the decisive impetus to the unprecedented international career of another Schwarzenberg. When asked, who should be chosen as chairman of the Helsinki Federation, the international human rights organisation based in Vienna, he proposed the great-nephew of the ambassador Prince Karel von Schwarzenberg, the scion (and at that time already head) of one of the most famous aristocratic families in central Europe. He had been known in Austria merely as a rich forest owner and carefree friend of the bohemians. Using this new position (1984–91), he has done more than anyone else for human rights and opening up of central Europe, which had been closed off by the communists.

Until the collapse of the Eastern bloc, most Austrian newspaper readers and TV viewers had taken "Kary", as the prince has always been called by friends, for a bon vivant, a whimsical millionaire who owned large estates. After his expulsion at the age of eleven along with his family from Czechoslovakia, Schwarzenberg lived in Austria for 41 years, always modestly describing himself as a "farmer and forester". At the beginning of his political career he was already 52 years old. It was only when he became head of cabinet and closest advisor to president Václav Havel (1989–92) in Prague that the general public realised that, despite his roots in Austria, he had a Swiss and a Czech passport, but never an Austrian one. He is "one of the greatest Europeans of our time", Havel said of Schwarzenberg, who he had first met in 1987 as the most active president of the Helsinki Federation. "He is an extraordinary Czech, an extraordinary European and an extraordinary human being. Although he was forced to spend most of his life outside his homeland, he has always remained a patriot. Although he was born an aristocrat, he is a staunch democrat and fighter for human rights".[9]

After the break-up of Czechoslovakia into independent Czech and Slovak states, Schwarzenberg also left the presidential office, following Havel's resignation. Then, to everyone's surprise, he managed to win a seat in the Czech Senate in 2004. There was, of course, considerable opposition to his political involvement, in part because of the return of a relatively small portion of the large family fortune. Greater media coverage was triggered by President Václav Klaus' attempt in 2007 to refuse the swearing-in of Schwarzenberg, proposed by the Green Party as foreign minister, on the grounds that he was half Austrian and would not "adequately defend Czech interests" because of his proximity to Austria.

As a senator in the Second Chamber of the Czech Parliament and twice foreign minister (2007–9 and 2010–13), this exceptional politician has become a symbol of the now endangered Europeanisation of the post-communist reform states. He co-founded a new, moderately conservative pro-European grouping, TOP 09, and was elected to the Chamber of Deputies in 2010. In 2013, he almost became president of the Czech Republic. In the runoff election, thanks in part to his playing the "German card", Socialist Miloš Zeman won. Schwarzenberg's outspoken criticism in interviews and speeches, both of EU foreign policy toward Russia and Eastern Europe and of the ambivalent attitude of Austria's two Kurz governments in recent years, has engendered strong international echo.

Even if he did not run in the parliamentary elections in October 2021 for reasons of age and health, he remained true to the family tradition to the end: "The Schwarzenbergs never stood apart; they were marshals, cardinals, prime ministers. We learned to put ourselves out there where we could make a difference".[10] The dictum also applies to Schwarzenberg's fascinating life story: "Homo sum, humani nihil a me alienum puto" ("I am a human being, nothing human is alien to me").

It was a stroke of luck that I was able to attend the solemn ceremony awarding Karel Schwarzenberg the Marietta and Friedrich Torberg Medal by the Jewish Community of Austria at the Belvedere Palace. This honour is awarded to personalities who have taken a stand against anti-Semitism, racism and neo-Nazis. In his laudatory speech, Israeli historian Prof. Shlomo Avineri thanked the prince for his humanitarian commitment to Judaism and Israel. "Your ancestors were and you are defenders of human rights, fighters for freedom and peace. Like us Jews, you knew exile and dispossession, persecution and humiliation. But, like us Jews, you also experienced redemption and triumph".[11]

Unlike other aristocrats (gathered in the "German Club" in Vienna), the Schwarzenbergs were courageous opponents of the Nazi regime. Diplomat Johannes Schwarzenberg fled to Geneva shortly after the Anschluss; he received several honours for his efforts as director of the Red Cross for Jewish victims, also in Budapest. After his death in a car accident in 1978, a crumpled photo of a pile of corpses from the Mauthausen concentration camp was found in his wallet, which he had apparently always carried with him.

Another great uncle of Karel Schwarzenberg, Adolph Schwarzenberg, had even had a plaque with the inscription "Jews are welcome here" put up on the park of his Viennese palace after the Anschluss. He fled to the USA. His adopted son Heinrich was sent to the Buchenwald concentration camp on the orders of SS leader Himmler, and all his property was expropriated.

*Shadow of the ancestors*

Historians stressed that in its basic attitude, the Austrian nobility was incomparably more reserved towards National Socialism than the nobility in Germany. Nevertheless, even in the history of the Schwarzenbergs there are traces of the conflicts between the followers and the opponents of Hitler's reign of terror. The father of Karel Schwarzenberg's wife Therese (Johannes Graf Hardegg) was in fact an active Nazi. Unlike the other so-called "best families" with black sheep from the Nazi era, Therese Schwarzenberg never made a secret of her father's Nazi past. Incidentally, the latter was also one of the hundred or so aristocrats who were members of the "German Club" in Vienna. Its statutes in the 1930s club stated, "Members can only be Germans of Aryan descent who profess the principles of German National Socialism". Five members of the club were even on the ministerial list of the first "Anschluss Cabinet" planned after March 1938. A study on the "Austro-Nazis in the Hofburg" published in 2021 revealed the fact that 10 per cent of the members and 25 per cent of the board of the "German Club" were aristocrats.[12]

This recent book about the involvement of the aristocracy with the Nazi regime also surprised me personally, as I learned details about the father of a highly esteemed friend that were completely unknown to me. It featured a certain Karl Anton (Prince) Rohan, a journalist and author, who had been an active member of the German Club and a member of the National Socialist German Workers' Party since 1 May 1938. He had also written a contribution for the *Confession Book of Austrian Poets*, which enthusiastically welcomed the Anschluss. During World War II, Karl Rohan was active in the intelligence service and foreign propaganda of the Nazi regime. He was arrested in 1946, and after his release he wrote for the far-right magazines *Die Aula* and *Neue Ordnung*.[13]

In my obituary, I praised his son Albert Rohan as "the most important international diplomat of the Second Republic" and particularly emphasised his merits in Balkan policy and in the fight for freedom of the press in Eastern Europe. The information about his father was new to me, but it did not change my admiration for this friend at all. What amazed me, however, was the fact that in his memoirs he wrote a whole chapter about the "shadow of the ancestors", including the details of the persecution of his anti-fascist Hungarian uncle but did not write a word about his father's political past.[14] The German poet, Matthias Claudius (1740–1815) wrote about such a hole in memory, about the oblivion that is longed for, in the "Evening Song":[15]

> How is the world so still
> And in the twilight shell
> So mournful and so hold!
> As a quiet chamber,
> Where you of the day's sorrow
> Shall sleep away and forget.

3

# HITLER'S SHADOW, YESTERDAY AND TODAY

It is rare that the past holds the present in its spell after almost eight decades. This is true of the Shoah, the extermination of six million Jewish men, women and children by Hitler's Germany. Despite the publication of thousands of books listed under the term "Holocaust", despite a multitude of educational programmes and courses, despite new films and museums on the subject, the institutions of the European Union and international research bodies in the member states register a growing anti-Semitism. The pandemic has encouraged conspiracy myths, demagogy and irresponsibility everywhere. A deep political, economic and international crisis proves again and again how thin the varnish of civilisation is and how fragile the rule of law is. That is why the call "resist the beginning" is always, and especially today, timelessly valid. In order to understand the ever-present shadow of Hitler, one has to cast a glance at the difficult birth of the First Republic.

*Always "under observation"*

The book by the respected Austrian historian Manfried Rauchensteiner on the history of Austria since 1918 bears the

## AUSTRIA BEHIND THE MASK

unusual title *Under Observation*. The author explains in the introduction that after the collapse of the Dual Monarchy, Austria "went from being a European necessity to an elusive remnant, from an indispensability to an embarrassment".[1] The turbulent history of the failed First Republic and the successful Second Republic (which I was able to witness from the beginning of my stay in 1957) confirms his basic thesis: "From day one, the country was under observation. And it was not only friendly glances with which Austria was viewed. Concern, suspicion, pity, mistrust and greed were mixed with indifference, contentment and goodwill". From my own experience and observations, in the case of neighbouring Hungary, Czechoslovakia and Yugoslavia, countries that only gained their freedom in 1989, I would also add their citizens' envy of the prosperity and the fear of the then communist rulers of the example of the economically flourishing liberal democracy on the other side of the Iron Curtain.

The beginning of the direct and undisguised paternal control of the First Republic, which slid into hyperinflation in 1922, was marked by the loan of the League of Nations. Federal Chancellor Ignaz Seipel of the Christian Social Party had been able to convince the victorious powers of the consequences of an Austrian catastrophe. Great Britain, France, Italy and Czechoslovakia granted Austria a bond of 650 million gold crowns with a term of 20 years in October 1922. The League of Nations, which was liable for the sum to be raised, had attached the toughest conditions to this. The Dutch Commissioner General Alfred Rudolph Zimmerman, appointed by the League of Nations, had to supervise the whole issue at the head of the control committee of the donor countries. Austria had to accept a 20-year ban on annexation to Germany and pledge its tobacco monopoly and customs revenues as collateral for the bond. The radical austerity measures for rehabilitation included the dismissal of about 100,000 state employees, the restriction of health insurance, the increase of school and college fees, the closure of dispensable post offices and district courts, the restriction of trade promotion and unemployment insurance, the reduction of pensions and the partial abolition of tenant protection.

As spokesman for the Social Democrats, Otto Bauer described this form of international supervision as "foreign domination"; Austria had become a "colony of the Entente". However, the bond created the conditions for rehabilitation and, from 1 January 1925, the introduction of the new currency, the schilling. The first bailout was not large enough to permanently secure economic and social stabilisation. In 1932, the League of Nations was prepared to grant a new loan of 300 million schillings. One of the conditions was again the prohibition of annexation.

In addition, the country was again placed under supervision. Another Dutchman, Meinoud Rost van Tonningen, was to watch over the use of the money until 1936. As a result of the financial stabilisation, the schilling became so strong that it was called the "alpine dollar". The social consequences of the extraordinarily strict conditions of the League of Nations bonds were devastating and contributed significantly to intensified conflicts between the political camps against the looming shadow of the Third Reich. The second bailout package was approved in parliament only by a razor-thin majority of 81 to 80 votes. The radicalisation of the domestic political climate reached its climax in 1934 with the civil war and the establishment of the Austrofascist dictatorship by Federal Chancellor Engelbert Dollfuß.[2]

Incidentally, Austria repaid the League of Nations bonds. From 1923 to 1938 all interest and instalments due were paid on time. After the Anschluss, Nazi Germany confiscated the money and gold reserves of the Austrian National Bank, but stopped the payments. After the Second World War, democratic Austria was called upon at a conference of creditor states to settle the outstanding payments on the League of Nations bonds. These were largely repaid by 1973 and the remainder settled in 1980. Thus, although it took almost 60 years, none of the creditors lost on the loan.

The "Anschluss", the annexation to the Third Reich, turned the paternalism from the symbolic into the true eradication of Austria through the establishment of the so-called "Alpine and Danube Provinces". After Austria's rebirth in 1945, the country was divided into four occupation zones, but unlike Germany, free elections were also held in the Soviet occupation zone, thanks primarily to the statesmanship of President Karl Renner. The four-power occupation ended after 10 years. The State Treaty of 15 May 1955 permanently sealed Austria's independence and tightened the ban on annexation to Germany that had been imposed in 1919, 1922 and 1932. The Soviet government blocked Austria's full membership in the European Economic Community several times, alternately referring to neutrality and to the State Treaty, Article 4 of which prohibited Austria from joining Germany, including economically. And so, it is not surprising that Austria had to negotiate membership in the European Community for three decades. After the federal government had requested the opening of negotiations on membership in July 1989, the former Belgian Foreign Minister Mark Eyskens even reacted with the flippant suggestion that the European Community should now negotiate with the Soviet Union about Austrian neutrality. Austria finally became a member of the European Union in 1995, four years after the collapse of the Soviet Union.

Without this recollection of the past, when Austria was repeatedly subjected to critical scrutiny and paternalism, many things would be incomprehensible in the vicissitudes of the Second Republic's history, which was so successful on the whole, and in the consequences of observation, which can still be felt today. Events since the State Treaty have confirmed Manfried Rauchensteiner's assessment several times:

# HITLER'S SHADOW, YESTERDAY AND TODAY

The country was out of the woods. The embarrassment had suddenly become a factor of stability. One thing, however, remained the same: every time something happened in Austria, the country was under observation. And even then when nothing happened. Again and again it was seen as a problem zone, then again as a special case, as a model pupil and several times as the bad boy who should be watched very closely.[3]

## *Kurt Waldheim: balance sheet of a crisis*

I briefly return now to the time when people were racking their brains over whether Austrian President Kurt Waldheim, former Foreign Minister and twice-elected Secretary General of the United Nations, was rightly or wrongly accused of being a Nazi and a potential war criminal in the Second World War. The so-called Waldheim scandal remains perhaps the best evidence of how breathtakingly fast a shift can occur between highs and lows in the reputation of a country and its international figurehead. As the Austrian historian Michael Gehler noted, "There is only one head of state in the history of Europe about whose retention in office an international commission of historians tried to decide: it was about the wartime past of Federal President Kurt Waldheim, elected in 1986 with an absolute majority".[4] The entry ban imposed by the United States in April 1987 without evidence (not lifted until his death in 2007—he was put on the "watch list") on a sitting head of state who was elected in free elections and a former UN Secretary General was also unprecedented. All protests were of no avail; in 1992 Waldheim renounced his candidacy for a second term.

The man who had symbolised world conscience for 10 years as UN Secretary General was both directly and indirectly associated with Nazi war crimes all over the world, and Austria was identified with him or with the accusations made against him that were never proven. Younger generations can hardly imagine what the dynamics of this campaign achieved worldwide. In lectures about contemporary history, I sometimes told three stories from three countries to illustrate the sentiment. Wiltshire, a county in the heart of southern England: my English wife Margaret is asked at the hotel reception, after announcing her place of residence, in a tone of dry British humour: "You live in Vienna; did you also vote for Waldheim?"; Washington, DC: talking to the Indian taxi driver during a long drive to the residence of the Austrian ambassador, he asks me in a friendly way: "You are from Austria? You have a problem there with Waldheim, don't you?"; Istanbul: late at night at a dinner on the sidelines of a conference of the International Press Institute, the tipsy host, a Turkish publisher, attacks me jokingly "And you Austrians, with a known war criminal at home, keep accusing us of the Armenian thing!"

The international commission of historians appointed by the Austrian government announced in February 1988 that Waldheim had not personally been involved in any war crimes; he had, however, known what he denied knowing. His statement about the "fulfilment of duty" in the German Wehrmacht (later regretted and withdrawn) and his alleged ignorance of the war atrocities in the Balkans (for example, the deportation of Greek Jews from Salonika), which no one believed, had also caused widespread indignation. Heinz Fischer, as President of Federal Parliament, pronounced at the farewell ceremony for Waldheim at the end of his term of office that "injustice was done to the man and the Federal President Kurt Waldheim when he was accused of actions—even war crimes—which, according to all historical evidence, including the expert opinion of a high-ranking commission of historians, he did not commit". Waldheim's testament, published the day after his death, stated: "I deeply regret that I (...) took a comprehensive and unequivocal stand on Nazi crimes far too late".

The most informed account of the sad history of the Waldheim case can be found, interestingly enough, in Simon

# HITLER'S SHADOW, YESTERDAY AND TODAY

Wiesenthal's memoirs. What he relates in the chapter devoted to Waldheim confirms the assumption that the Social Democrat (SPÖ) election strategists or journalists and eyewitnesses close to them worked hand in hand with the top officials of the World Jewish Congress, who were blinded by the arrogance of ignorance, to detonate the "Waldheim bomb". Wiesenthal, who from beginning to end held the opinion that Waldheim was neither a Nazi nor a war criminal, was deliberately ignored by the masterminds of the campaign and later received foul-mouthed attacks and was even suspected of complicity with Waldheim and the Austrian People's Party (ÖVP).

As Vienna correspondent of the *Financial Times*, and later editor in chief and director of the Austrian Broadcasting Corporation (ORF), I knew the political actors of this drama well, above all Waldheim himself and Federal Chancellor Fred Sinowatz. Sinowatz indirectly became a political victim of the scandal because of an unfortunate and judicially confirmed "saga" about Waldheim's "brown past", which he denied. Be that as it may, the line from Hitler to Waldheim and later to the triad Hitler-Waldheim-Haider on the occasion of the EU sanctions ordered against the black-blue coalition was born at that time. It has also become an almost unavoidable accompaniment up to the present day whenever resentments going back a long way are brought up. The conclusion of the State Treaty with the Austrian nationalisation of the "German property" returned by the Russians without compensation for the German owners provoked the German Chancellor Konrad Adenauer to make the well-known statement that one would answer Austrian claims against Germany by restituting the bones of Adolf Hitler to Austria. This was later accompanied by accusations from German Social Democrats that Austria had swindled its way through common history and had succeeded in making Beethoven an Austrian and Hitler a German.

Particularly in view of these classic insinuations, which are also occasionally registered to this day, as well as of lapses by radical right-wing functionaries of the Freedom Party of Austria (FPÖ) and the Alternative for Germany, I find it important to emphasise at this point the characterisation of Hitler written by authoritative historians. For example, in his biography of Hitler, Peter Longerich, the internationally renowned expert on National Socialism, described him as "a person who, until the end of the First World War, was nothing more than a meaningless nobody" whose political career began in Munich in 1919.[5] After her analysis of Hitler's influence on the "capital of the Habsburg Empire, which he hated", the historian Brigitte Hamann drew the following conclusion: "Hitler's career cannot be derived, let alone understood from the conditions in Vienna. It was only in the Germany of the Weimar Republic that this Austrian made his career. He returned to Austria in March 1938 as up to then undoubtedly successful German Reich Chancellor".[6]

The Austrian writer Joseph Roth had memorably answered the question: Who owns Hitler? He had clashed often with German emigrants in Paris, after they had repeatedly reproached him, saying that Hitler was, after all, an Austrian: "With us Hitler could become nothing—with us he was a little rascal. With you he became great". Friedrich Heer, quotes this statement, adding: "I gave the same answer to my German friends then and later". Heer dedicates the last chapter to this great writer who died in Paris in May 1938, an "Austrian who was almost everything one could be as an Austrian patriot: Socialist, close to Social Democracy, close to Communism, legitimist, Catholic, Jew: Joseph Roth".[7]

I also ask myself whether, with 50 million dead from war and genocide that was caused by a dictator and his criminal regime that held power for 12 years in Germany and 7 years in Austria, the division of the periods in the formation of his personality could be so decisive. Between the millions of convinced National Socialists, willing helpers and opportunistic followers who served the "Führer" submissively until the end, there were hardly any

# HITLER'S SHADOW, YESTERDAY AND TODAY

differences, whether they lived in the German Reich or in the "Ostmark". Things differ between the two countries, however, when it comes to the consequences in post-war history and coming to terms with the Nazi era.

For me, precisely for this reason, the solemn and symbolic dedication of the Shoah Wall of Names in Vienna's Ostarrichipark on 9 November 2021 represented a very special highlight in the long process of remembrance work in Austria. The names of 64,440 murdered Jewish children, women and men from Austria are immortalised on the 160 Indian granite slabs, each over two metres high, which stand in an oval shape around a patch of lawn with trees. When I read the names with the respective year of birth below them—rows of names such as Polacsek and Leimdörfer—I had the eerie feeling that my grandparents and aunts, uncles and cousins, my 29 relatives from Transylvania, Slovakia and Budapest, of similar names, who disappeared without a trace, were also remembered there.

Whenever I stand in front of monuments or memorials in Vienna or in the small towns of Gunskirchen or Rechnitz, my own experience confirms what the philosopher Friedrich Nietzsche once pointed out: "Only what does not stop hurting remains in the memory".[8] This is probably why for us, the still living contemporary witnesses, the classic formula "remember, repress, forget" does not usually apply.

The walls of names recall the often-shown images from TV documentaries, the photos and books about the acts of violence against the Jews in the days of March 1938 after the Anschluss, welcomed by the vast majority of the population, and also the indelible image of Heldenplatz, where Hitler announced the return of his homeland to the German Reich in front of an immense, cheering crowd estimated to be 250,000 people. The German playwright Carl Zuckmayer wrote in his memoirs about the terrorist actions and the pogrom atmosphere as a prelude to the annihilation of the Jewish community, which numbered around 200,000, through murder and expulsion over the next few years:

> That evening all hell broke loose (... What was unleashed here was the uprising of envy, resentment, bitterness, blind, malicious vindictiveness—and all other voices were condemned to silence.... The dull masses, their blind destructiveness, and their hatred were directed against everything refined by nature or spirit. It was a coven of the mob and a burial of all human values.

Countless personal stories of those affected or of their descendants confirmed Zuckmayer's observation: "The underworld had opened its gates and let loose its lowest, most hideous, most impure spirits".[9]

After the decades of fomented anti-Semitism, the persecution of the Jews was accepted by the vast majority of Austrians and probably approved of in many cases—similar to what happened a few years later in neighbouring central and Eastern European countries. Weren't the demons that erupted from the popular soul of Budapest in 1944, which I witnessed as a 15-year-old, just as terrifying as those in Vienna in 1938?

*Late confrontation*

However, it must be emphasised that, in contrast to Hungary or Poland, the dark years in Austria are now being dealt with in an exemplary manner by scholars with official support. Suffice it to refer here to the 1,167-page anthology *Antisemitism in Austria 1933–1938*, published in 2018.[10] In this book, all facets of the "creeping", the "concealed", the "mendacious" anti-Semitism in the years of Austrofascism are analysed and consistently established as "precursors for the brutal extermination through the Nazi anti-Semitism".

The fact that the Nazi regime also meant a state-sponsored, systematic and organised robbery and theft of Jewish property through Aryanisation and coercive measures in Austria, and that this was eagerly supported unhesitatingly to the last moment between 1938 and 1945 by a huge crowd of willing helpers and opportunistic hangers-on, could only be learned by the next generations and the general public, after a delay of 40 to 50 years. The so-called victim myth was destroyed only later as a result of the Waldheim affair, to be discussed subsequently. Under the cloak of blanket distancing from Hitler's Germany, with reference to the proof of innocence provided by the State Treaty, the full truth about Austria's own past was kept under wraps for far too long.

The history of the Shoah Wall of Names is also impressive proof of how strong the silence and repression are in Austria, even in the twenty-first century, and how long it takes for the political elite to face the past with all its horrors. The astonishing thing about the government policy, so often prone to mendacious self-sanctification, was that it was prepared to credit one person alone, namely the 91-year-old Holocaust survivor Kurt Yakov Tutter, for the erection of the Shoah Wall of Names.

A native of Vienna, who has lived in Canada since 1948 and is a retired computer scientist, fought for this memorial for over 20 years.[11]

He had fled to Belgium with his family in 1939. Three years later, during a raid by the German Wehrmacht on their flat in Brussels, 12-year-old Yakuv and his little sister were hidden at the last minute by their mother in an attic room. After many dangerous situations, the children eventually ended up with a Catholic family in Ghent; their parents were murdered in Auschwitz. The idea for a memorial wall occurred to Tutter on a trip to Brussels in 1974, when he visited the memorial that had been erected there shortly before. Here, among the 26,000 names engraved on granite slabs, were the names of his parents as well as those of 800 other Austrians who had sought refuge in Belgium and were deported from there.

## AUSTRIA BEHIND THE MASK

In his speech at the ceremonial opening of the Wall of Names on 9 November 2021, on the eighty-third anniversary of the November pogroms, and in interviews, Tutter made no secret of the fact that he had long met with great disinterest on the part of the city and the federal government with his efforts for the memorial: "In Austria, the authorities had for many years been more concerned with concealing the atrocities of the Shoah and presenting themselves as the first victims of fascism. A memorial for murdered Jews was therefore undesirable".

It was only in the commemorative year of 2018 that his plan fell on receptive ears. Tutter had written to Federal Chancellor Sebastian Kurz at the beginning of 2018 to ask for support. After talks in the Chancellor's Office, Kurz decided that the federal government would finance the bulk of the 5.3 million euros total cost. The decision was supported by all parties and the provinces. The implementation of the memorial began in November 2018 and was completed in autumn 2021.

In retrospect, it also seems particularly important to me that at the inauguration all official speakers openly acknowledged the failures of the past without any ifs or buts and paid tribute to Kurt Yakov Tutter's pioneering initiative. The fact that Ronald S. Lauder, President of the World Jewish Congress and US Ambassador to Vienna 1986–1987, in his message in the printed programme for the inauguration of the Shoah Wall of Names even described Austria as a "pioneer in preventing and combating anti-Semitism in Europe" and explicitly praised the measures taken to remember the victims of National Socialism, is noteworthy because he had previously reminded the audience of the "very late acceptance of responsibility for the Shoah". Other Jewish personalities, such as the presidents of important institutions like the European Jewish Congress and Yad Vashem, also emphasised in their greetings Austria's contribution to the Europe-wide fight against Jew-hatred.

# HITLER'S SHADOW, YESTERDAY AND TODAY

The belated confrontation with the past is also reflected in the farewell to the victim myth in the redesign of the memorial site in Auschwitz, which was originally erected in 1978. The new memorial displayed Austria's complicity and responsibility in the crimes of National Socialism. At the opening of the new exhibition on 4 October 2021, Federal President Alexander Van der Bellen, accompanied by a large, high-ranking delegation, declared:

> Auschwitz did not fall from the sky. Anti-Semitism and racism had been "very present" in Austrian society even before March 1938. The ground was prepared, the seed sown—and sprouted. Even though Austria no longer existed as a state, but had been part of the so-called Third Reich as the "Ostmark", many people from our country were among the perpetrators of this extermination programme, partly in leading positions.[12]

*From historical memory to historical consciousness*

Despite the sincere confessions about the past, even today one must be afraid of stumbling over all that has been swept under the carpet in this country for so many years. For example, the newspaper *Der Standard* reported on the eve of the ceremonial opening of the Shoah Wall of Names that a company whose former owner had employed Hungarian-Jewish forced labourers in 1944 was also involved in the construction of the foundations of the stone tablets on which the names of those murdered were engraved.[13] The current management of the company, which was founded almost 150 years ago, had never dealt with this chapter of the company's chronicle, it said. The paper quoted the words of Wolfgang Sobotka, President of Parliament on the occasion of the start of construction: "Whoever does not face history, history faces him".

There were also critical voices both on the aesthetics of the Wall of Names and on the fact that there had been neither a call for tenders nor a social debate in the run-up to the construction. The writer Doron Rabinovici and other critics also complained about the absence of the names of the murdered Roma and other victim groups. Since the decision on the project had been taken in March 2018 by the ÖVP–FPÖ coalition government, accusations of instrumentalisation were also raised. In any case, Kurt Yakov Tutter was probably right when after his decades-long struggle for the Wall of Names he indignantly rejected as "cheap contempt" the various accusations raised under the protection of anonymity.

Rabinovici wrote, among other things: "The Freedom Party probably thought they could use the commemoration to forget how deeply rooted was anti-Semitism in their party". Similar criticism was triggered in 2017–19 by the trips of Chancellor Kurz and FPÖ Vice-Chancellor H-C Strache to Jerusalem. In this context, with regard to the strange legacy of this coalition, I would like to quote the great German poet Friedrich Schiller (1759–1805): "... that the selfish man may pursue base ends, but unconsciously promotes noble ones".[14]

I characterised the large compensation package, passed by the ÖVP–FPÖ coalition government under Federal Chancellor Wolfgang Schüssel, for former forced labourers and Holocaust victims in 2000–1 with the same quote in my previous book on Austria. Without that ÖVP–FPÖ government, however, hardly any MPs would have approved the belated but all the more important international Washington Agreement. After all, the reconciliation fund law passed in July 2000 was for a total amount of 436 million euros. Stuart E. Eizenstat, the chief US representative at the negotiations with Austria on the "settlement of issues of compensation and restitution for victims of National Socialism", which resulted in the so-called "Washington Agreement" in 2001, wrote in his book *Imperfect Justice*: "Schüssel was confident that he could strengthen the moderates in the FPÖ by giving them a stake in power and thus isolate them from the radical wing of their party. Subsequent events proved that he was right".[15]

# HITLER'S SHADOW, YESTERDAY AND TODAY

I will come back to the radical right tendencies in the FPÖ and the role of the so-called Burschenschaften (Fraternities) in a later chapter. What mattered for me 20 years ago, and matters now, are not the motives in the decision-making by the ÖVP-FPÖ coalition governments, but their results and their longer-term effects. The dismal record of dealing with the Nazi past and its historical roots teaches us that we must turn historical *memory* into an Austrian historical *consciousness*. It is precisely the encounter with the Shoah Wall of Names and other memorials that reminds us of the words written by the German scholar, Harald Weinrich: "You would like to forget, but you are not allowed to".[16]

The fact that on the very day of the inauguration of the Shoah Wall of Names, the authorities announced for the third time in a year the discovery of a huge weapons cache and neo-Nazi materials underlines the great danger stemming from the extreme right-wing milieu. Ten days later, in a concerted action, 20 right-wing extremists had their houses searched in seven provinces. All of them were charged with neo-Nazi activities. Without underestimating the threat of Islamist terror, the fight against the networks of old and new neo-Nazis, who used the coronavirus demonstrations as a stage, must be intensified nationally and internationally. The reports on the mass demonstrations show how people repeatedly compare themselves to Holocaust victims, wear Stars of David or compare coronavirus vaccines to Zyklon B, the nerve agent used in Auschwitz, on social networks. The flourishing conspiracy theories, only some of them Israel-related, have acted as catalysts for Jew-hatred since the beginning of the pandemic. The Jewish community reports a rapid increase in various incidents, especially as a result of the coronavirus demonstrations. In the first half of 2021 alone, there were 562 incidents, twice as many as in the same period the previous year. According to the report, the number of unreported cases is also likely to have increased.[17]

# AUSTRIA BEHIND THE MASK

"The womb is still fertile from which this crawled!" These final words by the German poet Bertolt Brecht in the epilogue to his play *The Unstoppable Rise of Arturo Ui* are still relevant today. The reason why I do not have exclusively negative expectations despite worrying statistics and despite incidents that have become internationally known, such as the damage and destruction of several portrait photos of Holocaust survivors at an exhibition on Vienna's Ringstraße or an act of vandalism against the mobile Jewish prayer house erected by artists in Innsbruck, is as follows: In contrast to the decades of repression and concealment before the ground-breaking speech by Federal Chancellor Franz Vranitzky on Austria's complicity in July 1991, official Austria today professes unreservedly, without ifs and buts, to work on the indispensable memory and to close ranks with the small Jewish community and civil society on a "National Strategy against Anti-Semitism". The 180-page catalogue of measures published at the beginning of 2021 is an impressive and credible proof of this.

4

# THE ROLLERCOASTER RIDE OF THE FPÖ
## FROM FRIEDRICH PETER TO JÖRG HAIDER

The first visit of an Austrian head of government to Czechoslovakia since the Second World War, in February 1976, was, in the words of Chancellor Kreisky "a special event", far more than a superficial protocol event. The Chancellor began his impromptu dinner speech at the banquet with a personal remark: "For someone who is already so old that he can still remember the time when we all lived in one and the same state, tonight and this whole stay in Prague is an event of a special kind". Alluding to the dispute over who played Smetana or Mozart better, the Austrian musicians or the Czechoslovakians, he spoke of a "musical closeness in which we find ourselves". However, the conflicts that broke out between Prague and Vienna the very next year because of the brutal repression of the human rights movement Charter 77 confirmed Kreisky's warning at the end of the same speech: "This must not remain a policy of fine words, it must be a policy of sober deeds".[1]

In front of the Austrian officials and the journalists reporting on his trip, the Chancellor reminisced about the year 1934, for example, when as a young socialist activist he had witnessed a meeting in this city between Otto Bauer, the exiled leader of the Austrian Socialists, and the Soviet theoretician Nikolai Bukharin (later executed after a Stalinist show trial). He also recalled his first post-war stay on the way from Stockholm to Vienna, when the Austrian legation in Prague was besieged by thousands of Austrians who wanted to return home. As with almost every visit Bruno Kreisky made to the then communist-ruled countries of the Soviet sphere of power, the amusing and the macabre lay close together, the change from comedy to tragedy was abrupt.

For me, the excursion of the Austrian government delegation to the Theresienstadt concentration camp has remained an indelible experience even after almost five decades. The delegation was large; apart from numerous journalists, the Chancellor was accompanied by the governors of Burgenland, Lower and Upper Austria, and the heads of the three parliamentary groups (Social Democrat (SPÖ), Austrian People's Party (ÖVP) and Freedom Party of Austria (FPÖ)).

But only two men carried the burden of the past here, invisible but omnipresent, in their luggage. Bruno Kreisky visited the concentration camp and incinerators of Theresienstadt, where among the 43,000 victims and the 90,000 deported to the Auschwitz extermination camp were 6,182 Austrian Jews, including close relatives of his. Controlled, but obviously deeply affected, he stood at the centre of the hosts' attention and laid wreaths.

Also standing there, pale and but showing no emotions, with his wife discreetly in the background, was Friedrich Peter, Chairman of the FPÖ. He did his service as Obersturmführer with the 10th Regiment of the 1st SS Infantry Brigade, which committed numerous war crimes at the time when Jews, as well as many anti-fascists of non-Jewish origin, were deported to Theresienstadt. Shortly before, Simon Wiesenthal, the director of the Jewish Documentation Centre, had revealed this fact at a

# THE ROLLERCOASTER RIDE OF THE FPÖ

press conference, provoking years of passionate debate with Kreisky and the SPÖ. Many felt it would have been more tactful and dignified if the FPÖ chairman had not been present.

There were weird moments: a German cameraman shadowed Peter in whichever direction he turned to film his facial expression. All this took place in the courtyard of the camp complex. Some young Austrian reporters visibly enjoyed Peter's discomfort. The remembrance of the tragic fate of Jewish victims merged with a painful episode of Austrian domestic politics.

Peter told me at the reception in Prague that evening that the Federal Chancellor had advised him to accompany him despite the press attacks. Kreisky explicitly confirmed this to me and added: "Where did the allegedly new evidence against Peter disappear?" The FPÖ chairman, boycotted by the journalists in Prague, complained bitterly in conversation with me: "Your colleagues treat me as a leper, although I had led my party away from Nazism to democracy!" In his memoirs, Heinz Fischer wrote that Friedrich Peter had been "deeply impressed and affected" by the visit to the concentration camp. He added that "his attitude to democracy, Second Republic and especially also to the crimes of the Hitler era was impeccable". At that time and afterward when talking to him, I was also convinced of his transformation into a democratic politician; admittedly, I had known nothing about the details of his service in the Waffen SS unit.[2]

*Verband der Unabhängigen, FPÖ: the founding years*

The outstanding, overarching theme in looking back on these experiences in Theresienstadt and Prague is the roller-coaster-like history of the FPÖ, the so-called "third camp", since the end of the Second World War. It has been full of twists and turns, of ups and downs and vicissitudes, which, especially since the year 2000, have happened at an increasingly rapid pace. The vicissitudes, from time to time with breath-taking moments, were always symbolised and marked by striking personalities, from Friedrich Peter to Jörg Haider, from Heinz-Christian Strache to Herbert Kickl.

One has to keep in mind the legal end of "denazification" in 1947 and the amnesty in 1948 to understand the wooing of the two big parties ÖVP and SPÖ for the votes of almost 500,000 new voters. The initiative to found a collective party of those excluded from the electoral process on account of their Nazi past since 1945 had been taken by two well-known journalists on the staff of the *Salzburger Nachrichten*, Viktor Reimann and Herbert Kraus, who professed to be "liberal". Both journalists owed their popularity to their criticism of the denazification measures and their advocacy of the less-incriminated National Socialists.

The "Verband der Unabhängigen" achieved great success in the 1949 parliamentary elections with 11.7 per cent of the valid votes (479,000 votes) and 16 mandates, especially in Upper Austria, Salzburg and Styria. After setbacks at the elections in 1953, conflicts between the so-called "nationalists" (i.e. the convinced former National Socialists) and the party leadership appearing as "liberal" split the Verband der Unabhängigen and finally led to the founding of the FPÖ in 1956. The ousted leader Kraus spoke publicly of a "long prepared seizure of power by a small circle of right-wing extremists and Nazi leaders". He and Reimann resigned from the party. The election of the prominent National Socialist German Workers' Party (NSDAP) functionary and SS brigade general Anton Reinthaller, after many years in prison, as the first chairman of the FPÖ was a confirmation of the shift to the extreme right.

I would like to turn briefly to the enigmatic figure of Viktor Reimann (1915–96), who I got to know as spokesman of the state theatre administration and then as a long-time columnist for the mass circulation popular daily, the *Kronen Zeitung*. What seemed incomprehensible to me was the fact that someone who was sentenced to 10 years in prison for "preparation for high treason" in December 1943 and who completed 4 years of his sentence, nevertheless consistently expressed understanding for the Nazi regime and pan-German nationalist views both in politics as a Verband der Unabhängigen member of parliament (1949–56) and in his long post-war journalistic career. While it is true that Reimann joined the NSDAP as early as 1938, he had contact with the Catholic resistance group led by Roman Scholz, a priest friend of his. Scholz was executed as a resistance fighter in May 1944. Reimann's life was therefore not free of contradictions. Among these was his lifelong admiration for Bruno Kreisky. Almost at the same time as the presentation of the volume of essays on Kreisky written by me and Karl Heinz Ritschel, the editor-in-chief of the *Salzburger Nachrichten*, Reimann also presented a factual and sympathetic biography of Kreisky in autumn 1972. Almost two decades later, Reimann published a 40-page text in an anthology based on ten conversations with the seriously ill, half-paralysed and almost blind Kreisky during the last year of his life. This time, too, the author let his unbroken esteem for the Jewish statesman be known. But who can forget that in 1974 the same Viktor Reimann wrote a controversial, ambivalent series about "Jews in Austria" in 42 episodes in the mass newspaper *Kronen Zeitung*, which also triggered a flood of anti-Semitic letters to the editor? His special relationship with Kreisky can probably be interpreted only in psychological terms.

*Friedrich Peter: agile turncoat or genuine democrat?*

At this point, I return to the important political role of Friedrich Peter, who after Reinthaller's death was party chairman of the FPÖ from 1958 to 1978. The shifts in the political attitudes as well as in the personality of the FPÖ leader were profoundly influenced by his personal relationship with Bruno Kreisky as a Foreign Minister and then Federal Chancellor.

For his offensive South Tyrol policy, which ultimately laid the foundations for the agreement with Italy, Foreign Minister Kreisky (1959–66) also wanted to win the support of the opposition, and therefore informed the FPÖ about the most important foreign policy issues and also met Friedrich Peter from time to time. In the course of time, a closer contact developed between the two men. The Freedomite chairman, who came from an Upper Austrian social democratic family of railwaymen, may have convinced the foreign minister about his change from his Waffen SS past and pan-German nationalist sentiments to a sincere commitment to democracy, Austrian statehood and the Second Republic.

When the SPÖ under Kreisky's leadership surprisingly won the parliamentary elections in March 1970 with 81 seats to 78 ÖVP seats and 6 FPÖ seats, Chancellor Josef Klaus provided a second surprise. He stunned me and the other journalists present on election night in the large hall of the Ministry of the Interior and (secretly) outraged his Vice-Chancellor Hermann Withalm and many party grandees present when he, in front of the television cameras, succinctly rejected a "coalition of losers" (i.e. an option for the FPÖ). After all, an ÖVP–FPÖ coalition would have had 84 mandates against 81 for the SPÖ, but, Klaus said many years later in an interview, he would never have done that, it would have been "indecent".

With this unusually rapid and unequivocal renunciation, without consulting the party bodies (for Withalm it had been "like a bolt from the blue"), of a perfectly possible powerful card in the forthcoming coalition negotiations with the SPÖ, Klaus unconsciously and unintentionally set the course for 13 years of a single-party socialist government. On election night, Peter Jankowitsch, Kreisky's head of the cabinet office, telephoned the

# THE ROLLERCOASTER RIDE OF THE FPÖ

FPÖ leader to say that Kreisky wanted to meet with him. Peter appeared just before midnight at the already deserted SPÖ headquarters for a confidential four-eyes meeting with the election winner. There were no written agreements, but Kreisky reiterated, in response to my repeated questions as I wrote his biography, that there was an "informal understanding" about the possibility of an SPÖ minority government, tolerated by the FPÖ parliamentary group, in exchange for an electoral reform that would put an end to the disadvantage of the smaller parties. Both sides were true to their word: the FPÖ was rewarded with the long overdue electoral law reform in exchange for the promise to agree to the 1971 budget.

The Waffen-SS Obersturmführer with a dubious war past became a key figure of the Second Republic, twice shaping history at decisive moments. In 1970, Kreisky owed Peter his chancellorship. It was an irony of fate that the government participation dreamed of by the FPÖ leader vanished into thin air as a result of the absolute SPÖ majority in the early elections on 10 October 1971. Thanks to the electoral law reform, the FPÖ was at least able to increase the number of its mandates from 6 to 10 despite a stagnating share of the vote.

As a foreign correspondent, I was able to observe the upgrading of parliament and Peter's politics as FPÖ chairman and agree with the assessment of historian Friedrich Weissensteiner: "Friedrich Peter distinguished himself as an opposition politician and developed into a parliamentarian respected by all parties with trenchant, well-prepared and brilliantly delivered speeches".[3] He undoubtedly set liberal and pro-European markers despite pressure from the nationalist wing. As already mentioned, there had been considerable domestic controversy since 1975 over Simon Wiesenthal's revelations about Peter's role in the Nazi era. I have dealt with the alleged motives for Kreisky's passionate attacks against Wiesenthal and his partisanship on Peter's behalf at length in an earlier book.

For the second time, Peter set the course in domestic politics after the 1983 parliament elections, in which the SPÖ lost its absolute majority. Although he had not been party leader since 1978, he remained head of the FPÖ group in parliament and again played a decisive role together with Kreisky as architect of the first "red-blue" SPÖ–FPÖ coalition. At the head of the coalition government, however, were two other persons: Fred Sinowatz as Federal Chancellor and Norbert Steger as Vice-Chancellor from the FPÖ. His election as deputy president of the parliament failed because of his Nazi past: its mortgage and consequences "I carry to the edge of my grave", Peter said literally.

Peter's break with the party that he had led for two decades can be seen as part of his complex personality. After Jörg Haider's takeover of the party leadership in 1986, Peter withdrew from politics. Six years later he resigned from the party altogether because of Haider's "shameful gaffe" with his statement about the "proper employment policy in the Third Reich". "Nevertheless, it can be considered a historical merit of Friedrich Peter to have anchored the FPÖ and thus the third camp as a stable factor in Austrian domestic politics", states the official curriculum vitae on the website of the Freedom party. However, one must not forget that: "Kreisky was an important pace maker for the FPÖ. To put it bluntly, without Kreisky there would perhaps be no Haider today", I wrote at the time of the formation of the black-blue coalition government by Wolfgang Schüssel.[4]

*Jörg Haider: the virtuoso of demagogy*

The most successful and contradictory Freedomite party leader, Jörg Haider, was the one I knew best of all FPÖ politicians. Since 1990, I had the opportunity to meet him on two TV discussion programmes I chaired as well as several times in one-on-one conversations. In his rhetoric, in his political style, in his attitude towards consensus as the guiding principle of the Second Republic and above all in his attitude towards the Nazi past, he was a unique figure in Austria's post-war history. The political scientist Anton Pelinka aptly stated: "Haider was able to reconcile a pan-German Freedom Party with an Austrian patriotism without the core forces of pan-German nationalism—the Burschenschaften and Corps, the Turnvereine and Landsmannschaften—turning their backs on him because of it".[5] However, I do not at all share his view that he was merely a "political pause clown in Austrian politics". His political successes and his importance in setting the political course cannot be trivialised or merely attributed to exaggerated media coverage.

Haider, who was born in Bad Goisern in 1950, was able to double the votes for the FPÖ and increase the number of seats from 12 to 18 in the early elections called immediately after Chancellor Franz Vranitzky's break with the SPÖ–FPÖ coalition following Haider's seizure of the FPÖ leadership in the autumn of 1986. With his aggressive and uncompromising opposition policy, irrepressible energy, rhetorical brilliance and unhesitating agility, Haider was already then attacking non-stop migration policy and the excesses of the fossilised proportional representation system. The "postmodern Robin Hood" (Rudolf Burger) was able to increase his votes and mandates by leaps and bounds from election to election: from 9.73 per cent in 1986 to 16.63 per cent in 1990, to 22.5 per cent in 1994 and finally to a record 26.91 per cent of the popular vote in 1999. For the first (and so far the last time), the Haider party even received more votes than the ÖVP, albeit only by 415, and thus became the second strongest party after the SPÖ and soon after the ÖVP's partner in the coalition government formed by Wolfgang Schüssel.

It was an unprecedented and, for many observers, worrying rise of a right-wing populist party internationally discredited for right-wing extremist and Nazi nostalgic slips. Coming from a

Nazi family and raised in a radical right-wing student milieu, Haider catered to the shrinking group of old Nazis and the steadily growing group of radical xenophobes with numerous faux pas, from praising the "proper employment policy in the Third Reich" to a speech for Waffen SS veterans that hailed them as "decent people who have character", to playing down the Nazi extermination camps, which he described in parliament as "punishment camps". The "anti-foreigner petition" he invented received 416,531 signatures in January 1993 and provoked the "sea of lights" at Heldenplatz, with around 300,000 demonstrators holding candles against xenophobia; the largest political rally in the history of the Second Republic.

At the same time, Heide Schmidt, former General Secretary and deputy of Haider, FPÖ presidential candidate in 1992 and Third President of the Parliament, and four other MPs broke with the FPÖ for reasons of principle. They founded the pro-European Liberal Forum which, after initial successes, failed to clear the four per cent hurdle in the 1999 general elections.

The setting up of the ÖVP–FPÖ coalition on 4 February 2000 was an unprecedented success for ÖVP chairman Wolfgang Schüssel who, thanks to a deal with Haider, became Chancellor despite his party's third place in the election, despite his threat of going into opposition if the ÖVP became number three and also despite the public disapproval by Federal President Thomas Klestil. At the same time, the black-blue coalition of course meant a personal triumph for Jörg Haider, although he also remained as governor in Carinthia out of consideration for how it appeared internationally. Nevertheless, he led the coalition negotiations for the Freedomites and appeared alongside Schüssel at the press conference for international media (rather than the designated Vice-Chancellor Susanne Riess-Passer) to announce the coalition deal.

In my previous book on Austria,[6] I dealt in detail with the consequences of the outrage at home and abroad caused by the

## THE ROLLERCOASTER RIDE OF THE FPÖ

coalition with the Haider party and the temporary symbolic sanctions of the other 14 EU states. I also quoted there my statements in print and in television interviews condemning the hypocritical, unjustified and counterproductive international measures taken against Austria. Above all, I wanted to emphasise that Haider had won not because of anti-Semitic statements but as a result of his justified, albeit often unscrupulous attacks against the mendacity and corruption due to the fossilised proportional share out of positions under the SPÖ–ÖVP coalition system. Thus, by 1999, thanks to this virtuoso of demagogy, the FPÖ had won the majority of the working class and almost half of all voters under 30 years old. The hysterical demonisation of a provincial politician and his supporters worked to the benefit of those it was actually meant to harm.

*Soaring and crashing*

In retrospect, seven years later in a long conversation with me, Haider saw the formation of the black-blue government as "certainly the greatest success of my political life, becoming stronger than the ÖVP and achieving from the position of strength a government participation". Why then, after their "greatest victory" within two and a half years, did he and his party suffer, as early as November 2002, the greatest defeat of a political party in the history of the Second Republic—a crash from 27 per cent to 10 per cent and the loss of two thirds of their 1999 voters?

The architect of the defeat was the same politician who had made the turnaround possible in the first place, namely Jörg Haider. At the time, he told me in his casual way, that his decisive mistake had only been the handing over of the FPÖ party chair to Vice-Chancellor Susanne Riess-Passer after the electoral victory in February 2000. "It had been just too much for her to lead the government faction and the party", Haider said with apparently unbroken self-confidence.

After two decades, one has to recall the prehistory of this dramatic turn of events. Already in February 2002, the inner-party rift had become evident when Haider, without saying a word to the FPÖ cabinet ministers, flew to Baghdad and met Saddam Hussein, at exactly the same time as Riess-Passer made her first official visit to Washington. This was followed by the sharp criticism of the ministers of his own party under a flimsy pretext. On 1 September 2002, a Saturday, internal tensions reached a climax at a meeting of FPÖ delegates loyal to Haider in the small Styrian town of Knittelfeld. On the following Sunday evening, Vice-Chancellor Riess-Passer, Minister of Finance Karl-Heinz Grasser and FPÖ parliamentary group chairman Peter Westenthaler announced their resignation in front of TV cameras. Schüssel reacted immediately by terminating the coalition with the FPÖ and set the course for new elections. The ÖVP won the biggest election victory in its history, jumping from 27 to 42 per cent and gaining 800,000 votes. For the first time since 1966, the ÖVP was again the strongest party and increased the number of its seats from 52 to 79, while the FPÖ shrank from 52 to 18 mandates. Never before had a party been able to win so much at a parliamentary election as the ÖVP, and never before had a grouping lost so much as the FPÖ.

Before and after the demolition of the black-blue coalition, Haider repeatedly played with fire and took destructive actions. These included the founding of the new party BZÖ (Alliance for the Future of Austria) in 2005 and the break with the FPÖ. The fact that he was still able to win over many people, especially in Carinthia, despite astounding negligence and repeated capers, was shown by his success in the 2004 provincial elections with 42.5 per cent of the vote and the tripling of the BZÖ seats in parliament in the 2008 parliamentary elections. At 58, Haider once again projected a completely new image: he seemed almost statesmanlike, not as ruthlessly aggressive as his new rival at the

# THE ROLLERCOASTER RIDE OF THE FPÖ

head of the FPÖ, Heinz-Christian Strache, who was almost 20 years younger.

Back to the question: why did Jörg Haider blow up the coalition he initially praised so effusively? Over the years I have talked to him and his closest associates, as well as to Wolfgang Schüssel and other observers, about his possible motives in order to plumb the depths of this torn personality. At the time, Schüssel and Riess-Passer, in line with the majority of commentators, said that Haider had not been able to stand the popularity advantage of the FPÖ representatives he had appointed, Riess-Passer and the young star at the time, Finance Minister Karl-Heinz Grasser. Riess-Passer added that Haider had been a "brilliant opposition politician", with "provocation and polarisation" as decisive features.

I, too, have experienced this dazzling and contradictory personality at several encounters in various phases of his meteoric rise and abrupt fall. In private conversations, Haider always seemed sympathetic, interested and respectful. Once, after an event in the Carinthian capital, we flew to Vienna together and he questioned me at length about the situation in Bosnia and Kosovo. There is no doubt that he sometimes played down the Nazi past in Austria; he was a ruthless populist, but not a neo-Nazi. I met him for the last time in Klagenfurt's largest bookshop, "Heyn", in the autumn of 2007 at the presentation of my book on Austria. I had personally left an invitation for him with the porter of the provincial government. To general astonishment, he appeared shortly after the event began. After the discussion, I presented him with a copy of the book with a dedication. He stayed longer over a glass of red wine, and after talking to me, he chatted with people in a dazzling mood. I recalled that Haider had told me that he had seriously wanted to become an actor in his early youth. He always played the game in different roles—gambler and provocateur, taboo breaker in an encrusted system and symbol of an aggressive narcissism, still with a youthful image and great skill.

Barely a year after our last meeting, on Saturday 11 October 2008, governor Jörg Haider drove home alone and drunk at 1:15 am at 142 km/h, twice as fast as permitted on this stretch of road near Klagenfurt. His car went off the road and overturned. Observers saw in his death a "cruel inner logic" of his always "restless and restless life". He had died as he had lived: "Always full throttle, always over the limit. He was the greatest political genius since Kreisky, but also the greatest possible destroyer", the various obituaries said.

The night-time tragedy shook the whole country, especially Carinthia. The funeral service a week later, broadcast live by ORF, was attended by 25,000 people, including the social democratic Federal President and all the country's leading politicians. Diocesan Bishop Egon Kapellari paid tribute to the deceased at the requiem in Klagenfurt Cathedral, saying he had been "a person on fire". Chancellor Alfred Gusenbauer paid "respect and tribute" to Haider at the public ceremony. His successors as provincial governor (Gerhard Dörfler) and as BZÖ leader (Uwe Scheuch) promised: "We will take care of your Carinthia".

Quite apart from the fact that Haider's legacy also included the enormous scandal surrounding the Hypo Alpe Adria banking group, both successors, Dörfler and Scheuch, were sentenced to terms of 8 and 6 months' conditional imprisonment, respectively, and fines for embezzlement and taking advantage. As far as the "hero worship" with which Haider was sometimes treated after his death is concerned, perhaps Werner A. Perger (himself Austrian) put it best in his commentary in the German weekly, *Die Zeit*:

> "In the hours and days after Haider's accident, political dignitaries of the republic and journalists who consider themselves as such lied more unrestrainedly in Austria than ever before (...). The high point or rather low point of this hype of the obituaries was the emotion

# THE ROLLERCOASTER RIDE OF THE FPÖ

with which they declared Jörg Haider to be the exceptional figure of Austrian politics and elevated him to the same level as Bruno Kreisky".[7]

Perger, who is also the author of a biography of Kreisky, added, "The only permissible analogy is the fact that both were well-known and effective beyond the borders of their country. One as a democrat, the other as a demagogue".

5

# SCHÜSSEL'S DANGEROUS EXPERIMENT

Perhaps the most significant political difference so far between Germany and Austria has been the treatment of the extreme right. In Germany, after the "refugee autumn" of 2015, the Alternative for Germany, founded in 2013 and now dominated by right-wing populists and right-wing extremists, experienced an enormous upswing in votes in the following years. It now has strong parliamentary groups in the Bundestag and the state parliaments. Nevertheless, it has not yet been represented in any government.

In Austria, however, as already mentioned, the Freedom Party of Austria (FPÖ) became socially acceptable through the Kreisky–Peter Pact in 1970 and, after the Social Democrat (SPÖ) party losing its absolute majority in 1983, even became "fit for government" again thanks to Kreisky. The Freedom Party, with Norbert Steger (who for a time was considered a liberal figurehead) as Vice-Chancellor and Minister of Trade, also provided the Minister of Justice and the Minister of Defence and three Secretaries of State. The "liberal interlude", which even led to the admission of the FPÖ to the Liberal International in 1979, finally collapsed in 1986 when Jörg Haider came to power. After his German-nationalist start in the extreme right-radical fraternity Silvania Vienna, he later changed the party line to a populist, Austrian-patriotic course.

The black-blue government of Schüssel was just as much a "fall from grace" in the view of the former high-ranking Austrian People's Party (ÖVP) minister Heinrich Neisser as the last SPÖ–FPÖ coalition government formed by Sinowatz in 1983 under pressure from Kreisky was in the eyes of left-wing critics. Neisser is one of those very few ÖVP dignitaries who were not blinded by the electoral successes of the two Chancellors Wolfgang Schüssel (2000–06) or Sebastian Kurz (2017–21). His harsh criticism of the black-blue government sounds impressive even in retrospect:

> Any association with Haider is an infectious disease, makes you sick. I am convinced that the ÖVP has been damaged, it was not a success, this period 2000–2006. The ÖVP has made a shift to the right, which I personally cannot support at all. The ÖVP has partly adopted his political manners. Haider has done unbelievable damage to this country, that has to be said for all his political successes. I have seen how he attacked and ruined people, systematically. He was one of the most unscrupulous power politicians.[1]

Fifteen years later, he expressed himself even more harshly about Sebastian Kurz's hanky-panky with the FPÖ: "Personally, I am glad that the Kurz era is over, because it did not do Austrian politics any good. My problems with Kurz are rooted precisely in the fact that he caused a shift to the right in the ÖVP and one had the feeling that there was an ideological unity between it and the FPÖ".[2]

In retrospect, however, it has to be said that the two coalition governments led by Wolfgang Schüssel, especially since 2002, can be characterised more by the bizarre dilettantism of most blue ministers than by the radical right-wing slogans of FPÖ MPs loyal to the government. Schüssel's most significant international achievement was undoubtedly the agreement on compensation for former forced labourers and Jewish Holocaust victims. However, this very belated coming to terms with the Nazi past could not erase the damage caused by the taboo-breaking of the pact with Haider and its consequences to the image of our country, which since 2000 has again been "under observation" caused by heightened suspicion. However, all positive and negative facets of the Schüssel era were overshadowed a decade later and up to the present day by the corruption scandals triggered by the former young superstar Finance Minister Karl-Heinz Grasser.[3]

*The rise of the right*

In this chapter, my primary aim is not to take stock of the first centre-right government since 1945, but to describe the processes of change in the so-called "Third Camp". Under the leadership of Haider's 20-year-younger successor, the dental technician and professional politician Heinz-Christian Strache as federal party leader, the FPÖ was able to overcome the consequences of the split, first in Vienna and a few years later in the federal government. It succeeded in exploiting the stagnation and disputes of the red-black coalitions under Chancellor Werner Faymann and achieved unexpected successes on the core issues of foreigners, security, integration and jobs. As the top candidate at the local elections in Vienna, Strache won 25.8 per cent of the vote in 2010 and 5 years later almost 31 per cent. In the 2013 parliamentary elections, the FPÖ won over a fifth of the votes cast. The federal presidential election on 24 April 2016 marked the Freedom Party's greatest electoral success in Austria's post-war history. Their candidate, Norbert Hofer, third president of parliament since 2013, won in the first round of election with 35 per cent, ahead of the Green candidate, Alexander Van der Bellen, who with 21.3 per cent had only just beaten the surprise independent candidate Irmgard Griss, who achieved 19 per cent. The dramatic decline of the two major parties was shown by the share of barely 11 per cent for their respective candidates. Hofer, an aeronautical engineer and FPÖ politician, had trained in communication and rhetoric courses and later became a seminar trainer himself. This stood him in good stead in the TV debates. In the run-off election on 22 May he won 49.65 per cent and lost to Van der Bellen by a razor-thin margin of 31,000 votes. The enormous upswing of the FPÖ candidate can only be grasped if one remembers that none of the FPÖ candidates had scored more than 17 per cent at the previous presidential elections.

It was an irony of fate that the FPÖ was able to successfully challenge the run-off election at the Constitutional Court. Due to formal deficiencies in the counting of postal votes, a new ballot was ordered for 4 December 2016. Van der Bellen then won the second run-off election more convincingly with 53.8 per cent. In the relatively long period between the two run-off elections, a large coalition had emerged across party lines in favour of Van der Bellen. Vice-Chancellor and ÖVP chairman Reinhold Mitterlehner, ex-ÖVP Vice-Chancellors Erhard Busek and Wilhelm Molterer publicly spoke out in his favour. Several statements by Hofer contributed to the mobilisation of his opponents. Above all, Hofer's remark at the Austrian Broadcasting Corporation (ORF) candidates TV round table debate on 21 April 2016 about his understanding of office as a possible federal president triggered widespread concern: "You'll be surprised what's possible for a president!"

Following the impressive prestige success of the Freedom Party candidate, the Strache-led FPÖ achieved the second-best result in the party's history at 26 per cent at the parliamentary elections in October 2017, despite the rise of the "New People's Party" led by Sebastian Kurz. The share of the vote increased by 5.45 per cent compared with 2013, and the number of MPs by 11 to 51. Politically even more important than the electoral suc-

# SCHÜSSEL'S DANGEROUS EXPERIMENT

cess was the blue breakthrough to executive power thanks to the decision of the future Chancellor Kurz. In the coalition government with the ÖVP, the FPÖ succeeded in winning, among other things, such key portfolios as the interior, foreign and defence ministries, control over all secret services and the post of governor of the National Bank. No other right-wing populist party was able to gain comparable strategic positions of power at that time in a democratic state in Europe. In contrast to the successes of the 1990s, which were marked by the personality of Jörg Haider, the rapid rise in 2016–17 was mainly the consequence of global migration. A large part of the millions of refugees passed through Austria, and the flow of refugees had an increasing political impact. The number of asylum seekers reached 88,000 in 2015. The occasional comparison of Syrians and Afghans with the Hungarian refugees in 1956 made by some observers was historically and politically incorrect. To understand this, it is enough to recall the historical kinship until the collapse of the Dual Monarchy, the drama of the invasion of a neighbouring country only one year after the attainment of their own freedom through the State Treaty, and the common cultural roots. Nevertheless, the willingness of thousands of people to help was able to prevent a humanitarian catastrophe. However, the belated measures to control the massive migration movement led to ever greater fluctuations between compassion and xenophobia, between openness and isolation.

The undisputed beneficiary of the long uncontrolled influx was clearly the FPÖ. The conspiracy theories that became louder and more aggressive during the presidential election, the nationalistic and anti-Semitic remarks made by some FPÖ candidates, as well as Hofer's speculation with confrontational tactics against "Brussels" also caused a stir internationally. Austria was in the spotlight, particularly in those countries where in 1986 (Waldheim) and 2000 (the first black-blue coalition) Austria was portrayed as the last nest of national socialism. Especially in the exciting months between the two run-off elections, international public opinion became more and more interested in the neck-and-neck race between Hofer and Van der Bellen. The Czech ex-Foreign Minister Karel Schwarzenberg did not only speak his own mind when he warned that Austria would inevitably be "under observation" again if Hofer won.[4] The election result was received with a certain relief not only in Austria.

The moment the so-called Turkish-Blue coalition government was formed by Sebastian Kurz and Heinz-Christian Strache on 18 December 2017, it risked jeopardising the reputation that had been built up within the European Union since 2002 after Schüssel's break with Haider. Aware of the danger of European isolation and Israel's expected reaction, Kurz and Strache enshrined in the coalition agreement a "commitment to Israel as a Jewish state". In addition, the government pledged to extend dual citizenship to descendants of Nazi victims. Strache had personally tried again and again to "normalise" relations with Israel and the Jewish Community in Vienna before a possible participation in the government. He visited Israel and the Yad Vashem memorial in Jerusalem several times. In April 2016, he even went to Israel with the FPÖ vice governors of Upper Austria and Burgenland to visit Yad Vashem.

It is not without irony that Heinz-Christian Strache, federal party leader of the FPÖ (2005–19), who symbolised an Israel-friendly turn, was himself a member of the extremist Vandalia student fraternity at the age of 15 and for years had been involved in neo-Nazi and right-wing extremist circles. For the FPÖ, as for the other right-wing populist parties in France, Italy and the Netherlands, the influx of refugees made radical Islam the absolute enemy. In view of the strength of the national core groups around the fraternities, Strache also gave ambivalent signals within the party. On his first visit to Yad Vashem, for example, he wore the cap of his fraternity instead of a kippa. As late as

# SCHÜSSEL'S DANGEROUS EXPERIMENT

2012, he posted an anti-Semitic caricature on his Facebook page. His later emotional speeches and unequivocal statements against anti-Semitism, even at the Vienna Academic Ball of the Burschenschaften in January 2018, attracted attention. With his pro-Israel course, the FPÖ chairman was obviously concerned with portraying his party as moderate and capable of governing.

I have had no contact at all with the FPÖ leadership team since Haider's departure. Only at the events that have been held for some years at the Federal Chancellery on 8 May to commemorate the liberation from national socialism and the end of the Second World War did I also meet some FPÖ representatives. In 2012, I had the honour of giving the commemorative lecture on that day. In view of my naked survival as a 15-year-old school boy after fleeing from the death march towards Austria, this lecture entitled "Europe's End and Europe's Departure" was also a very personal confession.[5] Back then, Strache shook my hand after the lecture. Seven years later, in 2019, on this Remembrance Day, before the appearance of a Holocaust survivor, the mother of a well-known Austrian journalist, Chancellor Kurz and Vice-Chancellor Strache gave short ceremonial speeches. The entire FPÖ leadership was there. While Kurz, routine and smooth as ever, read out his text, Strache gave a free, very emotional commemorative speech, with several references to his visits to Yad Vashem. This time I shook his hand and only remarked: "You still have a lot to do in your party in terms of your lecture". I recounted the proceedings to my wife afterwards, adding with a touch of derision: "His words sounded almost like the appeal of the head of a philosemitic association".

*The songbook scandal*

There was never another opportunity to more closely examine the credibility of Strache's apparent personal turnaround. Nine days later, on 17 May 2019, the bomb of the Ibiza video dropped destroying his political career and putting an abrupt end to the coalition (the political consequences of the scandal will be analysed in a later chapter on the Kurz era).[6] Despite the pro-Israel statements of the party leader, the decision of the state of Israel and the Jewish Community not to maintain relations with the FPÖ remained unchanged until the end. Regardless of whether Strache's stand was dictated by political calculation or not, a long series of anti-Semitic incidents confirms the unchanged ideological core of the FPÖ precisely during Strache's chairmanship.

The Mauthausen Committee has produced documentation on the right-wing extremist activities of FPÖ politicians in three reports since 2013, entitled "Many individual cases = one pattern". A total of 169 individual cases have been documented since the beginning of 2013, which, according to the authors, prove that the FPÖ has not really changed its character even as a governing party (for 1 year and 151 days). Only a few weeks after the formation of the ÖVP–FPÖ coalition, the songbook scandal shook domestic politics. Five days before the Lower Austrian regional elections, the weekly Falter reported on the 300-page songbook of the Burschenschaft Germania zu Wiener Neustadt, published in 1997 in its third edition, which contained a number of anti-Semitic and racist song texts. For example: "Then the Jew Ben Gurion stepped into their midst: 'Step on it, you old Teutons, we'll make the seventh million'". The FPÖ's top candidate in Lower Austria, Udo Landbauer, then 32 years old, had been a member of this extremist fraternity since the age of 15 and was most recently its deputy chairman. In a revealing interview on Austrian television on 24 January 2018, the moderator confronted him with these questions:

> Now you said yesterday in your first reaction: 'I have not perceived even the slightest degree of xenophobia or anti-Semitism either in the FPÖ or in my fraternity in the many years I have been active.' Two months ago, a Lower Austrian FPÖ functionary had to decline his Federal Council mandate because he was shown in a photo with

# SCHÜSSEL'S DANGEROUS EXPERIMENT

> the Hitler salute. Three weeks ago you had to expel a functionary because he liked a neo-Nazi song on Facebook. Your Lower Austrian colleague calls asylum seekers earth and cave people. You call Lower Austria Governor Johanna Mikl-Leitner 'Muslim mama'. In parliament sits the FPÖ MP Zanger, who thinks, and I quote: 'Of course there were good sides to National Socialism, it's just that we no longer hear them today'. And, and, and. You have never perceived anything anti-Semitic or xenophobic in your time in the FPÖ?

After Landbauer affirmed that he had not known about the texts, he was again asked:

> But on page 198 there is the national song of the Bund Deutscher Mädels. On page 217 there is the 'Fallschirmjägerlied' from the Second World War. On page 221 there is the song of the 'Legion Condor', which was the first song of the German Air Force under Hitler. There is an incredibly racist song on page 140 called 'Negro Uprising in Cuba'. I'm not quoting anything from it because it's so disgusting. It was all blacked out? ... Now, as you say yourself, you have been a member of this fraternity since you were 15—that is, for 17 years. Member of this fraternity. You were also deputy chairman for several years. And you never asked why pages were blacked out or torn out in the official songbook of the Burschenschaft?

Landbauer kept answering, "Since I was a member, both I and everyone who was active at the time were never involved with such song texts and they were never sung".

The Austrian writer, Franz Schuh summed up the songbook story aptly:

> The reaction of the mentally exposed, of those unmasked on the basis of their library, whose family secret suddenly became public, was classic: firstly, they had known nothing about it and secondly, what they had known about it had not been meant that way, besides, they had blackened the lines, thirdly, they had also sung the words in question themselves, but at a time when they were not yet 'sensitive' to such things.[7]

Landbauer spoke out in favour of a judicial investigation, but under public pressure he resigned from all his political functions on 1 February 2018. The case against the four publishers of the 1997 songbook was dropped in Wiener Neustadt in August 2018 for lack of evidence. Landbauer was only questioned as a witness. In August, he returned to politics and was elected Executive Party Chairman of the FPÖ Lower Austria, and one day later, under heavy protest from other parties and organisations, Executive Chairman of his party in the provincial diet. By the summer of 2019, he had already risen to the position of Lower Austrian FPÖ party chairman. His career reached a new peak when he was appointed one of Herbert Kickl's six deputies at an extraordinary party congress in Wiener Neustadt in June 2021. He was showered with praise by Kickl: Landbauer had "not only political experience, but also things that already make him a great one: Empathy, your heart is in the right place and you are not a coward. All these are things that the provincial governor does not have", said the federal party leader. Referring to the songbook affair, Kickl said, "Udo, you've bathed in dragon's blood, nothing will knock you down that quickly".[8]

Incidentally, the district court of Wiener Neustadt had already provided a happy ending to the songbook affair. Dissolution proceedings against the Burschenschaft Germania were discontinued at the beginning of 2019. The public prosecutor's office had demanded the destruction of the songbooks, which the Burschenschaft Germania had opposed. The district court ruled that the pages with anti-Semitic texts be removed. On the morning of 30 April 2019, the chairman of Germania cut out the incriminated pages of the 19 confiscated songbooks at a hearing, in the presence of a representative of the public prosecutor's office in Wiener Neustadt and under the supervision of a judge. The hearing ended with the decision that the songbooks would be returned to the Burschenschaft. Even the scissors to remove

# SCHÜSSEL'S DANGEROUS EXPERIMENT

the pages were provided by the court. The spokesperson of the court justified this by saying that none of the summoned persons should bring scissors. Weapons are not allowed in courts.[9]

*A timeless warning*

I have told this sad story in detail because it showed with impressive virtuosity that tradition of mendacious self-promotion that the writer and social psychologist Manès Sperber (1905–84) described thus in his recollections of interwar Vienna: "'Eh scho wissen' was a key word barely accompanied by winks. It implied that everything, everything was comedy. 'Gar net ignorieren', was the demand to ignore the unpleasant".[10] Even in such a haunting "individual case", with texts of abysmal cynicism, the "almost gigantic concealment of one's own part" ultimately triumphs.[11]

The Landbauer case is politically symbolic. Firstly, one can see the importance of the fraternities and secondly, the practice of seemingly compromised FPÖ politicians rising again after a short political abstinence. At the regional elections in January 2023 in Lower Austria, the FPÖ headed by Udo Landbauer increased its share of the votes by almost 10 per cent to 24 per cent. Landbauer, whose mother is incidentally a migrant from Iran, again engendered widespread protests soon after the poll for speaking out against the Austrian state helping the victims of Russia's war against the Ukraine and of the devastating earthquakes in Turkey and Syria.[12] Nevertheless he even became deputy governor of Lower Austria after a coalition deal with the ÖVP.

It is one of the interesting phenomena that precisely during the officially pro-Israel course of Strache, the percentage of MPs who belonged to pan-German national fraternities rose sharply. Whereas the percentage of fraternity members after the last two general elections under Haider was a mere 5.4 and 6.3 per cent, in 2017 and 2019, 31 per cent and 33 per cent of FPÖ MPs were extreme right fraternity members. If all members of pan-German fraternities are taken into account, 40 per cent of FPÖ parliamentarians already belong to this category. In his fundamental work of over 600 pages, political scientist Bernhard Weidinger described "pan-German-ethnic nationalism as the core of fraternity ideology".[13]

Even before the formation of the ÖVP–FPÖ government, the FPÖ expert and author of several works on right-wing extremism and neo-Nazism, Hans-Henning Scharsach, warned in his last book (2017) of a "silent seizure of power". With his research, he uncovered the unknown structures and widely ramified power positions of the numerically tiny pan-German extremist fraternities. The total number of members is estimated at around 4000 (0.04 per cent of the population). Nevertheless, at the time the Scharsach book went to press, two-thirds of the members of the FPÖ party executive were fraternity members, and after joining the right-wing conservative Kurz government, they ended up as ministers, secretary generals, cabinet chiefs, supervisory board members, and so on—key positions in the Republic.[14]

In a brilliant speech on the parliament's day of remembrance "against violence and racism in memory of the victims of National Socialists" on 4 May 2018, the writer Michael Köhlmeier exposed the hypocrisy of the FPÖ, "some of whose members repeatedly, almost on a weekly basis, issue pro-Nazi or anti-Semitic racist messages, either openly in public or hidden in social media". Can such a party, Köhlmeier asked after enumerating outrageous "individual case", "at the same time set itself up as defenders and protectors of the Jews? One can. I am dismayed by the one, but I don't believe the other. Whoever believes that is either an idiot or pretends to be, in which case he is a cynic".

This short speech, delivered in the ceremonial hall of the Hofburg, in the front row with Strache and others from the FPÖ

## SCHÜSSEL'S DANGEROUS EXPERIMENT

leadership, was rightly a drumbeat with strong resonance. It contained a timelessly valid warning, even after the disappearance of the Freedomite government faction, to those who have allowed themselves to be blunted by the "individual case": "People never came to the big evil with one big step, but with many small ones, each of which seemed too small for a big outrage. First it's said, then it's done".[15]

After the fall of Heinz-Christian Strache and the rapid dimming of his successor Norbert Hofe's star, Herbert Kickl is the first man in almost 40 years at the helm of the party who has never belonged to a pan-German nationalist extremist fraternity. Nevertheless, this same politician, who since Jörg Haider is tactically the most capable, rhetorically the most brilliant and, even during the pandemic, the most unscrupulous in his methods, seems to be prepared to do anything to win power for his party. Due to inflation and the record influx of migrants, the FPÖ scored major successes at the regional elections in three provinces in the spring of 2023. As this book goes to press, the FPÖ is the frontrunner in the opinion polls with almost 30 per cent of the popular vote. Parliamentary elections are due to be held in the autumn of 2024. FPÖ Chairman Herbert Kickl already claims to be recognised as the future Federal Chancellor. He wants to convert Austria into "a fortress in the pattern of Viktor Orbán's Hungary". Attacking Federal President Van der Bellen for being a "senile mummy" behaving as if he were the head of a NATO state, Kickl rejects the EU sanctions against Russia. Thus Austria could again and all too easily come "under scrutiny".

6

# KARL RENNER AND BRUNO KREISKY
## TWO GREAT PERSONALITIES OF SOCIAL DEMOCRACY

Few people in our country today know what a great international reputation Austrian social democracy enjoyed both in the interwar period and after the Second World War, especially during the 13 years of the Kreisky era. This was particularly true for the neighbouring Eastern European countries, where liberal democracy was only a pipe dream under the pressure of totalitarian dictatorships.

Due to the media's focus on the almost weekly popularity polls, the complex political developments and also the lessons of the past are often overlooked in journalistic snapshots. The chequered history of the Second Republic and in particular of Austrian social democracy confirms the role of personalities at crucial moments.

*Karl Renner's historical achievement*

Thus, for example, it remains a mystery to this day how and why a 75-year-old retired Austrian politician was able to emerge from obscurity one April morning in 1945 in Gloggnitz am

Semmering and become a key figure in the re-establishment of the Republic. The man who wanted to protest to the local Russian command against the encroachments of Soviet soldiers was Karl Renner, who had already been state chancellor of the first republic in 1918–19 and chairman of the last freely elected parliament in 1933 before the Dollfuß dictatorship. Even if some details of the adventurous story of the contact with Stalin by letter remain disputed, it is certain that a political commissar who was present finally realised who he was dealing with. In his personal letter to "Dear Comrade, His Excellency, Marshal Stalin", dated 15 April 1945, Renner declared his willingness to speak for the Austrian people as the last president of the then still free parliament and also to establish the public administration as the first chancellor. As early as 19 April, Stalin is said to have given the order to entrust Karl Renner with the formation of the government. And on 27 April 1945, the world was taken by surprise by the establishment of a Provisional State Government headed by Renner.

The details of the course of Renner-Stalin contact, which were not so well known at the time, were told to me by Renner's first biographer, the long-time editor of the *Arbeiter Zeitung*, Jacques Hannak, during our frequent informal meetings. The author, who had only returned to Vienna in 1946 after emigration to France and the US, told me details about the political and ideological conflicts in the Austrian social democracy before and after the Second World War.[1]

Jacques Hannak, this unusual colleague, was actually my first left-wing "Austria teacher" (the right-wing one was my friend Kurt Vorhofer of the same age).[2] As described in my autobiography, I was a left-wing socialist already as a schoolboy and student, naturally loaded with prejudices against the right-wing social democrats, also in Austria, who (among them Renner) had already been eloquently insulted by Stalin and Lenin as "traitors to socialism" and "lackeys of German imperialists". Although I never became a member of a political party again, my close relationship with Bruno Kreisky and the knowledge of contemporary history I acquired later helped me to quickly throw off the ridiculous dogmas spread by the communists and to recognise the historical significance of Austrian social democracy.

Of decisive importance for the future of Austria, according to Hannak and all other observers, was Renner's action from the beginning when he demanded that his government be recognised by the four occupying powers (Soviet Union, France, Britain and the USA) as being responsible for the whole of Austria. The fact that Renner was able to win the approval of the Russians for free elections on 25 November 1945 in the whole of Austria was, of course, also related to the boundless overconfidence of the communists. They deceived themselves and the Soviet occupying power about the real feelings of the Austrian people: instead of the expected 25 per cent, the Communist Party of Austria (KPÖ) received only 5.4 per cent and thus 4 seats compared with 85 mandates for the Austrian People's Party (ÖVP) and 76 for the Social Democrats (SPÖ). The enormous significance of the free elections and the recognition of a government for whole of Austria is demonstrated by the fate of divided Germany until 1989 and the tragedy of the central and Eastern European states, which were reduced to Soviet satellites by the communists.

The triumph of Renner's tactics, who was elected Federal President by the Federal Assembly after the general election, was indeed a unique historical achievement: he founded two republics in his own lifetime as State Chancellor, in 1918 and 1945, and he was regarded as an integration figure admired by all sides at home and abroad until his death at the end of December 1950 after his 80th birthday. Renner was, of course, also in charge of formulating the Austrian Declaration of Independence, with the Austrian doctrine of victims without any complicity, without dedicating a word to the murdered Jews and Roma, the victims in concentration camps or those forced to leave their homeland.

## Karl Renner's commitment to the Anschluss

Even the shadows of the past do not change Karl Renner's lasting historical merit. However, the memory of his behaviour in 1938 and as head of government and state after 1945 undoubtedly weighs heavier today, after freer access to the digitalised archives, than it did in the post-war period. This also applies to the attitude of the top politicians of the two major parties, Federal Chancellor Leopold Figl, Vice-Chancellor Adolf Schärf and Minister of the Interior Oskar Helmer, towards the former Nazis and the Holocaust survivors. The question of how and why the explosive issue of restitution of Jewish property (or its compensation) was put on hold for decades was first answered by the British historian Robert Knight in his ground-breaking book on the relevant verbatim records of the federal government from 1945 to 1952. The very title of his work, quoting Interior Minister Oskar Helmer (dated 9 November 1948), "I would be in favour of dragging this out", is deeply symbolic and applies to the stalling tactics of many years beyond the period he covers (up to 1952).

But back to the enigmatic and fascinating founding father of the Second Republic, whose deeds and motives continue to divide his biographers and cause debate to this day.

It is undisputed that Karl Renner made a public, not forced, commitment, explicitly "as a social democrat and thus as a champion of the right to self-determination, as the first Chancellor of the German-Austrian republic and head of the Austrian delegation to the peace treaty talks at St. Germain" to the "Anschluss" and to a "yes" at the referendum ordered by Hitler. His statement was published in the *Neues Wiener Tagblatt* (New Vienna Gazette), a daily that was controlled, as all Austrian newspapers, by the Nazis. There was of course always much speculation about the motives, among other things, because of his concern for his Jewish son-in-law and the "half-Jewish" grandchildren. But he always emphasised that he had acted without compulsion and out of conviction. His pan-German conviction, which was also influenced by his Southern Moravian descent, was expressed in a long study, "The Anschluss and the Sudeten Germans", which only existed as proofs and was, fortunately for his post-war career, never published. In this study, he rejected the Czechoslovak state and thus basically justified the Nazi war policy. As a result of the break-up of Czechoslovakia, the 87-page document was overtaken by events. The explosive text was found and published, but luckily for Renner's reputation, only half a century later.

What is certain is that at that time, in 1938, and even during the war years, almost all leading social democrats were in favour of annexation to Germany. When I was working on my Kreisky biography in the early 1970s, I received documents from him about his correspondence with Oscar Pollak (later editor-in-chief of the *Arbeiter Zeitung*), who had found asylum in Britain during the war years. These letters and other documents show that Kreisky, despite his admiration for Otto Bauer, never accepted the Anschluss. In his memoirs, he also dealt with the case of Renner:

> It was inconceivable to him that during his lifetime anything would change in the facts created by Hitler. History had spoken and one had to bow to it, he said, almost like a reed in the wind. To what extent personal motives, fear for his son-in-law and the like, played a role in this, I do not know. There are many reasons for a certain political behaviour, subjective as well as objective, and in any case it seemed to me that Renner always let himself get involved in a given situation (...) The Nazis had left him completely alone (...) why should we reproach Renner for something that many others also did, just not in such a prominent position as he did.[3]

Renner was obviously underestimated by both sides, by Moscow and by the three Western allies. The role of his style and personality was described at the time by a British journalist in the *Observer* in London:

> (...) this time the Russians had chosen the wrong man. Renner was mild, friendly and obliging, even willing to leave some ministerial posts to the Communists, but quite capable of keeping the reins in his own hands. He meekly resigned himself to being called a Russian puppet by some of his foreign friends; he caused no offence to the occupying power, he was agile, polite, charming. But the point on which he insisted with determined calm was the need for general elections (...).

After this appreciation of Renner's "brilliant move" to win the consent of the Soviet occupiers and probably Stalin to the creation of a federal government resulting from free elections, the *Observer* article concluded with an almost prophetic prediction: "If this second Austrian republic remains successful, it will be Dr Renner's monument".[4]

*The SPÖ's hypocrisy towards Jewish comrades*

Given the changes in the attitudes of most Austrian voters between 1938 and 1945, the historian Oliver Rathkolb probably correctly surmises that Renner was the perfect personification of typical Austrian behaviour and thus also an integration figure. In Vienna in 1945, those who had remained silent and those who had fought, those who had come out of the prisons and concentration camps and those who had come to terms with the brown rulers (always "on behalf of the party", of course) met in the newly formed socialist leadership bodies. Together with the leading figures of the Austrian People's Party, they all achieved great things during the critical years of the occupation. It must be noted, however, that there was not too much willingness in the socialist leadership to bring back the emigrants.

## KARL RENNER AND BRUNO KREISKY

The Social Democrats were not only the oldest, but also repeatedly the strongest party in the Second Republic, with over 40 per cent of the vote at the general elections and with 700,000 members. After 11 years underground, and after the murder and expulsion of many leading functionaries, the SPÖ, unlike its coalition partner the ÖVP, emerged from the Second World War in 1945 with few suitable personalities. The new leadership, headed by Vice-Chancellor Adolf Schärf and Interior Minister Oskar Helmer, were practically unknown in 1945. The lack of personnel for the party elite was also the result of its particular structure. The founder and legendary leader from 1889 onwards was Viktor Adler, a doctor, who was a Jew, as were many other leading figures in the interwar period, headed by the most outstanding Marxist intellectual Otto Bauer. In order to counter the anti-Semitic agitation against the SPÖ as "the Jewish party", it was not Bauer who had been chosen as the party leader, but Karl Seitz, who also held office as mayor of Vienna.

In his memoirs, the theatre director and author Ernst Lothar, who had returned from American exile as a US cultural officer and had decided to resign and to stay in Vienna, wrote in a bitter note: "There was no desire for returnees, least of all for recognised figures, although this was not admitted officially; they wanted to remain among themselves and spare their bruised consciences".[5] The scope and acuteness of the anti-Semitic sentiment in the black-red coalition government with regard to Jewish survivors at home and abroad and the restitution of looted property only became properly known after free access to the verbatim minutes of the federal government and SPÖ executive committee meetings. In view of the fact that in the first freely elected government 12 out of 17 government members were former concentration camp prisoners, the demonstrative indifference to the tragedy of Austrian Jewry mixed with barely concealed anti-Semitism seems worthy to be noted.

## AUSTRIA BEHIND THE MASK

Here are, for example, a few short quotations from the minutes of the Council of Ministers meeting on the request of the Jewish community to create a fund for impoverished Jewish repatriates dated 9 November 1948:

> Minister of Agriculture Kraus (ÖVP): "(...) but I do not know how just now one race should get special privileges. Others who didn't leave don't get any support, but the Jews should get one".
>
> Minister of Trade Kolb (ÖVP): "(...) the injustice done to the Jews was not done to Austria. Austria and the Greater German Reich, there is a difference".
>
> Minister of the Interior Helmer (SPÖ): "What was taken away from the Jews cannot be ascribed to the 'Greater German Reich'. A large part taken was due to our dear fellow citizens. (...) But I see only Jewish expansion everywhere, as in the medical profession, in trade, especially in Vienna (...) Everything was also taken away from the Nazis in 1945 (...) I would be in favour of dragging the matter out".
>
> Federal Chancellor Figl (ÖVP): "The motion will not be approved in the Council of Ministers (...) Moreover, a contrast, a difficult situation with the National Socialists would be created here".[6]

At the time of the meeting, a total of 9,000 Jews were living in Austria, many in temporary transit camps. The Council of Ministers did not extend the deadline for filing claims under the Restitution Act. In his candid and knowledgeable book on the shabby treatment of emigrants and Jewish victims, published in 2021, the author Herbert Lackner also exposes the repulsive hypocrisy of Chancellor Figl. At the "Mourning and Commemoration Ceremony" of the Jewish Religious Community, he had recalled in a speech on the occasion of the tenth anniversary of "Kristallnacht" in the sense of the "victim theory" that "all these crimes and atrocities were conceived and organised beyond our border" and that the "government from the very beginning did everything (...) to help the spirit of humanity, justice and morality to break through again in our state".[7]

## KARL RENNER AND BRUNO KREISKY

Lackner also describes, with hitherto unknown statements by Karl Renner, Adolf Schärf and Oskar Helmer, the consistent refusal by the SPÖ leadership to bring back or invite prominent emigrants, not least the humiliating stalling tactics in the case of Bruno Kreisky, who repeatedly tried to return to Vienna from Sweden despite several offers by his wealthy father-in-law to join his company in Sweden.

I had the good fortune to be able to observe Bruno Kreisky at close quarters for 30 years thanks to his trust, to have numerous private conversations with him and to publish dozens of interviews. I received many documents and much information about his life during the 12 years as an emigrant in Sweden and as a diplomat for free Austria. In the course of the preparations for my Kreisky biography in 1972 and also during our conversations in the following two decades, however, he never told me details about the disappointing indifference of the SPÖ leadership towards his wishes for an early return. Nor did he say a word about possible anti-Semitic motives in the process of his return, which dragged on for years. Nor is there any reference to this in his autobiographical writings. What I and the other authors of the first Kreisky biographies received from him at the time was merely a copy of his letter of 1 April 1946, one month before his first trip to Austria, written to Frieda Nödl, a resistance fighter and member of the Viennese parliament: "One thing is certain, however, I will not impose myself very much. The Party has no obligations towards me, nor has it made much effort to make my return possible".

*Kreisky's relationship with Judaism and Israel*

However, the fact that it was only at the beginning of 1951, a few days before his fortieth birthday, that he managed to enter the economic policy department of the Foreign Ministry, which at that time still belonged to the Federal Chancellery, as a "third-class legation councillor" speaks volumes. It was the surprising victory of the 78-year-old mayor of the city of Vienna, Theodor Körner, in the presidential election on 27 May 1951 against the ÖVP candidate Heinrich Gleißner that suddenly cleared the way for Kreisky to enter the innermost leadership circle of the SPÖ. He became foreign policy advisor to the Federal President in the rank of cabinet vice-director.

In dealing with Bruno Kreisky, it is not my intention to outline the stages of his rise to SPÖ chairman on 1 February 1967 and to Federal Chancellor 3 years later, but to describe in him, as an important symbolic figure, as perhaps the greatest paradox of Austrian post-war history.

Many influential comrades knew very early on that Kreisky, with his outstanding intellect, his political ingenuity, his tactical talent even in sensitive foreign policy issues, as demonstrated in the case of South Tyrol, would be an ideal leading figure for opening up the party after the last crushing defeat in 1966. Nevertheless, despite all his political ambitions, he himself wanted to remain "in the second row" for a long time. He faced a seemingly insurmountable barrier: can, may and should a Jewish emigrant and intellectual from an upper middle-class background become party leader and candidate for chancellor in this country of deeply rooted anti-Semitic prejudices, felt in all strata of the population and in all parties, including his own?

When, still as Foreign Minister, he told me confidentially over a cup of coffee in a tiny room next to his office on Ballhausplatz after the overwhelming election victory of the People's Party in 1966 about party friends from the provinces who wanted to put him on the ticket, I could not hide my doubts either. After all, he had repeatedly been the target of subtle and crude anti-Semitic attacks. Most recently, during the 1966 election campaign, the president of the Lower Austrian Chamber of Agriculture and

## KARL RENNER AND BRUNO KREISKY

long-time MP of the ÖVP, Alois Scheibenreif, had called him a "dirty Jew". The same appeal to anti-Semitic feelings was the motive in the 1970 parliamentary elections when Federal Chancellor Klaus was placarded as "A real Austrian". Until the very end, Kreisky, like most observers (including myself), did not believe that a change of power was possible. Thus, on the evening of 1 March 1970, when we heard the first vote projections in the ballroom of the election centre, we journalists, too, sensed that we were witnesses of a turning point in the history of the Second Republic.

Half a century after that day and 30 years after his death, the fascination with Bruno Kreisky and the "golden era of social democracy" symbolised by him is unbroken and even stronger than ever. He was above all the victor who led his socialist party to a series of five electoral victories, unique in European history, to winning an absolute majority of mandates and (for the first time) of electoral votes three times. He became the longest-serving chancellor in a rather conservative country and for 16 years was the leader of the SPÖ, a party that was also prone to anti-Semitism.

Given the attitudes cited, it is fair to ask: how was he able to reduce prejudice and win the affection of the Austrians? How can it be explained that over time he always did better in the ratings than his party? Certain psychologists claimed from the beginning that Kreisky benefited from latent anti-Semitism, from repressed guilt complexes and from the fact that broad sections of the population regarded him with personified authority and credibility, precisely because he so obviously did not have those characteristics that anti-Semitic propaganda attributes to the Jews.

However, one must also openly state the fact that the passionate and increasingly hateful conflict with the undoubtedly rather ÖVP-friendly Simon Wiesenthal after his revelations, first about an SS man as Minister of Agriculture, then about four former National Socialist German Workers' Party (NSDAP) members in the first SPÖ government, both harmed and benefited him. Many democrats, by no means only Jews, were stunned that Kreisky, who had lost 21 relatives in the Holocaust, appeared as a vocal defender of all those former Nazis who had become "good democrats". Kreisky has always held the opinion that "even an NSDAP member or an SS man must be allowed to hold any political office in Austria as long as no crime is proven against him".[8]

This attitude, which was sometimes harshly condemned internationally, and his often heavy-handed statements regarding Israel and Judaism strained relations with the USA, Israel and Jewish organisations for years to come. His amazingly tolerant treatment of the Nazis was too much influenced by his personal experiences, especially the joint imprisonment of the National Socialists and the Social Democrats at the time of the Austrofascist state. One must also add the fact that, being in exile, he had experienced the very worst time "at second hand".

What the former ÖVP Vice-Chancellor Erhard Busek said in a conversation with me in retrospect about the Kreisky–Peter Pact (1970–1) is a cynical but probably accurate assessment: Kreisky had "de-Nazified" Peter and Peter had "freed Kreisky of Jewishness" for a certain group of voters. In a certain sense, this also applied to the reconciliation Kreisky always advocated with groups that had previously been considered enemies or opponents, without abandoning his own social democratic values. One of his biographers, Werner A. Perger, put it less provocatively than Busek: Kreisky had "quieted the public conscience of the country" with his understanding attitude. In any case, I can confirm on the basis of many personal conversations that nothing gave him such deep inner satisfaction as the irrefutable fact that the Austrian people voted again and again with a large majority for him, the disenfranchised, outcast and persecuted in the past.

# KARL RENNER AND BRUNO KREISKY

Despite all his outbursts of rage against Israeli attackers and against his Jewish critics, Kreisky never denied his affiliation to Judaism as a community of destiny. In a remarkable, long interview, the only one about his relationship to Judaism, years after his resignation, he said: "The knowledge of Auschwitz is the only thing that unreservedly binds me to my Jewish origins. Without Auschwitz, my relationship to Judaism would not commit me to any particular behaviour or attitude. Auschwitz is the fate of the Jews, which even those who consider their Jewish ancestry to be more or less arbitrary cannot escape. We have all been lumped together by a strange cruel quirk of history".[9]

Unfortunately, it must be noted that the politician Kreisky probably also chose the controversial path of (often rotten) compromises, (often undifferentiated) reconciliation and (often unforgivable) repression out of sober calculation and electoral considerations. It was a stroke of luck that (unfortunately much too late) a non-Jewish Social Democratic Federal Chancellor, Franz Vranitzky, found those clear words in Vienna and Jerusalem about Austria's co-responsibility for the National Socialist crimes that Kreisky, who was so directly affected personally and through his family, did not want to or could not say out of domestic political considerations and probably also out of inner conflict.

## *The beginner and the finisher*

In historical retrospect, even in international comparison, there is hardly another phenomenon as surprising and as contradictory as the rise of Bruno Kreisky and his winning streak. Georgi Valentinovich Plekhanov (1856–1918), the "father of Russian Marxism" and a bitter opponent of Lenin, wrote in his famous work *On the Role of Personality*, in 1898:

> A great man is great not by the fact that his personal peculiarities give an individual stamp to the great historical events, but by the fact

that he possesses peculiarities which make him most capable of serving the great social needs of his time, which have arisen under the influence of general and special causes. In his well-known work on heroes, Carlyle calls the great men beginners. This is a very felicitous term. The great man is precisely a Beginner, because he looks further than the others and wants to be stronger than the others.[10]

In this sense, Bruno Kreisky was also a "beginner" as party leader and Federal Chancellor. He wanted to destroy the taboos inside and outside his party, the relics of the authoritarian state along with its mentality, as a belated finisher of liberal reforms. He considered it a great good fortune that "of the liberal heritage, which has in part become ownerless property, Austrian social democracy, perhaps also through my participation, is getting a larger piece". Kreisky reconciled his party with the intellectuals and with the youth, with the Catholics and with the aristocracy, with the left, and with the Nazis. He also wanted to and was able to win over those who "wanted to go a bit of the way with us". His memorable motto was: "The courage to go unfinished".

At the end of my Kreisky biography, I indirectly quoted the great Basel historian Jacob Burckhardt from his *Weltgeschichtliche Betrachtungen* with a question mark about Kreisky's historical position: "Only from a distance will it be possible to see whether Bruno Kreisky will go down in Austrian history as a 'momentary greatness' in which a brief phase of history is condensed, as a 'relative greatness' springing from the weakness of others, or as a 'historical greatness' whose criterion is not merely a shift in power but a fundamental change in social structures and social consciousness".[11]

I had written these lines at the end of the third year of the Kreisky era, after his achievement of an absolute majority. In the following decade, an astonished public witnessed a series of corruption scandals and a years-long fight for better or worse between the old and sick chancellor and his impatient and brilliant crown prince, Hannes Androsch, who was 27 years younger. When on the evening of 24 April 1983, the loss of the absolute majority was certain (after losing 3.4 per cent or five seats), the chancellor resigned immediately. On that day, the SPÖ had 47.6 per cent of the vote; a share that it has not even dreamed of since and that it will unlikely to ever win in the future. The questions I asked in 1972 about Kreisky's legacy were unanimously answered in the affirmative by critical and independent observers even before the turn of the millennium in terms of the historical course set. Norbert Leser, the critical historian of Austrian social democracy, wrote of an "epoch-making phenomenon" in Austrian history and international socialism. The top Catholic journalist Kurt Vorhofer, the inventor of the attributes "journalist chancellor" and "sun king", spoke of Kreisky at a discussion event in May 1995 shortly before his much too early death, thus: "Like a freak of nature—something intangible in talent endowment—half a dozen capable politicians could live comfortably on his talent endowment". According to the liberal author Armin Thurnher, Kreisky was "the most important politician that Austria of both republics has produced". Both after his resignation and after his death, numerous international personalities stressed that Bruno Kreisky had given the Republic of Austria as Foreign Minister and as Federal Chancellor an international splendour that it had never had before.

*Fred Sinowatz, the failed heir*

In view of the state and character of the SPÖ and the attitude of its leading bodies, the phenomenon of Bruno Kreisky was, in my opinion, the most convincing proof of how aptly the title of Oliver Rathkolb's well-known work characterised Austria: *The Paradoxical Republic*. And now we can add to the Plekhanov quote on the role of personality, the question: who gambled away the leadership role and the chancellorship of the social democracy and why did its share of the vote fall from almost 48 per cent to just over 20 per cent at the last general elections in 2019?

The glorious Kreisky period was followed by the personal tragedy of Fred Sinowatz, his successor as Federal Chancellor and party chairman, whom even political opponents appreciated in retrospect as a very decent personality in terms of character and humanity. He was one of the most underestimated politicians as a result of his clumsiness in his encounters with the media and of the sometimes deliberately misinterpreted shortened speech quotations. The politician, who came from a Burgenland-Croatian family, was an extremely successful and popular Minister of Education and Culture for almost 12 years, implementing numerous important school policy reforms. Preferred by Kreisky as his successor after the passionate conflict with Androsch, the modest and principled Social Democrat obviously did not want to be first choice, and it was no secret that he only accepted the honourable task out of party discipline.

I only came to know and appreciate him more closely as head of government when I accompanied him on trips to Moscow and Budapest and during meetings in Vienna. Therefore, it was possible for me to observe at close quarters the unbroken streak of bad luck that led to his inexorable fall in the polls and finally, after 3 years, to his resignation.

At the time, as editor-in-chief of the Austrian Broadcasting Corporation (ORF) for Eastern Europe, I was personally impressed how firmly the Chancellor rejected Soviet attempts to intimidate the Austrian media. For example, he flatly stated in November 1984 that he would only accept a Soviet invitation to pay an official visit travel to Moscow if all Austrian journalists registered for the trip were granted visas. It was really an issue only about me, since I had been blacklisted in Moscow and

Prague 2 years earlier because of a "provocative indiscretion". Sinowatz always defended uncensored reporting on the communist world. Thanks to his backing, the ORF was the first Western media company to broadcast a Club 2 programme from Moscow, with critical comments.

A government reshuffle, with the replacement of a Kreisky confidant in the Ministry of Finance by the successful bank director Franz Vranitzky and in the Ministry of Foreign Affairs by the popular Viennese Mayor Leopold Gratz, was seen as a sign of his emancipation from the patriarch and strengthened the position of the chancellor. However, this momentary success was overshadowed by the series of political, economic and international crises that marked the short era of the Sinowatz cabinet. To name but a few: the abandonment of the planned Danube power plant in Hainburg forced by the Green environmentalists and a whole series of speculation, bribery and arms export scandals in nationalised industry and surrounding the construction of the new Vienna General Hospital. But it was his involvement in the Waldheim affair, which I described in the previous chapter, that sealed the inglorious end of Fred Sinowatz's chancellorship. One day after Kurt Waldheim was elected Federal President, Fred Sinowatz resigned as Federal Chancellor and 2 years later as SPÖ party leader.

A particularly sad aftermath of the Sinowatz drama was his conviction for false testimony, also in the second instance, to a fine in 1991. He also claimed to me until the end that he had not made the statement about addressing the "brown stains" in Waldheim's past before the election campaign began. I spoke to him from time to time even after his retirement from politics. He was a hapless, failed and, despite the tragic end of his career, generally appreciated heir to an extraordinary personality.

7

# GREED INSTEAD OF PRINCIPLES

## THE DECLINE OF SOCIAL DEMOCRACY

Since a famous (and incorrect) diagnosis by Ralf Dahrendorf—"Social democracy is at the end of its term"—written more than three decades ago, the crisis of social democracy seems to have become, along with the pandemic, climate change, digitalisation and artificial intelligence, one of the most discussed topics in the media and political science.[1]

The apparent or temporary flourishing at the end of the twentieth century reflected the fact that Social Democrats provided 11 out of 15 heads of government in the EU and two partners in coalition governments. Tony Blair, Gerhard Schröder, Lionel Jospin or Romano Prodi were the symbolic figures of a triumphant "third way". The creeping decline was then interrupted by brilliant recovery phases. Confronted with the danger of a catastrophe of the uncontrolled financial system, however, in 2008 the celebrated "third way" turned out to be the way "into the descent society".[2]

Social scientists spoke of the end of the "social democratic solidarity society", of the "aloof" versus the "excluded" or of "the new underclass". The German political scientist Franz Walter, one of the most perceptive analysts of social democracy, stated: "The social democrats missed a historic opportunity in these years of the third way".[3] Sociologists and political scientists pointed out that young middle-class voters who were ecological or feminist or who supported human rights were looking for new political representatives. They gave a sustained boost to the new green groupings everywhere.

The massive political alienation of the Austrian Social Democrats (SPÖ) from their traditional supporters of the poor, uneducated and socially risk-prone classes was already becoming apparent at the end of the last century. In the 1979 election, two-thirds of the working class still voted for the Kreisky SPÖ; 20 years later, this proportion was reduced to one-third, while Haider's Freedom Party of Austria (FPÖ) was able to win 47 per cent of workers and almost half of all voters under 30 years of age. In the 2017 parliamentary election, 59 per cent of workers already voted for the FPÖ and only 19 per cent for the SPÖ. The term labour force, however, hides the fact that it has always consisted of different parts, with noticeable differences between sectors and regions, between rural and urban communities, between resident and immigrant first- and second-generation workers, and exacerbated by the dynamics of globalisation and massive migration.

Nevertheless, the fact that this is by no means a brand new phenomenon is proven to me by the following observations from a speech given by the philosopher Theodor W. Adorno on "Aspects of the New Right-Wing Radicalism" half a century ago(!) in Vienna:

> The tendency of capital to concentrate means (...) the possibility of the permanent declassification of strata which, according to their subjective class consciousness, were quite bourgeois, who would like to hold on to their privileges, their social status, and possibly strengthen it (...) That in spite of full employment and in spite of all

these symptoms of prosperity, the spectre of technological unemployment continues to haunt us to such an extent that in the age of automation, which is still behind us in Central Europe but is undoubtedly being caught up with, even those people who are involved in the production process already feel potentially superfluous, actually feel potentially unemployed.[4]

The social preconditions of right-wing radicalism he outlined have been tremendously reinforced in recent decades by the upheavals in the capital markets. While the sense of insecurity and vulnerability as a result of loss of status is by no means new, the crucial question remains whether "social democracy's historic task of acting as an advocate for a justified fear of citizens is being fulfilled". The British contemporary historian Tony Judt (1948–2010) also saw in this the chance for social democracy's continued existence in the twenty-first century, which he foresaw as an "age of chronic insecurity": "If social democracy has a future, it is as the social democracy of fear".[5]

*Franz Vranitzky's political achievements*

The basic problem of the SPÖ has remained unchanged: the distance of the decision-makers from the people for whom they claim to make policy. All this, of course, also shaped the era of Franz Vranitzky, who was undoubtedly the most successful Federal Chancellor in the post-Kreisky era (June 1986 to January 1997) and SPÖ Federal Party Chairman (1988–97). I got to know him as *Financial Times* correspondent during the Kreisky government in the cabinet of Finance Minister Androsch and later in his function as head of the nationalised Länderbank. Closer personal contacts only developed during his time as Federal Chancellor, and even after his resignation I continued to meet him from time to time.

The more time passes, the more I regard Franz Vranitzky as an authentic and calm stabiliser in the period of upheaval in foreign and domestic policy between 1985 and 1996. No one can deny him two great achievements in state policy: the clearing of debris in the complex relations with Austrian Jewry and Israel together with the impetus for the long overdue reckoning with the victim myth through trend-setting speeches, and his leading role in setting the course for Austria's accession to the European Union. His third act, which was particularly explosive in terms of domestic politics, though the most controversial, was his break with the FPÖ after Jörg Haider came to power, thus ending the red-blue coalition. In his political style, in his attitude to consensus as the motto of the Second Republic and above all in his ambiguous attitude to the Nazi past, Jörg Haider embodied the absolute antithesis to Franz Vranitzky's person, politics and attitude.

In retrospect, one must also acknowledge Vranitzky's steady hand in financial and economic policy, thanks also to the productive cooperation, free of ulterior motives, with his long-time, capable Finance Minister, Ferdinand Lacina, and the stabilisation of the crisis-ridden nationalised industry. In foreign policy, too, Vranitzky was able to fill the vacuum created by Waldheim's international ostracism. The occasional friction with Federal President Thomas Klestil over protocol issues because of the professional diplomat's jealousy should hardly affect Vranitzky's track record.

Things are different with regard to his activity as SPÖ party chairman, which was critically assessed by independent observers. Vranitzky could not put a brake on Haider's rise. The FPÖ leader often made justified attacks against the high number of insurance companies, against multiple salaries of chamber and trade union officials, pension abuses in the nationalised companies and other undesirable developments of the proportional representation system. Of course, one should not forget that in his heyday Haider was the most rhetorically and dramatically gifted opposition politician of the Second Republic. This is probably why the

## GREED INSTEAD OF PRINCIPLES

FPÖ's share of the electorate rose from 5 to 22 per cent between 1983 and 1994 and the number of MPs from 7 to 42. In the same period, the SPÖ's share fell from 43.1 per cent to 34.9 per cent. Although Vranitzky succeeded in winning back six seats in the early election of 1995, the FPÖ reached its peak in 1999 under Viktor Klima's chancellorship with 26.9 per cent and 52 MPs.

In view of the orientation of many FPÖ leadership figures and functionaries described in the chapter "Under Observation", there is no doubt today that such a party cannot and must not have a place in the government of a liberal democracy without radical, comprehensive and credible changes. So even from today's perspective, Vranitzky's decision to end the coalition with the FPÖ in 1986, after Haider's takeover of the party, was the right one. The accusations, for example by Norbert Leser, that he was the main culprit in the decline of the party, in the "transformation of a community of ideas into a special-purpose association", are a completely different matter.[6] Hannes Androsch, who had turned from his former boss into an irreconcilable enemy, was the harshest judge: "He ruined the party in terms of content, morals and finances because it didn't interest him".[7]

If one takes a closer look at the phase in SPÖ history after Vranitzky and compares him with his three successors, Alfred Gusenbauer, Werner Faymann and Christian Kern, these sweeping judgements, probably also made for personal reasons, seem unfair. What is true is that Vranitzky did not make the decisive career leaps before becoming chancellor in the party apparatus, but in the National Bank, in the Ministry of Finance and in banking. The appearance of the tall, successful basketball player (in the national team) as an elegant "socialist in pinstripes" was also deceptive. He came from a poor background, his father was a communist iron founder, he himself worked as a construction worker in the summer holidays so that he could graduate from the College of World Trade. He was neither a party employee nor a professional politician and only joined the SPÖ when he was an employee in the National Bank. Unlike many SPÖ functionaries, he thus had flawless proletarian roots. In meetings with voters or workers, Vranitzky appeared more authentic than most of his colleagues in the government or in the party executive. He thus had a double public image simply because he socialised so well in the course of his professional rise that he completely lost the socialist "barn smell" to the outside world.

*Viktor Klima, a footnote in the history of the SPÖ*

The fact that he made a serious mistake in choosing Viktor Klima as his successor is no longer denied, even by Vranitzky in private, even if the public and also inner-party popularity of the former personnel manager of the Austrian Mineral Oil Administration Stock Company (OMV), confirmed by surveys, is cited as a counter-argument. The duo of Viktor Klima as party leader and Andreas Rudas as central secretary failed, despite the massive support of the *Kronen Zeitung*, with an election campaign devoid of concept and content against the triumphant Jörg Haider and was also paraded, outmanoeuvred and toppled soon afterwards by Wolfang Schüssel, the most capable conservative power politician of the Second Republic since Julius Raab.

I will write about Schüssel's role in another chapter, but as far as Viktor Klima is concerned, I once contradicted the publicist Anneliese Rohrer in the past after she wrote that Viktor Klima would not even be a footnote in the history of the Second Republic. Today, I am inclined to agree with her harsh judgement. He is one of those figures in the chequered history of social democracy who have disappeared into oblivion, who became a symbolic figure by chance. What remains of him?

His name appears from time to time in the domestic media only because of the social life of his former wife. She publicly supported the Lower Austrian Austrian People's Party (ÖVP) under the retained family name after leaving the SPÖ and was appointed director of the Spanish Riding School by the supervisory board in January 2019 against the recommendation of the advisory board, albeit only for one term. Klima headed the Volkswagen subsidiary in Argentina from October 2000 to November 2011 after leaving politics. He reportedly lives an hour from Buenos Aires with his third wife and three children and owns a farm with 240 hectares of land and 200 cattle. What a peaceful happy ending after failure in Austrian politics and what a contrast to the adventurous life of his dazzling successor Alfred Gusenbauer at the head of the SPÖ.

*Alfred Gusenbauer: from revolutionary to businessman*

The changes and upheavals in Alfred Gusenbauer's career, which have been documented many times in the media, could be taken from the script of a political thriller. Apart from the long-time British Prime Minister and Labour leader Tony Blair and the former German Chancellor and friend of Putin Gerhard Schröder, I know of no former top politician, even from a small country, who has worked so intensively and so successfully as a lobbyist, advisor, director or head of a supervisory board, almost worldwide, as the former SPÖ Federal Chancellor, who is now 63 years old.

Born in St. Pölten in Lower Austria, his father was a worker and his mother a cleaner. He earned a doctorate in political science and philosophy at the University of Vienna, and in a conversation with me one, he was quite proud that the ailing Bruno Kreisky had attended his graduation ceremony. The stages of the storybook career of a young socialist from a poor family were: Federal Chairman of the Socialist Youth (SJ), Vice-President of the Socialist Youth International, Chairman of the SPÖ and head of the SPÖ parliamentary group. Behind these posts lies an extraordinary talent and an unlimited thirst for recognition. He became an outstanding intellectual, able to communicate effortlessly in English, French, Spanish and Italian.

His hour came when, after Klima's departure in 2000, two former SPÖ interior ministers, one from the right wing, the other from the left wing, were the candidates to succeed him at the party helm. The deciding factor was the powerful Viennese mayor and kingmaker Michael Häupl. In his autobiography, he tells how he "invented" and enthroned Gusenbauer as a man who did not tear the party apart but brought and held it together. Häupl praises the new party leader (2000–08) and opposition leader to the skies: "He was one of the most intelligent people I ever met. An incredibly educated man". As a top candidate, Gusenbauer had been "enormously hardworking and also enormously clever". After the surprisingly victorious election against Wolfgang Schüssel in 2006, he was, according to Häupl, "rightly considered a hero, a star".[8]

What happened to cause the triumphant election winner to be replaced by Werner Faymann at the head of the party and the federal government after barely two years and causing him to leave politics? What Michael Häupl does not say in his memoirs, confirmed by all sides and denied by him, is the fact that he not only "invented" Gusenbauer but also destroyed him politically 8 years later. Gusenbauer himself told me this in the summer of 2008, while he was still chancellor, together with the information that he had parted company with his long-time press spokesman because of disloyalty. I will come back to the role of Häupl and Faymann, but the reasons for Gusenbauer's quick fall still need to be explained.

Wolfgang Schüssel had narrowly lost the elections but clearly won the coalition negotiations with the SPÖ candidate for chancellor on the composition of the new government. The key port-

## GREED INSTEAD OF PRINCIPLES

folios—finance, foreign and interior ministries—remained with the ÖVP, which also prevented the abolition of tuition fees promised by Gusenbauer. The new chancellor, despite his flawless proletarian roots, quickly alienated himself from the party base due to a lack of social intelligence, a pretentious and aloof attitude. More and more mistakes were made by him in inner-party communication and public relations.

A key role was played by the conflict with the trade unions. A former top social democratic functionary, who knew Gusenbauer from the youth movement, sees the basic error in the dispute over the privileges of political trade union representatives not in the substance of Gusenbauer's arguments but in the arrogance with which he spoke to trade unionists. She and another leading Social Democrat have declared, in almost identical words, that he had put on an armour of prepotency as a shield and tried, possibly from a childhood trauma of discrimination, to prove himself over and over again. Does his boundless thirst for recognition in the economic and financial world in which he now works also go back to the wounds he suffered in 2009 when he returned for a few months to a low-ranking job in the regional office of the Chamber of Labour, his original employer in 1990–9 and the mocking remarks that went with it, which were not only in the media? Did he want to compensate for the new wounds and take revenge on the "ungrateful" party, so to speak, by his quick enrichment? This is considered a quite probable assumption by some insiders.

It would go beyond the scope of these reflections to try to describe in detail Gusenbauer's glittering track record and international network as a businessman. Hapless as chancellor, he invented himself a second time. He occasionally hinted in interviews that his decades of contacts through the Socialist International proved extremely useful for his entry into the world of the lobbying elite. The now defunct magazine *Addendum*, in a three-part investigation, detailed, among other things, his connections to a Canadian mining company with a gold mining project in Romania, to a holding company in the Caribbean, to the Novia gambling fund in Malta and intermediary companies in Cyprus. Some of his highly lucrative contacts were with such evil figures as the dictator of Azerbaijan, Ilham Aliyev (120,000 euros in fees via front companies for consultancy) and dictator of Kazakhstan Nursultan Nazarbayev (400,000 euros a year as the head of an advisory board). Such details have been revealed in the reports of the Austrian and international media, based on the worldwide research of the Organised Crime and Corruption Reports Project.

As the alleged head of the so-called "Hapsburg Group" (as described in the files of the case against Paul Manafort, Gusenbauer's US client who was sentenced to 47 months in prison for tax and bank fraud), Gusenbauer was said to have worked as a paid lobbyist for Ukrainian President Viktor Yanukovych, who was overthrown by the Maidan revolution in 2014 and fled to Russia. This was only reported years later. According to court documents disputed by Gusenbauer, the "Hapsburg Group" allegedly received around 2 million euros from Manafort for lectures at conferences on Ukraine and the EU. For the SPÖ, it was particularly embarrassing that Gusenbauer conducted his business correspondence via the email address of the SPÖ's Renner Institute, where he served as president between 2000 and 2017.[9]

"I have a clear conscience", Gusenbauer affirmed in an interview about his involvement in Kazakhstan, adding, "we are not working for a dictator, but for the government, for the progress of this country. And progress is visible". He did not dispute the annual fee of 400,000 euros. However, he said, he pays tax on all his income, including from abroad, in Austria. In addition, the ex-chancellor also acts as an advisor to the Serbian government, which is strongly criticised internationally for authoritarian tendencies, in the EU accession negotiations, and he has also worked for the notorious gambling company Novomatic in Latin America and Eastern Europe. In Austria, he chairs the supervisory board of the concern owned by the industrialist Hans Peter Haselsteiner and of three companies controlled by the controversial real estate billionaire René Benko.

As far as the moral imperative for social democracy repeatedly invoked by Kreisky is concerned, Gusenbauer obviously has no problem with it, since he has always denied any wrongdoing and has never had any fear of contact with regimes like those of Kazakhstan and Azerbaijan. In Georg Büchner's play Woyzeck says: "Morality, that is when one is moral. It is a good word ... There must be something beautiful about virtue". Accordingly, to the astonishment of many observers and comrades, Gusenbauer received the Viktor Adler plaque, the highest SPÖ award, at a festive reception in autumn 2021, with reference also to his victory in the 2006 election and the recapture of the federal chancellorship. At the same time, the report published in the news magazine *Profil* on the secret flow of 120,000 euros from the authoritarian regime of Azerbaijan, sarcastically stated: "Since his abrupt departure from top politics at the end of 2008, however, he has made more headlines with his business activities as a lobbyist than with social democratic initiatives". Gusenbauer, who has so far not been proved to have done anything illegal, was nevertheless visibly proud at the celebration and gave encouragement to the party functionaries present that the SPÖ was far from being a discontinued model.

*Werner Faymann, the administrator of the quiet decline*

Since his successor as Federal Chancellor and SPÖ-Chairman, Werner Faymann, was also present at this celebration, it is a good point to now look at his time in office. In contrast to the glory and downfall of Gusenbauer, the rise and fall of the "Federal Chancellor without qualities" were very special, both at the beginning and at the end. It was actually a unique letter in the political history of the Second Republic that indirectly paved the way for Werner Faymann's leap to the top of the government.

One week after Gusenbauer had to hand over the party chairmanship to Faymann, the latter's first official action as acting party leader was to write a letter to the "Dear Editor" of the *Kronen Zeitung*, Hans Dichand, together with the still-Chancellor Gusenbauer on 25 June 2008. The two top politicians promised nothing less than a 180-degree turnaround in Austria's EU policy, even before they informed the executive board of their own party, the coalition partner ÖVP or the Federal President Heinz Fischer. They promised in the letter that every change to the EU Treaty that has a significant impact on Austria should be submitted to a mandatory referendum in future, following the Irish model, and that the opening of the labour market towards the East would also not take place. All this was in line with the aggressive anti-EU line of the *Kronen Zeitung* (with a relatively short exception during the EU accession campaign) and meant a radical change of course without a party or government decision.

Gusenbauer told me in an interview that the letter had been suggested by Faymann, but that they had discussed it in the party leadership and that afterwards "everyone" had been "surprised". I could not interview Werner Faymann because, despite repeated attempts, he was the only Austrian politician who was never willing to have a background talk with me for this book (even 15 years after his resignation). In any case, Gusenbauer's trivialising version was not confirmed by any side; even Häupl says in his memoirs quoted above that he had only read the "fatal letter" in the "Krone".

# GREED INSTEAD OF PRINCIPLES

The media echo was disastrous. The *Salzburger Nachrichten* printed a a cartoon of the "populist" Faymann on the front page crawling into a butt. Other media stated Alfred Gusenbauer and Werner Faymann were lickspittles (*Salzburger Nachrichten*) of the tabloids, throwing themselves in the dust in self-deprecation (*Die Presse*) with circus-like contortions (*Vorarlberger Nachrichten*) and indescribable callousness (*Kurier*) before Hans Dichand (*Oberösterreichische Nachrichten*). The conclusion of the *Kleine Zeitung*: The SPÖ no longer knows any shame. The party leadership is for sale. Even an SPÖ MP complained that the skin of an eel was rougher compared to Faymann. But all this did not harm Faymann. On the contrary, the whole machinery of the highest-circulation Austrian newspaper, at that time with 3.8 million readers, was set in motion by the 87-year-old owner, "Uncle Hans" (as Faymann had called Dichand) to defend Faymann and to build him up as a shining beacon of hope as successor to the hapless Gusenbauer at the head of the party and later the government.

The "first violin" in the orchestra of the largest newspaper, *Kronen Zeitung*, measured in terms its circulation compared to the size of the Austrian population, was played by its "house and court poet" Wolf Martin with his almost daily hymns of praise for Faymann. His effusions read like this: "Smooth is Faymann like an eel?/No, he is courageous and social (...) With clear words and an open mind/He makes the best policy".

Not only the rhymes, but also the comments and the daily letters pages of the *Krone* warmly recommended Faymann as favourite for the chancellorship after ÖVP Vice-Chancellor Wilhelm Molterer dissolved the coalition government at the beginning of July 2008 and Faymann was nominated as SPÖ top candidate in the elections. Before we turn to his political career, it is therefore essential to look at his relationship with the *Kronen Zeitung* and Hans Dichand. All leading politicians, from

Bruno Kreisky to Wolfgang Schüssel, have tried with more or less success to win Hans Dichand's favour. In his memoirs, Franz Vranitzky, as chancellor, called the effort to bring his political messages on certain issues closer to the powerful publisher, a line of "pragmatic discourse".

However, Faymann's relationship with Dichand cannot be compared at all with the latter's usual contact with politicians. The publisher and half-owner of the *Kronen Zeitung* (the other half belongs to the German Funke Group and the Austrian investor René Benko) had already actively supported Faymann as a young chairman of the tenants association and SPÖ member of the municipal diet as Vienna councillor (1985–94). He was allowed to give tips to readers of the *Krone* who were in conflicts with powerful landlords. When he was city councillor for housing and urban renewal (1994–2007), the so-called "media cooperation" flourished with personal appearances by Faymann on social housing projects in the form of a column entitled "The direct line to the city councillor", paid for by the City of Vienna through an advertisement. When Faymann became infrastructure minister at the beginning of 2007, he immediately placed a series of advertisements in the *Kronen Zeitung*, which cost the Federal Railway Administration (ÖBB) 500,000 euros. Every two weeks, double-page advertisements appeared that were only marked as "reportage". Because of several advertisements by ÖBB and the motorway company Asfinag, a parliamentary investigation committee was set up in 2011 following a complaint by the FPÖ. The Office of the Public Prosecutor for Economic Affairs and Corruption initiated proceedings against Faymann, and thus for the first time against a sitting Federal Chancellor. Faymann and his Secretary of State Josef Ostermayer were accused of having forced the companies ÖBB and Asfinag, which are subordinate to the Ministry of Infrastructure, to place advertisements in the tabloid newspapers *Krone, Österreich* and *Heute*. The investigations by the public prosecutor's office against both politicians were discontinued in November 2013.

However, the special relationship between Dichand and Faymann was not primarily about money, but about a close friendship that had developed between the old publisher and the ambitious city politician, who was 40 years younger. They met regularly for confidential chats in a café and were even spotted on holiday together in Venice. The closeness was such that it was said in Vienna that Dichand was Faymann's father. Dichand took the rumour so seriously that he denied it in an editorial and stated that Faymann was not his son. Even the question of whether Faymann called his old friend "Uncle Hans" or just "Hans" was discussed in the media.

In his memoirs, former Vienna mayor Michael Häupl provides convincing evidence that Faymann had originally sought his succession as mayor and thus confirms the rumours that he had for this reason, as a precaution, supported Faymann's move into government and ultimately also his ambition to be chancellor. Häupl describes at length Faymann's "very personal way of doing politics. He tried to create loyalties through conversations, personal relationships and by building a kind of friendship". And then Häupl correctly states: "Faymann's problem was that the SPÖ did not win any elections during his time in government, not even in the provinces (...) And then it is relatively irrelevant whether the arguments put forward against you are correct or merely pretended. If you don't succeed, after a certain time you can forget everything".[10]

The balance sheet of Faymann's eight years as chancellor (2008–16) confirms the assumption that the always friendly, affable and non-committal professional politician is likely to go down in contemporary history as the quiet administrator of the SPÖ's inexorable decline. Of the 20 elections that have taken place during his tenure at the helm of the party, 18 have ended with heavy losses of the SPÖ. In the first round of the presidential elections in April 2016, the party's candidate only won a miserable 11.3 per cent of the votes and ended up in fourth place. This election was, so to speak, the culmination of the massive alienation of social democracy from its traditional supporters and an alarming triumph for the unrestrained social demagogy and xenophobia of the FPÖ.

Apart from the economic crisis of 2008–09, which the country survived relatively well, there was a steadily growing, comprehensive lack of orientation during these years. Under Faymann, who the German weekly *Die Zeit* had already described as a "Teflon politician" in the very first portrait after his election as party leader, the SPÖ was not at all capable of playing a leading role. The permanent crisis of the SPÖ, which Kreisky had once called "a party in the historical sense", developed not only from the structural changes in society but also and primarily from years of chronic weakness and confusion, from years of massive misjudgements and aberrations on the part of its leaders. If one asks the question of how Faymann was able to stay at the top for so long, seemingly unthreatened, despite two parliamentary elections with heavy losses and despite the SPÖ's never-ending electoral defeats, the explanations are basically similar, tuned according to personal sympathy: "An intriguer and schemer, only interested in his position" (Gusenbauer), "a very calm, stable leader, did not seek confrontation" (Doris Bures), "maintained very good relations with the trade unions and with the pensioners, with the boulevard papers" (Brigitte Ederer), "a skilful media networker; highly friendly press releases on his person (not on the SPÖ in general); solidarity with the trade unions and the pensioners' association" (Oliver Rathkolb). In the rather sceptical profile of Faymann in his work *The Paradoxical Republic*, written long before the fall of the chancellor, Rathkolb notes: "Faymann will probably never get rid of this symbolic genuflection [before the

## GREED INSTEAD OF PRINCIPLES

*Krone* with the letter mentioned above] (...) he has the image of a chancellor who depends on the favour of the *Kronen Zeitung*".[11]

I would mention two more factors that both indirectly and in the long run contributed to the stability of Faymann's position. First, the performances of the ÖVP vice-chancellors in his government (Spindelegger, Pröll and Mitterlehner) were similarly dismal, so that the SPÖ was always able to narrowly defend first place and thus the position of chancellor. Secondly, Faymann had a rare stroke of luck in the person of Josef Ostermayer, his closest collaborator over 20 years, as head of cabinet, secretary of state and chancellery minister. "He was the highly intellectual alter ego of Werner Faymann and he is really good. Everyone can only be happy to have him as a collaborator and comrade-in-arms", Michael Häupl said in his memoir.[12] After three conversations with Josef Ostermayer and similar positive remarks even from political opponents, I can only confirm these words, adding the remark that Ostermayer, beyond intellectual substance, possesses a particularly rare quality in political life, namely full loyalty to his superior.

Faymann's reaction to the regional election flops was always in line with political jargon: the election had been a regional poll and only marginally concerned the federal party, sometimes with the equally usual additional phrase: "We didn't manage to present our policies properly...". He held onto this fictitious self-image until the end, that is until 1 May 2016, because he had no feeling for the realities of life in society. The demonstration on that day against Faymann with catcalls and banners at a festive event in front of the town hall was of course not a spontaneous outburst of rage by young socialists but was organised, allegedly by the left wing, although there is no credible information on this, just contradictory speculations.

Less than a week later, Faymann resigned as chancellor and SPÖ chairman, citing a lack of support. Faymann himself has not said a word in public since leaving politics and has concentrated entirely on what appears to be the highly successful development of his real estate company operating in Austria and abroad. His complete silence since his resignation and his refusal of all requests for interviews are reminiscent of the attitude of Chancellor Josef Klaus after his defeat in 1970. He, however, published his memoirs a year later. I also think the former ÖVP party leader Josef Taus a a comparable example of a failed top politician who never spoke out on current political issues after his resignation and did not address any unsolicited public advice to his party. The departure of the third-longest-ruling social democratic chancellor, followed by a quick but ultimately disastrous succession with Christian Kern, has made obvious the deep crisis of identity in Austrian social democracy, still in existence at the time this book went to press.

*Christian Kern: loser of the chancellorship*

After Faymann's fall in May 2016, the previously hidden rivalry between Christian Kern, the general director of federal railways, and Gerhard Zeiler, the most internationally successful Austrian media manager, was decided in 3 days. After all provincial organisations, with the exception of the Viennese SPÖ, had spoken out in favour of Kern, he was proposed and appointed as Federal Chancellor and Party Chairman by the federal party executive. After losing the parliamentary election in October 2017, Kern declared in September 2018, as leader of the opposition in parliament, his resignation from the party chairmanship, without a prior knowledge of the party leadership. At the same time, he announced his intention to run exclusively as the SPÖ's top candidate in the EU election, which was not due until May 2019, as well as his intention to also gain the position of the top candidacy of the European Social Democrats. The party leadership, as well

## GREED INSTEAD OF PRINCIPLES

as the entire public, learned all this from the media. After chaotic days, the former health minister Pamela Rendi-Wagner was nominated by the SPÖ presidium as Kern's successor at the party leadership. The role as opposition leader had not suited him, he had other skills than the domestic political "nitty gritty", Kern explained. In his memoirs, Häupl openly describes Kern's pursuit of the top candidacy of the European Social Democrats as "completely crazy, because [it was] hopeless". Two weeks after this "communication-strategic disaster" (Peter Kaiser, SPÖ governor of Carinthia), the next surprise in Kern's failed melodrama followed: after the wave of indignation of many party functionaries and members, Kern announced his final departure from politics, referring to "constant petty intrigues from here and there". He wanted to devote himself to the "economy and entrepreneurship".

After this chaotic resignation in instalments, I asked a number of authoritative social democratic interlocutors the theoretical question: wouldn't Zeiler have been a better choice and why did Kern fail so quickly and so dramatically? The first question was clearly answered in the affirmative by the majority, and by others as irrelevant, but all agreed that in retrospect Christian Kern was a disastrous miscast. Häupl's personal responsibility because of his belated and lukewarm commitment to Gerhard Zeiler was also broached by some. A long conversation I had with Kern, apart from reproaches to the "dried-up SPÖ without talent" and to the "scheming saboteurs from the ÖVP against the coalition government with the cooperative Vice-Chancellor Reinhold Mitterlehner", did not contribute anything to my clarification of his motives for the hasty resignation. It is possible that his wife's wish was indeed decisive for his departure from politics, as hinted at by him in an aside as well as by friends.

Be that as it may, the main reasons for his fiasco, according to the general opinion of party friends and staff, were the following: he was a dazzling communicator, but two good speeches could not make up for the lack of strategy and the divided team. He had been volatile, erratic, immensely vain, "like a princess", not resilient, always focused on the beginning but not the end of a project, resistant to consultation and sometimes taking idiosyncratic decisions without discussion with the campaign team. Some observers see one of the main reasons for the defeat in the fact that Kern had not forced an early new election after his "Plan A" speech in January 2017, which was very well received by the media. Thus, after Mitterlehner's resignation in May, Foreign Minister Sebastian Kurz was able to continue his long-prepared secret project to take over the ÖVP, to end the coalition and to gain early elections.

However, there were still two factors that contributed significantly to the election victory of the "New ÖVP": 1) The SPÖ's chief campaign advisor, Tal Silberstein from Israel, who had been recommended by Gusenbauer, was arrested in the middle of the Austrian election campaign in his home country for bribery and money laundering in Romania. His case became a nightmare for the SPÖ after the discovery of the smear campaign he ran against Kurz on two Facebook pages. 2) The second factor was the role of Silberstein's interpreter. Kern told me that this woman had been a friend of a close relative of a leading ÖVP politician at the time and had immediately passed on to him her notes on the conversations with Silberstein. The internal deliberations on the SPÖ's election strategy, which were widely reported in the media, repeatedly triggered tensions within their campaign team because Kern's staff blamed each other for the indiscretions. These disputes produced headlines again and finally led to the resignations of the SPÖ executive director and the campaign manager during the intensive phase of the election campaign.

In my above-mentioned conversation with im, Kern indirectly hinted that he regretted his resignation after his wife had mentioned a week before our meeting that it was "actually a pity that he had left politics". This impression is confirmed by several newspaper interviews that have appeared in the meantime. For example, Kern consistently avoided answering the question whether his chosen party leader, Pamela Rendi-Wagner, was suitable to become candidate for the chancellorship at the next election. The SPÖ had many suitable candidates who were "full of energy waiting in the wings", he remarked once.

After his resignation, Kern became one of the twelve supervisory board members of the Russian State Railways, until he resigned from this post on 24 February 2022 after Russia's attack on Ukraine, and remains president of the European China Business Council, the business association with around 2,000 of China's largest companies, which is linked to the Beijing government. Kern had criticised the EU sanctions against Russia at the St Petersburg Economic Forum while still Chancellor in June 2017. Based on his various public statements even on the eve of war against the Ukraine and after the practical takeover of Hongkong by China, the former chancellor can be seen as one of the advocates in Austria of the policy of appeasement towards both autocratic regimes.

The uncertain future of Pamela Rendi-Wagner

Kern undoubtedly promoted Pamela Rendi-Wagner, a medical doctor, as his successor and the first woman to head the SPÖ party. He had already put her as minister of health in second place after him on the federal candidate list in the 2017 parliamentary elections. Michael Häupl characterises her in his typical enigmatic way:

> Pamela Rendi-Wagner was not his logical successor, but she was a universally appreciated suggestion because she was simply the first woman in the history of social democracy to become federal party leader. She had cut a very good figure as Minister of Health, but of

course she was not a woman who had been washed in all the waters of social democratic politics and bureaucracy (....) In my estimation, she is a really clever woman who also has a high sensitivity for what social democracy has to implement, especially in difficult times ... In terms of the subject matter, she is doing it really well and she is also getting better and better rhetorically (....) I stand by that: Pamela Rendi-Wagner is a good chairperson.

She joined the SPÖ only a few days before her inauguration as Health Minister in March 2017, but had already been a member of the BSA, the Social Democratic Academic Association, since 2012. After all better-qualified candidates, first and foremost former long-time SPÖ managing director, ex-transport minister and second president of parliament, Doris Bures, and some others had dropped out, Rendi-Wagner was elected as party leader at the party congress in November 2018 with 97.81 per cent of the delegates' votes. In the general election in September 2019, the SPÖ obtained 21.18 per cent of the votes with her as the top candidate, a loss of 5.7 per cent compared with the previous election, the historically worst result in a parliamentary election in the party's history. In order to strengthen her position, she organised a controversial internal party survey on her chairmanship for the first time ever in spring 2020. Only 41.3 per cent of the members answered the questionnaire; 71 per cent were in favour of her continuing as party leader. A year later, in June 2021 at the SPÖ party congress, only 75 per cent of delegates voted for her as party leader. She surmised in a background interview with me that organised action from Burgenland and Lower Austria was taken against her, which was also noted by most independent observers.

At the time of writing, Austrian Social Democracy is in the throes of a disastrous internal crisis. The SPÖ has become deeply split between the nominal party chairwoman, Pamela Rendi-Wagner, and her two rivals who forced an internal party survey

# GREED INSTEAD OF PRINCIPLES

before an extraordinary party congress in June. These rivals are Hans-Peter Doskozil, governor of Burgendland, the smallest region with only 300 000 inhabitants and a hard-liner in migration policy, and Andreas Babler, the demonstratively left-wing mayor of Traiskirchen, a small town with 18 000 inhabitants, some 20 miles from Vienna. However, it is likely that none of the three candidates on the list presented to the 150 000 registered SPÖ members for a choice will achieve a convincing victory. This could provoke the emergence of new challengers at the party congress or even on the eve of the next general election. Without unity on the political line and the issue of leadership, the SPÖ can be no longer a credible alternative to the center-right ÖVP or to the far-right FPÖ. Even the launching of a new left-wing group cannot be excluded.

8

# THE ÖVP, THE MOST UNUSUAL CONSERVATIVE PARTY IN EUROPE

The Austrian People's Party (ÖVP), founded on 17 April 1945 in Vienna, is a unique phenomenon in the European party landscape. Even the founding of the ÖVP was unusual. Firstly, the three confederations, the Business Confederation (led by Julius Raab), the Farmers' Confederation (by Leopold Figl) and the Workers' and the Salaried Employees' Confederation (by Lois Weinberger), were founded before the party itself. It was more than a symbolic act and indicated their decades-long, sometimes decisive importance in shaping the overall party priorities. The primacy of these bodies as constitutive elements of the party depended, of course, on the personalities at the top. Secondly, it was also important, that the leaders in Vienna were quickly able to establish contact with Christian social politicians in the western regions across the demarcation lines of the occupying powers. It was the young resistance fighter and medical student Herbert Braunsteiner who, in the evening hours of 20 May 1945, swam across the ice-cold Enns River and, with a letter from Cardinal Innitzer, established contact with the distrustful bourgeois politicians in Innsbruck as a messenger of the executive committee. This marked the first step towards the formation of the ÖVP as a national party, active over the whole country and thus also in the three occupation zones of the Western allies. It was not until October, however, that the misgivings of the western provincial organisations against the Renner government and the Viennese party leadership were completely dispelled. The danger of a division of the country was overcome and appropriate conditions created for the decisive free elections on 25 November 1945.

This party, divided territorially and functionally, was one of the essential architects of the Second Republic and has played a key role in politics over the last 75 years up to the present day. It has provided the federal chancellors from 1945 to 1970, from 2000 to 2006 and since 2017. Not only through my journalistic work, but above all thanks to personal contacts with three party chairmen and leading journalists, I have been able to gain an insight into the complicated structures and personal rivalries over the course of almost six decades.

*Leopold Figl and Julius Raab: architects of the Second Republic*

I will always regret that I did not personally know two key figures—the first two ÖVP Federal Chancellors, Julius Raab and Leopold Figl. Raab was undoubtedly the key figure setting the course for the State Treaty in Austria. Before all other politicians, he had recognised and seized the opportunity when the Soviet Foreign Minister Molotov proposed direct Austrian–Soviet negotiations in February 1955. Raab also proved to be a strong personality in domestic and economic policy. As the chairman of the ÖVP for many years, he was responsible for the particularly strong role of the business confederation and, through an agreement with the then trade union leader, Franz Olah, also for the organised form of social partnership through the establishment

# THE ÖVP

of the joint commissions of representatives of employers and employees. Nevertheless, it was Leopold Figl, former prisoner of the Dachau Nazi concentration camp and after 1945 the first ÖVP Federal Chancellor, who is still considered one of the most popular Austrian politicians due to his direct and winning personality. Leopold Figl crying on the balcony of the Belvedere Palais the words "Austria is free!" has become the indelible symbolic figure of the State Treaty in the memory of Austrians.

My best friend and "Austria teacher" Kurt Vorhofer, to whom I posthumously dedicated my first book on Austria, told me his impressions as a young journalist of Figl. At a New Year's Eve dinner in his flat overlooking St. Stephens Square in Vienna, sometime in the 1970s, he read me the touching Christmas message of Figl in 1945. At the time, it was an unforgettable speech for all those who had a radio set and even electricity, but also for those generations who later read the oft-quoted text: "I can give you nothing for Christmas. I can give you no candles for the Christmas tree, if you have one at all, no piece of bread, no coals, no glass to cut into. We have nothing. I can only ask you: believe in this Austria!"

His state funeral on 14 May 1965, one day before the tenth anniversary of the State Treaty, was marked by a funeral procession from St. Stephen's Cathedral to Heldenplatz. That rainy day was unforgettable for me, too. One felt what his biographer Ernst Trost later wrote: "The Austrians openly testified that they had lost a man and politician and human being who had been close to them all. They had often laughed about him, and now they were not ashamed to cry about him either".[1]

I did not know Raab himself, but I established a relatively close and friendly contact with the real mastermind of his economic policy, known as the "Raab-Kamitz course", namely Professor Reinhard Kamitz, during his long term as President of the National Bank (1960–8). Before this he had been minister of finance between 1952 and 1960. He was an independent and sovereign person who bluntly and frequently made known to me, the young foreign correspondent, his critical opinion of the financial policy of his successor, Josef Klaus, later chancellor. I had no idea at the time that this outstanding financial expert had already had a rapid career as a party member (and SS candidate) during the Nazi era. In the spirit of coalition harmony, the then minister of the interior, Oskar Helmer, is even said to have presented him with his "Gauakt" (i.e. the Nazi personal file on him) as a birthday present.

*The reformer Josef Klaus*

Alfons Gorbach (1898–1972) was the first Federal Chancellor I met as Vienna correspondent of the *Financial Times*. He was imprisoned in Dachau immediately after the Anschluss and in Flossenbürg from 1944 until the end of the war. I spoke to him several times during his tenure from 1961 to 1964 and reported on his activities. Under the leadership of this jovial politician, the ÖVP succeeded in winning the elections in November 1962, but the conciliatory negotiator was unable to achieve a breakthrough in the 5 months of talks with the SPÖ. Incidentally, the fuse of the Habsburg crisis also began to burn during his chancellorship.

After his brief tenure, the pair of reformers Josef Klaus (1910–2001), as Federal Chancellor, and Hermann Withalm (1912–2003), as Secretary General of the ÖVP, came to power. I got to know and appreciate both of them at close quarters. In retrospect, Klaus was probably, along with Fred Sinowatz, the most underrated or forgotten Federal Chancellor. To date, he is the only provincial governor ever to become federal chancellor in Vienna, in his case after 12 years in Salzburg.

On 6 March 1966, Klaus went down in Austrian history as the great victor: with him at the helm, the ÖVP won an absolute

## THE ÖVP

majority for the first time since November 1945. Before that, during the occupation, there was simply no alternative to coalition government. Of course, the ÖVP also owed its victory to the split in the SPÖ caused by the break with the popular trade unionist Franz Olah and to serious tactical mistakes by the party leadership. The shock of the election defeat sealed the demise of the coalition for the SPÖ after 21 years.

The Klaus government set the course in many areas of economic and media policy. Nevertheless, perhaps the chancellor's personnel policy had the most important long-term significance. No Austrian head of government has ever discovered and promoted so many young political talents as Josef Klaus. To name but a few: Thomas Klestil (Federal President 1992–2004); Alois Mock (Foreign Minister 1987–95), Heinrich Neisser (Second President of the National Council 1994–9), Josef Krainer (Governor of Styria 1981–96), Wolfgang Schmitz (Finance Minister 1964–8), Josef Taus (State Secretary, Chairman of the Supervisory Board of ÖIAG 1967–75, Federal Party Chairman of the ÖVP 1975–9).

Of course, it must also be emphasised that all those named were members of the Cartellverband (CV), the Catholic, colour-bearing university fraternities, which stand in sharp contrast to the right-wing radical, duelling fraternities described in an earlier chapter. This Catholic network with an esprit de corps was particularly strong in the 1960s, especially during the Klaus government, in the Federal Chancellery, in the Chambers of Commerce and Agriculture, and in some provincial and district administrations. After all, 23 per cent of the ÖVP parliamentarians belonged to the CV at that time. I owe the insight into the mentality and the atmosphere of the CV above all to my lifelong friendship with the journalist Kurt Vorhofer. He belonged to perhaps the most influential fraternity, the Norica, which counted Raab, Figl, Withalm and Mock among its members.

# AUSTRIA BEHIND THE MASK

The Federal Chancellors Gorbach and Klaus as well as Federal President Klestil and my close friend Josef Taus were also CVers.

Today, the CV no longer plays the formative role it did back then. One must also point to the growing influence of the Catholic Middle School Students' Association and the Catholic Student Youth (Katholische Studierende Jugend, KSJ) in elite education. Such important personalities as the former Federal Chancellor Wolfgang Schüssel, the ex-Vice Chancellors Erhard Busek and Josef Riegler, as well as the long-time Governor of Styria Josef Krainer Jr, were in the KSJ and not in the Cartellverband.

It is one of the strange details of a long life that, apart from the special case of Bruno Kreisky, who I also never called by his first name as a non-SPÖ member, I have at times formed closer bonds of friendship above all with ÖVP politicians, especially with Taus, but also with Klestil, Busek, Schüssel and (Erwin) Pröll. I owe to these friendships and close contacts of such authoritative social democratic figures as former Vice-Chancellor Hannes Androsch and former Federal President Heinz Fischer my background knowledge of Austrian politics and economics.

*Alois Mock: symbolic decency*

After Chancellor Vranitzky's break with the Haider FPÖ in 1986, the election results gave the ÖVP two options: the chance of a new small coalition with the sign reversed, namely under an ÖVP Chancellor Alois Mock, or entry into a grand coalition under Vranitzky. Mock, supported also by the Governor of Salzburg, Wilfried Haslauer, proposed the formation of an ÖVP–FPÖ coalition. He failed due to the resistance of the Wirtschaftsbund and the eastern provincial organisations. The offer to give him the foreign ministry and the post of vice-chancellor made it easier for him to give in, according to the history of the ÖVP.

# THE ÖVP

Here, for the first time, I would like to outline my personal memories of Alois Mock and my impressions from many years of friendly cooperation at some length. I not only met him quite often professionally as a journalist, but also gained many personal impressions of his human greatness through mutual friends and CV brothers such as Kurt Vorhofer and Josef Taus. In contrast to Sinowatz and Klaus, Mock was not underestimated politically, but as a human being he was sometimes seen wrongly, sometimes treated unfairly. He was a politician who somehow never had any luck in politics. He was not granted the chance to become federal chancellor. In addition, he had severe, incurable Parkinson's disease, which had already been diagnosed in his late fifties. Due to his illness, he had to retire from active politics much too early and could not really enjoy the greatest political triumph of his life, Austria's accession to the European Union.

What lies behind the dry dates of his political rise—in 1969, at the age of 35, Minister of Education in the Klaus government; in 1971–9 Chairman of the Österreichischer Arbeiter und Angestellten Bund (ÖAAB); and in 1979–89 ÖVP Party Chairman and 1987–95 Foreign Minister? It was neither intellectual brilliance nor stirring rhetoric, but iron adherence to principle and unwavering straightforwardness, sincerity shaped by Christian social teaching and unbroken loyalty to friends, tremendous diligence in the service of the homeland and deeply rooted sympathy for and solidarity with gagged peoples in Eastern and South-Eastern Europe, modesty in success and courage in defeat, and a never flagging sense of duty coupled with unparalleled enthusiasm for work that were his outstanding qualities.

Here is just one example of loyalty: the brilliant banker and then ÖVP Federal Party Chairman Josef Taus had no chance against the exceptional politician Bruno Kreisky. Moreover, this talented man was not popular even in his own party. What is more, he had wanted to push through his old idea of a radical party reform with the primacy of the federal party leadership over the three professional confederations and the provincial organisations much too late, after the second election defeat. Even a member of the reform commission opposed his proposals on the grounds that without the confederations the ÖVP would be "a party without people". The fact that Alois Mock was elected by the ÖVP deputies as executive chairman of the party was already seen as a preliminary decision for Mock as "ÖVP crown prince". Despite the alarm sounds of the media in this regard, however, he remained loyal to party leader Josef Taus until the end. To those who regarded Mock as a "dangerous leftist" because of his ÖAAB chairmanship, Kurt Vorhofer answered: "You have to be very narrow-minded or very far to the right, which often amounts to the same thing if you see Mock as a leftist. Alois Mock is an open-minded conservative of Catholic-bourgeois origin".

After Taus's resignation in the summer of 1979, Mock succeeded in breaking Kreisky's absolute majority as party leader, thanks in part to internal SPÖ antagonisms. But the turbulent election year of 1986 (Waldheim affair, resignation of Chancellor Sinowatz, bursting of the small coalition of the FPÖ–SPÖ) was dramatic politically and health-wise for Alois Mock. As he put it himself: "As party leader I went from minus 19 mandates to minus 11 and finally to minus three behind the SPÖ", and with reference to the changes from Kreisky to Fred Sinowatz and finally to Franz Vranitzky he added with resignation: "I couldn't cope with two new party leaders of the SPÖ, but I could have managed one".

The fact that his party, like so many predecessors (and successors), dismantled him was something he accepted outwardly without bitterness or rancour. He was undoubtedly a great integration figure, always seeking reconciliation and balance with political rivals in his own party. I know of no Austrian politician

# THE ÖVP

who would have formulated his state-political mission as Mock, still as party leader, did in an interview after massive losses in three state elections, visibly dejected:

> My most important concern is to realise my politics, my second most important is to win elections. But now I also have to realise that the second most important thing very often determines how a party views its leader, or how long-term a party can decide. After all, it has to win elections so that it can shape the future. And that is why it is a reciprocal effect. So, the second most important thing for me is to win elections. Only if I don't manage one without the other, then the point comes sooner that everyone is only elected for a time.[2]

## *Alois Mock: pacesetter for Balkan policy*

Alois Mock's international reputation was primarily the result of his commitment to the liberation of the peoples of Eastern and South-Eastern Europe from the double bondage of communism and foreign domination. In this sense, the 8 years at the head of the foreign ministry meant his immeasurable contribution to overcoming the division of Europe. I will not detail here his pioneering efforts to secure Austria's accession to the European Union and the symbolic cutting of the barbed wire between Austria and Hungary and between Austria and what was then Czechoslovakia, but rather his controversial role in the Yugoslav crisis.

His commitment to the independence of Slovenia and Croatia, and later also to the human rights of the Kosovo Albanians, seemed at the time incomprehensible to many party friends and even more so to many political opponents. Sometime in the late 1980s after his appearance on a TV programme, we were talking in the ORF canteen about the tensions in the multi-ethnic state of Yugoslavia, and I encouraged him in his critical stance with unusually frank advice: "Don't stop putting pressure on the SPÖ; you could even go down in Austrian history with a courageous stance in the Yugoslav crisis!" Our mutual friend Kurt Vorhofer, also confirmed him in this endeavour.

In an article, on account of his Balkan engagement, he was even personally attacked by the philosopher Rudolf Burger as a warmonger.[3] I have been involved with Yugoslavia for decades and published my first major book on nationalism in the communist Balkan countries, with a focus on Yugoslavia, as early as 1969. That is why I supported Mock's Balkan policy. As far as Mock's Yugoslavia initiatives are concerned, I agree now as I did then with the opinion aptly expressed by the commentator Peter Michael Lingens: "It was not the war that followed a hasty recognition, but a long-delayed recognition that followed the war already in full swing".[4]

For me, his role in the birth of the Europa Forum Wachau (from June 1995) as an international meeting place, which he co-founded despite failing health, remains unforgettable. The initiative came from him and Erwin Pröll, the Governor of Lower Austria. I consider Pröll the most important regional politician in the history of the Second Republic. Countless cultural initiatives and projects for the promotion of the arts and science are associated with his name as governor of the largest Austrian province for 25 years.

The impressive list of three dozen prime ministers, ministers and EU commissioners who have come to the Europa Forum at the Benedictine Abbey in Göttweig in the 25 years since 1995 provides a most convincing proof of the success of this experiment in the heart of Lower Austria to create a recognised, European discussion forum. Since Alois Mock's first major interview with the famous columnist and author Flora Lewis in the *New York Times*, the discussions at Göttweig Abbey have been echoed in the continent's major newspapers, from *Le Monde* in Paris to the *Frankfurter Allgemeine* and the *Neue Zürcher Zeitung*. The fact that I could contribute from the very beginning as co-

# THE ÖVP

organiser and moderator to the success of the Europa Forum Wachau is one of the great experiences of my life.

I will never forget when he explained the Austrian position in the discussion on European integration to Flora Lewis with his characteristic passion on the sunny terrace of the monastery restaurant in 1995, at the very first event. Shortly afterwards, he spoke in excellent French with Daniel Vernet, at that time *Le Monde's* Moscow correspondent (later its editor-in-chief), followed by a brief exchange of views, also in French, with the first foreign guest speaker, Jean-Claude Juncker, then Prime Minister of Luxembourg, later President of the EU Commission.

*The mysterious espionage case of Felix Bloch*

Alois Mock studied at the Bologna Centre of Johns Hopkins University in 1957–8 and at the Université Libre de Bruxelles in 1960–1, thanks to scholarships, and then worked at the Austrian OECD representation in Paris from 1962–6.

Mock's student days in Bologna were the reason why the name of this man of "unassailable integrity" (President Heinz Fischer in his obituary) inadvertently appeared several times on the sidelines of one of the biggest US espionage stories. In Bologna, a lifelong, close friendship developed between Mock, the US student Felix Bloch, and Bloch's future wife Lou (Lucille), who was also a student. Bloch had fled from Vienna to the United States with his parents as a 4-year-old child after the Anschluss, and after completing his studies he worked at the US State Department. After holding various diplomatic posts, mainly in Germany, he was transferred to Vienna in 1980, where he served first under the Austrian-born Ambassador Helene von Damm from 1983 and then under the billionaire Ronald Lauder for 7 years as number two in the rank of Deputy Chief of Mission, until the autumn of 1987. He spoke fluent German and, with his wife Lou, was part of a popular diplomatic couple in Viennese society. His long-standing close friendship with Alois and Edith Mock was common knowledge in town.

The news of Felix Bloch's unmasking as a spy hit Vienna like a bombshell on 21 July 1989. As was to be expected, Foreign Minister Mock was accused of having involuntarily become an informant. The Austrian diplomat Martin Eichtinger, Mock's secretary at the time, summarised it briefly as follows: "Mock categorically ruled this out, but was deeply affected by the American diplomat's breach of trust. Finally, Interior Minister Franz Löschnak confirmed that no Austrian security interests had been affected by Bloch's contacts with Austrian politicians". US newspapers reported the opposite version based on statements by Ambassador Lauder, namely that Bloch had allegedly divulged secrets from internal US documents to Austrian politicians, especially to his friend Alois Mock.[5]

A detailed article in the *New York Times*[6] rehashed a 14-hour interview with Bloch and many internal documents to conclude that the Bloch case remained unique: never before had a high-ranking civil servant been publicly suspected and labelled as a spy for the Soviet Union, shadowed for months by the FBI state police, TV stations and the press, but not formally accused, charged or tried. He was nevertheless dismissed from the service soon after, his pension rights were cancelled and he was ruined. What was the evidence? They had recordings from Paris and Brussels of Bloch's encounters with an alleged Frenchman, "Pierre Bart", who in reality, under the name Reino Gikman, was a KGB agent and had officially lived in Vienna as a technical employee for 7 years at the same time as Bloch. During the two filmed encounters in Paris and Brussels, Bloch handed him a small suitcase each time. According to Bloch, these suitcases contained only stamps or stamp collections. Bloch has always denied all accusations and claimed never to have met the agent in Vienna. In any case, no charges were ever brought against him.

# THE ÖVP

President George HW Bush publicly spoke of a "very serious case". However, this turned out to be an unprecedented loss of image for the FBI and probably also for the CIA, since a spy suspected of being in the public spotlight could never be convicted. Felix Bloch moved to Chapel Hill in North Carolina and found a job as a bus driver. According to a local newspaper, he was convicted of shoplifting in 1992. His wife Lou, who was unaware of his double life and only learned of his long-term sadomasochistic relationship with a Viennese prostitute from the newspapers, divorced him. His two daughters Kathleen and Andrea also had professional difficulties because of the media campaign.

And now we come back to the human greatness of Alois and Edith Mock: Lou Bloch, who had to fight over her pension rights with the State Department, came to Vienna a few years later, I think even several times. Where did she live? With the Mocks, who did not drop her in this crisis. This human reaction at the end of a puzzling and, for the innocent family, catastrophic case is what I wanted to describe here.

*1989–99: unlucky time for the ÖVP*

After the dignified departure of Alois Mock as party leader, his three successors at the top of the party, Josef Riegler, Erhard Busek and Wolfang Schüssel, had no luck in the decade 1989 to 1999 and could not stop the decline of the ÖVP. Josef Riegler, the likeable minister of agriculture from Styria, had not pushed himself forward as a successor candidate and only reluctantly allowed himself to be put forward. At the party congress in May 1989, Mock was elected honorary chairman to great applause. In order to understand this very structurally diverse party, it is useful to recall the warnings of Bertram Jäger, President of the Vorarlberg Chamber of Labour: "The way we treat our chairmen is a chapter in itself. I have experienced many party leaders.

People have cheered a party leader and it hasn't taken long for the criticism to start again. And not infrequently, the kingmakers were then also the king-killers, i.e. those who raised him up on the shield were the first to attack the new chairman". For the future, he said, the party should bear in mind Mark Twain's saying: "Before you start loving your enemies, you should treat your friends better".[7]

Riegler's term of office as party leader and vice-chancellor lasted only 2 years. After the crushing defeat in October 1990 with the loss of 9.2 per cent of the votes and 17 mandates, Riegler's star was extinguished, although his concept of the eco-social market economy, even if as a political slogan, proved to be surprisingly durable. His personal charisma deficits stood in stark contrast to Franz Vranitzky's presentation skills and Jörg Haider's seductive demagogy.

*Erhard Busek: the intellectual reformer*

I had already known his successor Erhard Busek well before this period of inner-party intrigues. He became a friend over the years. For him, perhaps more than for any other politician I know, Nietzsche's statement applies: "He who thinks a lot is not suited to be a party man; he thinks himself through the party too soon".[8] It was therefore almost a miracle that this man succeeded beyond his own party on the small stage of Austrian politics. Although he even rose to become party leader and vice-chancellor (1991–5), it was above all as Vienna's ÖVP chairman and vice-mayor in Vienna (1978–87) that he left his indelible mark on the intellectual climate in that city. During his 4 years as minister of science and research and minister of education and culture, Busek also gave Austria's role in Central Europe and the Danube region a distinctive character. In his flat in Vienna, in the 1980s, Busek and his wife Helga introduced countless

# THE ÖVP

impressive personalities, such as the brilliant thinker Leszek Kołakowski, the Montenegrin rebel Milovan Đilas, and the future presidents of Croatia and Hungary, Franjo Tuđman and Árpád Göncz, to Austrian journalists and cultural figures. Who could forget his contribution, unique in Austrian politics, to the liberation of the people east of the Elbe?

Erhard Busek was a person with extraordinary abilities as an intellectual networker and a thinker always open to new areas. In and outside Austria, Busek was always a tireless advocate against xenophobic and anti-Semitic tendencies. Until his death in March 2022, the former coordinator of the Stability Pact for South Eastern Europe (2002–08), the chairman (since 1995) of the Institute for the Danube region and Central Europe and the organiser of numerous cultural events exuded an unbroken capacity for curiosity and steadfastness. His stimulating books on Austria and the Danube region should not be overlooked either. His death is an irreplaceable loss for Austrian democracy. I also have personal reasons to be grateful to him, among other things for financing many years of the Hungarian edition of the *Europäische Rundschau* and above all for his two statements of solidarity with me during the defamatory attacks from Hungary after my first book on the worrying developments under the Orbán regime was published.[9] Busek defended me twice, once with a statement to the Hungarian news agency MTI and once in an article published in the newspaper *Die Presse*.[10]

It is actually incredible that Erhard Busek always had the reputation of being a failed ÖVP chairman. First, he had achieved singular successes in Vienna in the regional elections of 1978 and 1983, the last with a share of the vote of almost 35 per cent and 37 regional deputies. The invention of citizens' initiatives outside the traditional party organisation and the promotion of non-party cultural figures increasingly met with resistance from the party base. At the federal party congress in June

1991, Busek received only 56.4 per cent of the votes for the post of ÖVP federal party chairman, despite being confronted with a colourless opponent. This was an encouragement for his sworn opponents to start sawing away at his chairmanship immediately after his appointment.

Neither the breakthrough in the EU negotiations nor the surprising success of his proposed presidential candidate, the diplomat Thomas Klestil, could halt the ÖVP's uninterrupted decline. Despite the success of Austria's European policy associated with the name of Alois Mock, the polls signalled a further electoral drop to below 30 per cent for the ÖVP. I was present at the congress of the ÖVP in Linz in June 1994. Erhard Busek, then vice-chancellor in the grand coalition with Franz Vranitzky, ruled out the option of a small coalition with the FPÖ and spoke out "without ifs and buts" in favour of continuing the grand coalition. Although there were increasing doubts about the leadership quality of the federal party leader, Foreign Minister Mock, the party's most popular figure, demonstratively backed Busek after the EU success and because of his positioning in the Yugoslav crisis, saying that if the party did not have Busek, it would have to invent him.

At the parliamentary election in October 1994, both coalition parties lost massively. The clear winners were the FPÖ, Greens and Liberal Forum opposition parties. Election day sealed Erhard Busek's political fate. However, with a skilful tactic he managed to pave the way for his preferred candidate as federal party chairman, Economics Minister Wolfgang Schüssel, to win at the party congress in April 1995. Schüssel, his closest friend promoted by him so far, seemed to Busek to be the guarantor for a liberal-conservative, urban policy with a positioning in the centre of the political spectrum. Wolfgang Schüssel was elected party leader with 95.5 percent of the delegates' votes, almost exactly 50 years after the foundation of the ÖVP.

# THE ÖVP

Nobody suspected at the time, not even his inventor, that the 50-year-old new leader would lead the ÖVP on a rollercoaster to its greatest defeat and then to an unprecedented triumph.

9

# FROM WOLFGANG SCHÜSSEL TO SEBASTIAN KURZ

## FROM TRIUMPH TO CRASH

It was Friday evening, 17 May 2019, at a buffet dinner of the *Le Monde* correspondent in Vienna, when an excited colleague showed me short quotes on his mobile phone from a video about the Freedom Party of Austria (FPÖ) Vice Chancellor Strache. As my wife and I were going to Hungary very early the next day, we went home, and I did not realise the implications of the famous Ibiza video[1] until I was in the car. Then in Budapest, a Hungarian journalist from a news website called me and asked what I thought of the story. Without thinking, I said, "This is the happiest day of my life!" Afterwards, Austrian papers often quoted my spontaneous remark. Since then, I have always had to correct this absurd claim in interviews. If we speak about a "happiest day", then for me it would certainly have been rescue from certain death in February 1945 or release from the internment camp in 1953 in Hungary or arrival in Vienna in 1957 and not the completely surprising fall of the Austrian People's Party (ÖVP)–FPÖ Kurz-Strache government. My statement was nonsensical, yet psychologically treacherous: it showed how deeply I despised, perhaps even unconsciously, this government of Sebastian Kurz and Heinz-Christian Strache and at the same time how worried I was about Austria's future.

In view of the fact that more than two decades earlier I had publicly defended, both in print and on the screen, the first black-blue government under the chancellorship of Wolfgang Schüssel, which was so strongly condemned not only in Austria but also internationally, punished by sanctions and fought with mass demonstrations, my reaction after Ibiza might seem incomprehensible or even hypocritical to some. Therefore, I would like to start this second part of the ÖVP story with Wolfgang Schüssel and his government.

*Wolfgang Schüssel's "masterpieces"*

As explained in the previous chapter, the real dilemma of the ÖVP is in the structure of the party itself with nine provincial organisations, each with branches of the six confederations (employees, farmers, business, youth, senior citizens and women). The relationship of these governing bodies to each other and the mood in the provincial organisations have repeatedly confirmed Churchill's saying: "There is no friendship in politics, especially at the top". In this sense, the history of this Christian party is also that of un-Christian secret and open intrigues and struggles for top positions within the party.

Wolfgang Schüssel's wish had not been a secret from the beginning: in front of some 500 party conference delegates in the ballroom of the Vienna Hofburg, the former economics minister, who had just been elected federal party chairman with 95.5 per cent of the vote, had declared in April 1995 in a firm voice: "I want to become Federal Chancellor with your help". The informally dressed and talented draughtsman, football player and

# FROM WOLFGANG SCHÜSSEL TO SEBASTIAN KURZ

mountaineer, piano, guitar and also cello player became head of a party that had been struggling with its identity and leadership crisis since the Klaus government (i.e. for a quarter of a century). I had already known Schüssel well as the former secretary general of the business confederation and as minister of economics. Once he invited me to give a lecture on Eastern Europe to the officials of his ministry and even paid me a decent fee for it. I had met him several times in his office, which was furnished with modern furniture, in the early 1990s. He had been friendly and direct. I did not believe that he would pose a greater threat than Busek to Chancellor Vranitzky in his new position of party chairman and vice-chancellor. Like almost the entire public, I was surprised that Schüssel provoked new elections within the first 6 months of his appointment because of a dispute over the budget. The election result was a success for Vranitzky and a defeat for Schüssel: the SPÖ gained six mandates, the ÖVP only one. The next parliamentary election, on 3 October 1999, turned out to be a disaster for the ÖVP and its party leader. Jörg Haider's FPÖ overtook the People's Party for the first time, by 415 votes, as the second strongest party! With 26.9 per cent, the ÖVP achieved the worst result in its history and was in third place. The SPÖ, under Viktor Klima, landed at its historic low of 33.1 per cent but was still considered the clear winner. The situation was dramatic, however, because Schüssel had literally declared at the beginning of September 1999: "Under no circumstances will we participate in a government if we are not at least second". Chancellor Klima, on the other hand, who had been entrusted by Federal President Thomas Klestil with the formation of the new government, had from the outset ruled out a coalition with the FPÖ.

The strange thing about this seemingly hopeless situation was that, in retrospect, Wolfgang Schüssel's greatest political defeat formed the basis of his greatest personal success. As I have already described Wolfgang Schüssel's rise and fall in detail in my previous Austria book,[2] I would like to focus here on the question of why, after 7 years as chancellor and 12 years as ÖVP chairman, I take a more critical view of his personality and politics.

First a summary of the facts: against the resistance of the SPÖ (the party with the largest number of seats), the Federal President Thomas Klestil in the Hofburg, the *Neue Kronen Zeitung* (the newspaper with by far the largest circulation in Austria) and the 14 other concerned members of the European Union, Schüssel finally succeeded in doing what had seemed impossible before. As leader of only the third strongest party, he neither went into opposition (as promised before the election in case of defeat) nor into a grand coalition as a humiliated junior partner (as generally expected) but forced his appointment as chancellor of a coalition with the extreme right, against the opposition of a weak and erratic head of state.

The fact that Schüssel achieved the two "masterpieces", the formation of the government in February 2000 and the election triumph in November 2002, was not only due to his tactical skills and strong nerves. "Schüssel owed his rise above all to Haider's misjudgement of the situation and his personality", said former ÖVP chairman Josef Taus in a conversation with me. Haider had underestimated Schüssel; if Haider had stayed in the opposition for another period, he would have received 35 per cent the next time. For Schüssel, the coalition with the FPÖ was the only chance for his political survival. The philosopher Rudolf Burger saw the initial situation similarly: "The decision was fundamentally correct; it was the absolutely correct decision for the country (....) It was the only way to prevent Haider's triumph, even if it was not intended that way by Schüssel". In an exchange of letters with the former Federal Chancellor Franz Vranitzky, Burger wrote: "I consider the coalition unpleasant, but quite legitimate. After all, one cannot reproach Schüssel for being more intelligent than his opponents".[3]

# FROM WOLFGANG SCHÜSSEL TO SEBASTIAN KURZ

*The downfall*

As far as my own stance is concerned, I still stand firmly by what I said at the time in television interviews and wrote in commentaries in the international press. As a critic of the hectic EU boycott measures, I always emphasised that, in terms of democratic policy, questionable sweeping judgements and excessive steps against one of the most stable European democracies were counterproductive and could evoke the very danger they were trying to prevent. Even at international conferences, such as the German–Jewish Dialogues of the Bertelsmann Foundation, I refused to portray Jörg Haider, this virtuoso of right-wing populist demagogy, as a dramatic threat to Austrian, even European, democracy, despite unacceptable sayings about the Third Reich. Also in retrospect, I would like to emphasise that I have always been a supporter of a grand coalition or the single-party government capable of acting, but never a supporter of an experiment with the FPÖ.[4]

Today, however, I have to admit that Rudolf Burger's praise of Wolfgang Schüssel as the "dragon slayer" who sealed Haider's political fate, or my claim that after Schüssel's landslide victory in 2002 "Haider's FPÖ was most likely irreversibly destroyed" was completely exaggerated. As described in the chapter "The rollercoaster ride of the FPÖ", Schüssel's plan to weaken the FPÖ in the long run by bringing it into the government was a complete failure. Unfortunately, I have to agree with Oliver Rathkolb's conclusion at the end of his short profile of Schüssel, years before the formation of the Kurz–Strache coalition government. "What Schüssel did succeed in doing, however, was to further reduce the fears of contact of especially young voters towards aggressive election campaigners. After the FPÖ's participation in government in 2000–06, there is no longer an inhibition threshold".[5]

Even today, Schüssel claims that in 2002 he would have formed a coalition with the Greens, but their leaders had failed due to grassroots resistance. The extension of the coalition with the Freedom Party minus Haider and the use of the popular Finance Minister Karl-Heinz Grasser, who had "jumped ship" from Haider, as an image carrier turned out to be huge miscalculations. In retrospect, it was not the dreaded turn to the extreme right but big corruption scandals that overshadowed the image of the Schüssel government. Above all was the scandalous privatisation of 60,000 flats of the state housing company Buwog and the commissions of 9.9 million euros, which according to the first instance verdict (not yet legally binding) are said to have flowed to Finance Minister Karl-Heinz Grasser and his accomplices. The fact that the FPÖ ministers were frequently replaced due to obvious incompetence is an additional facet of the first "black-blue" experiment. That Schüssel still enjoyed international prestige despite the EU sanctions was shown by the two attempts of Angela Merkel, the German chancellor, to propose Schüssel as president of the EU Commission in 2004 and as president of the EU Council in 2008. The first time her proposal was torpedoed by French President Jacques Chirac, the second time by his successor Nicolas Sarkozy.[6]

Incidentally, a significant exception in the controversial line-up of ministers of the two Schüssel governments was Foreign Minister Ursula Plassnik. The politically independent professional diplomat from Carinthia was head of the chancellor's cabinet between July 1997 and January 2004 and was sworn in as foreign minister of the second Schüssel government in October 2004. She joined the ÖVP only a few days before her appointment. I got to know and appreciate her during these years as foreign minister and later as ambassador to France and Switzerland. She was one of the very few Austrian cabinet ministers who won their position through diligence and talent and not through party card or social networks. She remained in office in the Gusenbauer/Molterer government. Special attention was

# FROM WOLFGANG SCHÜSSEL TO SEBASTIAN KURZ

paid to the fact that she resigned in November 2008 in protest against the lukewarm EU policy of the new Faymann/Pröll government. She was not prepared to go along with the capitulation in European policy symbolised by the letter from Faymann and Gusenbauer to the *Kronen Zeitung* publisher Hans Dichand. She was personally attacked several times by Dichand for her pro-European line. I can only recall two cases where ministers resigned in protest: Josef Klaus as minister of finance in 1963 and Theodor Piffl-Perčević as minister of education in the Klaus government because he could not push through his demand for the 13th school year at secondary schools.

*Wolfgang Schüssel: an assessment*

As for my relationship with Wolfgang Schüssel, he was a superficial acquaintance, from the time when he took over the foreign ministry together with the post of vice-chancellor, but it turned into a close personal relationship. I was always impressed by his curiosity, openness and adaptability. Unlike most of his predecessors and successors, he was often interested in outside opinions, for example, with regard to Ostpolitik. Even as federal chancellor, he remained as relaxed, informal and open as before. He was the most intellectual and well-read federal chancellor since Kreisky. His "philosophical lunches" in the federal chancellery, organised on a case-by-case basis with a maximum of 15 to 20 people, were always controversial and stimulating. The fact that I had rejected the hypocrisy of the EU and the unjust and counterproductive foreign attacks against Austria further intensified the relationship. We also worked together closely at the Europe Forum in Göttweig Abbey. Although he was available to me for several interviews during the preparation of this book, Schüssel has completely stopped professional cooperation with me in his functions as President of the Austrian Society for International Politics, Chairman of the Board of Trustees of the Konrad Adenauer Foundation and Supervisory Board of the Bertelsmann Foundation. This happened after Viktor Orbán became Hungarian prime minister in 2010 and attacks were launched against me from Budapest. In 2009, I had presented his autobiography "Offengelegt" in Berlin together with Günther Nonnenmacher, then editor of the *Frankfurter Allgemeine Zeitung* (FAZ). However, since 2010 I have never been invited by him to a discussion or lecture at any of the three institutions mentioned, not even as a guest at the celebration of his 70th birthday with 650 guests, among them Viktor Orbán, at the Orangery in Schönbrunn in June 2015.

After his retirement from parliament and politics, after 32 years in the National Council and 18 years in government as minister and chancellor, Schüssel has taken on well-paid supervisory board positions in Germany (RWE and Bertelsmann Foundation) and in Russia: first in 2018 on the supervisory board of Russia's largest mobile phone company MTS, and then after a year he moved from MTS to the supervisory board of the Russian oil company Lukoil in 2019. He gave up this post after the Russian invasion of Ukraine, but only under strong public pressure.

The ex-chancellor has not forgotten that at the time of the total isolation by the EU, Viktor Orbán received him as prime minister in Budapest in 2000 with all protocol honours. He has also always defended Orbán publicly. In an interview with the pro-government Hungarian weekly *Heti Válasz*, Schüssel even jumped into the breach for Grasser, who was being "harassed" by the judiciary. Schüssel was also one of the three members of the so-called council of wise men set up in 2019 by the European People's Party to examine the situation in Hungary after Fidesz's membership was suspended over Orbán's anti-EU stance. In June 2020, the work of this panel of eminent persons was terminated without a final report because the members could not agree on what should happen to Hungary, said Belgian ex-prime minister

# FROM WOLFGANG SCHÜSSEL TO SEBASTIAN KURZ

Hermann van Rompuy. Wolfgang Schüssel, who was "quite disappointed", had obviously taken a rather pro-Orbán position.

All this does not change the fact that Wolfgang Schüssel has been the most successful ÖVP federal chancellor since Julius Raab in terms of power politics. In view of the (not yet legally binding) court ruling against Grasser, the media have recalled his failed attempt after the narrowly lost election in 2006 to promote the bright young star Grasser to the position of the vice-chancellor. Schüssel had wanted to install an unusual dual leadership in the ÖVP: "Karl-Heinz Grasser should head the government team as vice chancellor and finance minister, while Wilhelm Molterer should form a centre of power outside the government as party and club chairman". After complicated intrigues by Tyrolean ÖVP politicians, Schüssel's plan, invented along the lines of "do the unexpected", failed in the ÖVP party executive. Grasser withdrew and Molterer was elected party chairman, vice chancellor and finance minister.[7] At Molterer's request, Schüssel accepted the post of the head of the ÖVP parliamentary group. He resigned from this post after the election defeat in September 2008 and from parliament altogether in 2011.

During the long Faymann era, three ÖVP vice-chancellors were in office, who (although very different types) were seen only as transitional figures on the way to the exceptional Sebastian Kurz.

*In-between time*

Schüssel's direct successor at the top was Wilhelm Molterer. This amiable politician committed one of the most disastrous mistakes in recent Austrian history. With the now legendary words "Enough is enough!", he quit the coalition government with the SPÖ on 7 July 2008 and called for immediate elections, encouraged by the power struggle between Gusenbauer and Faymann and by internal polls favourable to the ÖVP. His own party was not at all prepared for the election campaign in the middle of summer: the posters came too late and were of poor quality and the awkward slogans and Molterer's colourless appearance did not arouse interest, let alone enthusiasm, even among loyal party supporters. Some powerful provincial politicians were completely against early elections for financial considerations and self-serving interests. Moreover, the *Kronen Zeitung* gave full flank protection to the SPÖ, now led by Faymann, the publisher's favourite. When Molterer consulted me about the situation in the Balkans sometime at the end of 2008, I asked him in between why he had actually provoked the elections. "I don't know", was his obviously honest answer. A former ÖVP minister recently told me, "Willy wanted to get out of Schüssel's shadow ...".

Be that as it may, Faymann's "election success" was a Pyrrhic victory with the loss of eleven mandates and the SPÖ's worst election result since 1945. But the hapless Molterer did even worse: the ÖVP lost 15 parliamentary seats; the worst result for the conservatives since 1945. Molterer resigned immediately and remained in parliament until 2011. Subsequently, he became one of the vice-presidents of the European Investment Bank.

His successor as vice-chancellor, Josef Pröll, nephew of the powerful governor of Lower Austria, moved from the ministry of agriculture to the key portfolio of finance. His time as a specialist minister without the relevant knowledge was marked by the luckless attempts to wind up the bankruptcy estate of the Carinthian bank Hypo Alpe Adria. As head of an internal perspective group, he at least tried to develop a liberal-conservative line. In the middle of the legislative period, he resigned for health reasons (a pulmonary embolism) at the age of 42. According to rumours circulating in insider circles at the time, his withdrawal from politics was also for private reasons. He was popular in his party because of his open communicative style. Even today, as chairman of the board of the Leipnik-Lundenburger

## FROM WOLFGANG SCHÜSSEL TO SEBASTIAN KURZ

food company, he does not mince his words when talking about the structural problems of the ÖVP.

His successor as party leader and vice-chancellor, Michael Spindelegger, belongs to the core stratum of the People's Party. His father was an ÖVP MP, he himself belongs to the elite CV fraternity Norica. Despite his prominent positions in the party and in parliament, Spindelegger was long considered only a man of second rank. Only after the resignation of Ursula Plassnik, for reasons of principle already described, did he get his chance as foreign minister in 2008. In contrast to his polyglot predecessor with an international network, Spindelegger was a colourless, friendly administrator of a well-rehearsed apparatus. His rise to party chairman and vice-chancellor in 2011 was seen by critical observers as confirmation of the Peter Principle, according to which people employed in any hierarchy are promoted until they reach a post in which they are incompetent. In 2021, I asked Wolfgang Schüssel how he explained Spindelegger's election as party leader. He answered drily: "He was the only one available...". The press soon criticised the new ÖVP chairman unusually harshly: "Apparently, Spindelegger is no longer trusted with much within the party. He hardly has any political ideas of his own, but runs after populist advances of others".[8] Karel Schwarzenberg, the former Czech foreign minister, was also not reticent with his opinion: "the Vice-Chancellor and Foreign Minister often had himself represented at EU Councils and acted reservedly when present there. I believe that Spindelegger is not really interested in foreign and European affairs", he added.[9] After losing the parliamentary election in September 2013, Spindelegger switched from the foreign ministry to the finance ministry, a move that was criticised within the party and served as a prelude to his fall in August 2014.

There are two reasons why I think Michael Spindelegger will go down in Austrian contemporary history despite his colourless tenure in government: He was the actual discoverer of the exceptional talent Sebastian Kurz. In a personal conversation, he enthusiastically told me how, as second president of parliament, he had repeatedly invited Kurz to his office as the head of ÖVP youth in Vienna and promoted him in various directions. As the new vice-chancellor, Spindelegger caused a real sensation in 2011 by promoting the 24-year-old politician to state secretary for integration affairs in the ministry of the interior, and 2 years later he helped to push Kurz through as the world's youngest foreign minister. For initiated circles in the People's Party, Spindelegger is also considered a kind of godfather of the Kurz group. Finance Minister Gernot Blümel had also spent many years in Spindelegger's secretariat, and the key figure in the "chat" scandal, Thomas Schmid, was also employed in his office. "Spindi", as he was known among his friends, first took him under his wing as press spokesman in the foreign ministry, then Schmid moved with him to the finance ministry as head of cabinet and later secretary general.

After the publication of the often intimately worded "chats" with emojis and smileys, rumours circulated in inner-party circles of the ÖVP about the sexual orientation of the young guard headed by Kurz and about their sponsor. In contrast to Germany, where the ex-mayor of Berlin, Klaus Wowereit (SPD), the late Foreign Minister Guido Westerwelle (FDP), the former Health Minister Jens Spahn (CDU) and the SPD's young star Kevin Kühnert openly live as homosexuals, the private lives of politicians in this country are hallowed taboos. The leading Green politician Ulrike Lunacek, who openly confessed to being a lesbian as early as 2005, remained an isolated case. It was not until 5 June 2021 that the young ÖVP politician Nico Marchetti (born 1990) sent an important signal in an ORF TV interview: "The ÖVP has no problem with homosexuality and it is perfectly normal to be gay".

# FROM WOLFGANG SCHÜSSEL TO SEBASTIAN KURZ

Back to Spindelegger. His most important function, also perceived internationally, after leaving politics was to head the controversial "Agency for the Modernisation of Ukraine". The fate of this project, which was presented with great international fanfare, began with a bang and ended with a whimper. Spindelegger presented a plan for a large-scale economic reform of Ukraine (300 measures were to be developed in 200 days) in front of international VIPs, among them the German ex-Finance Minister Peer Steinbrück and France's ex-Foreign Minister Bernard Kouchner.

The agency was invented and financed by one of the most controversial Ukrainian oligarchs, Dmytro Firtasch, who has not been allowed to leave Austria since 2014 because of a US extradition request.[10] The US accuses the Ukrainian billionaire, who made his fortune in Russian gas, of paying bribes of at least 15.5 million euros to Indian politicians in a titanium deal that never materialised. After his arrest in Vienna, the oligarch was released shortly afterwards on a record bail of 125 million euros. Since then, his numerous lawyers been successfully fighting his extradition to the USA until now. Firtasch, whose fortune was estimated at 10 billion dollars, has promised 300 million euros for the agency. Steinbrück and other renowned experts quit their cooperation soon after Spindelegger's presentation. They obviously did not want to serve as "useful idiots" of a shady oligarch wanted by the USA. Nevertheless, Spindelegger presented his report in autumn of 2015, which was ignored by the Ukrainian government and the international public. Firtasch's "Marshall Plan" for Ukraine had vanished into thin air.[11]

Spindelegger, however, got a full-time job soon after, with the help of the Austrian foreign ministry, as director general of the Vienna-based International Centre for Migration Policy Development. The representatives of, at that time, 19 states (apart from Austria, they were mostly from Eastern and South-Eastern Europe) entrusted him with a salary of 10,000 euros a month to run the organisation for 5 years from January 2016. When I met him in his office in Vienna,[12] the 61-year-old politician seemed in a good mood; he was appointed for another 5 years as head of the organisation, which is hardly known to the public. However, there is little sign of the greater "political weight" and "visibility" he promised 5 years earlier. He still held his former assistants in high esteem, above all Sebastian Kurz and Gernot Blümel, somewhat less so Thomas Schmid, although his homosexuality should not play a role, he said. As for his now ousted successor at the party leadership, he was moderate in his judgement. All in all, I got the impression from Spindelegger that he was happy person, content with himself and the world.

Spindelegger's successor as vice-chancellor and ÖVP chairman was Reinhold Mitterlehner, who had been minister of economics since 2008, and is also a member of a CV fraternity. He had already been considered a possible candidate in 2011. He was a convinced grand coalition advocate and, measured by ÖVP standards, the representative of a relatively liberal socio-political line. A total of 99.1 per cent of party congress delegates elected him ÖVP chairman in November 2014, the highest percentage in the last 30 years, reflecting a feeling of relief after the departure of the colourless predecessor. That Vice-Chancellor Mitterlehner worked well with the SPÖ Federal Chancellors Werner Faymann and especially with Christian Kern was explicitly confirmed to me by both him and Kern.

Driven by unbearable pressure and humiliated by the Kurz group acting with the precision of Swiss clockwork and abandoned by the ÖVP provincial leaders, Reinhold Mitterlehner resigned on 10 May 2017, clearing the way for Sebastian Kurz. Two years later, in an autobiography, he accused his successor of foul play and intrigue on his way to the chancellorship. During a three-hour conversation in my flat during the Covid-related lockdown, the former vice-chancellor described to me in detail

## FROM WOLFGANG SCHÜSSEL TO SEBASTIAN KURZ

his experiences dealing with Sebastian Kurz before and after his fall. He also recounted how Kurz had offered him the presidency of the National Bank in November 2017 but later declined due to alleged FPÖ demands, only to announce his loyal follower Harald Mahrer as president in 2018. Mitterlehner could not hide his contempt for the power games and intrigues of the ÖVP structures before the 2016 presidential election. In the run-off election, he himself had publicly supported Van der Bellen. All in all, he left the impression of a likeable, decent, but not very assertive politician of the "old ÖVP school".

*Personal encounters with Sebastian Kurz*

The story of Sebastian Kurz, the next Federal Chancellor, forms a special period in Austrian history. I met him for the first time at the Wachau European Forum in Göttweig Abbey in 2011, when he was secretary of state for integration in the ministry of the interior. He sat at the end of the table reserved by protocol for the domestic and foreign keynote speakers. A polite, friendly young man, but even then more preoccupied with his mobile phone than with his neighbours. Even during the speeches of the foreign dignitaries, he concentrated almost exclusively on his mobile phone.

We did not have any real conversations during this time. I found it strange that in 2016, at the Europe Forum in Göttweig, he told me that he did not want a personal introduction to his speech. However, for almost 25 years, this was precisely my role at Göttweig: to introduce the guests with a few personal remarks about them and to moderate the events. Kurz always wanted to deliver flawless performances, he never improvised and, in the end, did not even appear at the so-called protocol table in the abbey restaurant, but dined separately with the guests he considered important. I thought at the time that his aloof attitude was perhaps also influenced by a quote from *Spiegel*. The German news magazine had run a two-page story about the "world's youngest foreign minister" that was basically positive. "'He has an incredible feeling for publicity and the media', says Paul Lendvai, Social Democrat and one of Austria's best-known publicists", it stated. Since I have never belonged to any institution or party except the Austrian Automobile Club, I asked the author, albeit in vain, to publish a correction. I later suspected that perhaps Kurz had written me off as a "socialist".

Be that as it may, there was one exception in our relationship during the years of his ascent. As federal chancellor, he received me for a long one-on-one conversation in his office at Ballhausplatz on 10 April 2019, a week before the presentation of Reinhold Mitterlehner's critical book about him and barely a month before the bombshell of the Ibiza video exploded.

Among other things, I also asked him about the already published and planned focus on anti-Semitism in the *Europäische Rundschau*. As mentioned in the chapter "Hitler's Shadow", Kurz had personally ordered the funding of the Shoah Wall of Names and, for whatever motives, had always been active against anti-Semitism and for solidarity with Israel, including at a high-level international conference organised by the European Jewish Congress in Vienna in November 2018.

I asked him to promote the printing of an increased number of the issues on anti-Semitism and to help with the distribution by the federal chancellery and the foreign ministry. He responded positively, and I subsequently discussed the issue with the then government spokesman, Ambassador Peter Launsky-Tieffenthal. However, due to the disintegration of the ÖVP–FPÖ government and the new elections, the issue disappeared from the agenda, and a year later, I decided to stop publishing, after 47 years, the international quarterly *Europäische Rundschau* because of the chronic lack of funding.

# FROM WOLFGANG SCHÜSSEL TO SEBASTIAN KURZ

But our conversation was not just about the magazine or anti-Semitism. We chatted mainly about the risk of his government experiment with the Freedom Party. In this conversation, too, he sensed my deep mistrust of the Freedom Party. Kurz therefore naturally tried to convince me of good cooperation with the FPÖ and above all of the positive transformation of its top representatives. Self-confident and well-mannered, he even characterised and imitated the individual FPÖ ministers with a touch of humour. After the lively conversation, which lasted over an hour, he accompanied me down the stairs almost to the entrance of the chancellery. I thought of the experience of the great actor Otto Schenk, whom Kurz had chauffeured home in his official car after a reception for artists. On Schenk's birthday, the chancellor appeared at his flat with a large Sacher cake, accompanied by his court photographer and a TV recording team. In my case, there was no such gesture either then or later. I was never on his invitation list, even if a few hundred or almost a thousand guests were invited. So, our meeting was an exception. Nevertheless, I was, even if temporarily, impressed by his feigned or calculated friendliness, surprising after years of distance. After Kurz's departure from politics, an editorial in *Die Presse*, the Vienna daily, aptly described one key to his puzzling success: "The real talent of Sebastian Kurz was not in being intellectual or visionary. No, Kurz was a people catcher; he managed to win people over. He could win elections".[13]

*The beginnings of Sebastian Kurz*

So what was the start of this political career, unique in Austrian, even European, contemporary history? There have already been three biographies on Sebastian Kurz, a book entitled *The Rhetoric of Sebastian Kurz*, a book on his networks, a book on "his regime", a collection of interviews and two critical writings on his power politics. The long Wikipedia entry on Sebastian Kurz cites 214 individual references. Many of the 55 interviews I have conducted with Austrian politicians over the last 15 years also deal mainly or marginally with the personality and politics of the youngest "former chancellor" in Austrian history. In addition, there are hundreds of articles in the domestic and foreign press, television and radio recordings with or about Sebastian Kurz.

What I find particularly strange is how little material there is about his leap, after only one year, from 24-year-old member of the Viennese municipal diet to a government post as secretary of state for integration. After graduating from high school with honours and doing his military service, he dropped out of law school without graduating. Since then, he has been exclusively involved in politics, not working in any other profession. Since the age of 17, he was politically active, first in Vienna as head of the youth organisation of the ÖVP and from 2009 to 2017 as federal chairman of the JVP. With 105,000 members today, the Young ÖVP has been one of the party's six confederations since 1971.

The fact that Kurz has carved out a personal instrument of power for himself from the Young ÖVP is shown by the fact that he himself retained this position after becoming foreign minister and only gave it up when he took over the party chairmanship in May 2017. As is well known, the confederations have shaped the peculiar world of the ÖVP from the very beginning. The three most traditional confederations are the ÖAAB with around 250,000 members, the Wirtschaftsbund with 100,000 members and the Bauernbund with around 300,000 members, although farmers only make up four per cent of the population. The ÖVP Seniors' Federation has 300,000 members and the Women's Federation has 60,000. The chairpersons of the sub-organisations are members of the federal party executive.

Kurz thus already had the opportunity to forge regular contacts with the most influential ÖVP top politicians since 2009,

## FROM WOLFGANG SCHÜSSEL TO SEBASTIAN KURZ

and so he became a member of the provincial diet the very next year. He caused a stir in the 2010 Vienna election campaign with the "Schwarz macht geil" ("Black makes you horny") campaign launched in the "Moulin Rouge" nightclub and then cruising in the capital in a Hummer SUV described as a "Geilomobile". Although the ÖVP had the worst election result in Vienna at the time with a loss of five per cent, Kurz became one of the thirteen ÖVP members of the regional parliament. With his motion to lower the age for awarding decorations from the current 50 years and to allow awards also for young politicians, he has remained in the memory of the city's history only because of the cross-party laughter.

His appointment as state secretary at the age of 24 was a sensation in the small world of Austrian domestic politics. A whiz kid without a university degree, he was the youngest member of government in the history of the Second Republic and was initially greeted with derision in the media. In 2011, journalist Robert Misik was among those who mocked him, saying that "a completely clueless person who has not yet achieved anything recognisable in his life is entrusted with an important portfolio" with a salary of 15,000 euros per month. The picture changed abruptly, however, when a week later Kurz cut an "excellent figure" on television, according to Misik, and soon afterwards he self-critically admitted his mistake. He praised Kurz for having said "largely sensible stuff on immigration and integration, and even managed to express it eloquently". But that did not change the fact that Kurz presented himself, often with great skill, as a defenceless victim of the media because of this brief period of critical notes. Again and again he said in interviews: "I have experienced tougher phases than most others in politics. When I became Secretary of State at 24, the headwinds were so strong that it was a really terribly difficult time for my team, for my family and for me". A year and a half after his appointment as state secretary, he concluded at the end of a full-page interview, after the usual remarks about having been a "victim" of the media, that politics was "a world of total intrigues. A system where you have to fight to get things done for an issue".[14] Only 9 years later, it turned out that the young star, driven by an unconditional sense of mission and a will to remain at the top, became a true master in this "world of intrigues" stadium, supported from the very beginning by his sworn-in, tightly-knit team.

Contrary to his self-description as a naïve novice in the swamp of politics, on the night of 18 April 2011 when he accepted Spindelegger's offer, Kurz gathered a handful of talented and loyal aides around him in the ÖVP party headquarters, people who were to form the backbone of his system over the next 10 years. The young journalist Klaus Knittelfelder published an interesting collection of portraits about the members of this power circle and the birth of their networks.[15] The real brain of the whole group and the central figure behind the "chancellor's actor" was Stefan Steiner, who assisted Kurz as office manager, then as section head in the interior and foreign ministries and finally as chancellor's advisor with a monthly salary around 33,000 euros. Other hand-picked close advisors and collaborators were Cabinet Chief Bernhard Bonelli, spin doctor Gerald Fleischmann, press spokesman Johannes Frischmann, later Finance Minister Gernot Blümel, campaign manager Philipp Maderthaner, ÖVP Secretary General Axel Melchior and, in the decisive phase as Interior Minister, later as National Council President, Wolfgang Sobotka. The young Elisabeth Köstinger was important for Kurz above all as the female face of the ÖVP revival and as a representative of rural areas.

With the slogan "Integration through achievement", invented by mastermind Stefan Steiner, the state secretariat for integration carried out the campaign "Together Austria" with the Austrian Integration Fund and the ministry of education. So-called "inte-

# FROM WOLFGANG SCHÜSSEL TO SEBASTIAN KURZ

gration ambassadors" were sent into schools to discuss with migrants their attitudes towards Austria and to convey values and democracy. Other positive initiatives were the dialogue with religious communities and the proposal to introduce a second compulsory kindergarten year for children with language deficits.

## *The youngest foreign minister in the world*

The next career leap, which attracted a lot of international attention, was Kurz's appointment as foreign minister in December 2013, following Spindelegger, who moved to the ministry of finance. This time, too, his great patron "Spindi" had set the course. Several prominent ÖVP politicians told me in background talks that they had advised Kurz to finish his studies first and only then accept a ministerial post. In retrospect, they suspect that Kurz had in fact already made up his mind and he had asked them for advice for appearances' sake. He had even called former SPÖ-Chancellor Alfred Gusenbauer who was on a trip to Bangkok to ask for his advice on whether to accept Spindelegger's offer. Former Agriculture Minister and two-time EU Agriculture Commissioner Franz Fischler, whom Kurz had consulted often, saw him as a "talent of the century" but also as a man of "ice-cold calculation with several faces". For Kurz, the end always justifies the means, but at the same time he is sensitive, wants to be loved.[16]

As the youngest foreign minister in Austrian history and in the world, Kurz quickly became known internationally through interviews and magazine articles. An early description from the German magazine *Der Spiegel* read as follows:

> At first glance, Kurz does not seem ministerial, more like a model from the Hugo Boss catalogue (...) But if you listen to him talking and close your eyes, accompany him on business trips and talk to his advisors, then at some point you believe that he has been a minister not just for months, but for a very long time, that he

must somehow have been born as a politician. That's probably how he sees it himself.

The report also mentions that Kurz cannot remember which book he last read, while he proudly lists having written over 1,340 tweets.[17]

Perhaps the most important thing for his future career was what he did *not* do during his time as foreign minister. At the height of the asylum crisis, when most politicians welcomed refugees at some point at Vienna's Westbahnhof, Foreign Minister Sebastian Kurz, who was also responsible for integration, of all people, was absent. His chief advisor Stefan Steiner had strongly advised him not to go to the Westbahnhof and have his photo taken there in the refugee chaos because it would send the wrong signal. Kurz followed the advice. This became a mosaic tile in the later rejection of the so-called "welcome culture".

No former Austrian foreign minister is likely to have met as many foreign colleagues in a relatively short time as Sebastian Kurz. In striking contrast to his time as state secretary for integration, as foreign minister he took a hard line on refugee and integration policy in every respect. At every opportunity, he bragged about the successful closure of the Western Balkans route and downplayed the importance of the solution negotiated by Chancellor Angela Merkel with President Erdoğan in reducing refugee numbers. Merkel, however, had rejected Kurz's claims, repeated ad nauseam in the 2017 and 2019 election campaigns:

> If you ask me whether the closure of the Balkan route has solved the problem, I would clearly say no. In the weeks before the EU–Turkey agreement came into force, it did lead to fewer refugees arriving in Germany—but 45,000 in Greece. Converted to the German population, that would have been 360,000 new arrivals, almost twice as many as we had in the most difficult month of November.[18]

Some of the formulations of the resolute foreign minister, such as "it will not work without ugly pictures", also caused interna-

# FROM WOLFGANG SCHÜSSEL TO SEBASTIAN KURZ

tional surprise, even if they were enthusiastically received in right-wing Christlich-Soziale Union circles in Germany. Kurz repeatedly criticised the rescue operations of aid organisations as "NGO madness" because, according to him, these actions would lead to more refugees dying in the Mediterranean instead of fewer. At the same time, he called for the rescued refugees not to be brought to the Italian mainland, but to refugee centres outside the EU, following the Australian model.

The foreign minister took advantage of the chairmanship of the Organisation for Security and Cooperation in Europe in 2017 to raise his own profile and to exploit photo opportunities. The Austrian historian Michael Gehler has twice described (first in a shorter newspaper article while Kurz was still chancellor and then in a longer essay after his resignation) the rhetorical actionism and perfect media staging without any concrete idea behind the supposed foreign policy success of a "politician of the moment" who immediately seizes opportunities as they arise. The calculated rhetorical provocations in migration policy and in cutting reconstruction aid for coronavirus-damaged EU members, the high-profile actionism against Merkel's policies and the Franco-German projects served to increase Kurz's popularity ratings at home in the short term but undermined Austria's international credibility. What Professor Gehler said about Kurz as chancellor, applied already to the foreign minister: "The chancellor's foreign policy programme is Sebastian Kurz".[19]

*At the height of power*

The fact that Kurz and his team, led by Stefan Steiner, had already drafted a "Project Ballhausplatz" on 21 July 2016 to overthrow ÖVP leader Mitterlehner and conquer the federal chancellery was only revealed a year later by the weekly paper in Vienna, *Falter*.[20] The secretly drafted election programme was about

"FPÖ issues, but with a focus on the future". The targets of attack were foreigners, Brussels and "the system" (i.e. the SPÖ–ÖVP coalition and the social partnership). A year before Mitterlehner's fall, the Kurz circle was determined to take over the ÖVP, end the coalition with the SPÖ and win the chancellorship with new elections. The election campaign and the balance sheet of the first 100 days were prepared. Next to each of the 61 subtitles in six phases were abbreviations showing who from the Kurz squad was responsible for each task. Stefan Steiner, the head of the group was responsible for "planning the election campaign", "ministerial team", "government negotiations" and "government programme".

No wonder, by the way, that his sister-in-law, the Lower Austrian farmers' union director Klaudia Tanner, later became defence minister without any previous experience in military affairs and his brother Thomas Steiner became one of the directors of the National Bank. Kurz took over only one politician from the old ÖVP guard, the 30-year older former Interior Minister Wolfgang Sobotka, who, as his close confidant, played the role of public detonator in settling scores with Mitterlehner and toppling the Kern government. His reward was the prestigious position as president of the federal parliament.

After his election as federal party chairman on 1 July 2017 with 98.7 per cent of the delegates' votes, Kurz, heading the "List Sebastian Kurz, the new People's Party (ÖVP)", led the ÖVP after 30 years back to first place in October 2017 with 31.5 per cent of the votes. In December, he was sworn in as chancellor of the ÖVP–FPÖ coalition government: this made him, at 31, the youngest head of government in the world.

The coalition government did not last long: it disintegrated in May 2019 as a result of the revelations of the Ibiza video about the willingness of FPÖ Vice-Chancellor Heinz-Christian Strache and his club chairman Johann Gudenus to engage in

## FROM WOLFGANG SCHÜSSEL TO SEBASTIAN KURZ

bribery, corruption, greed for power and media control, to "Orbánise" Austria.

I would like to emphasise here once again that Kurz as Chancellor and Karin Kneissl as the non-party Foreign Minister nominated by the FPÖ have damaged Austria's international reputation as a pro-Western, neutral state. The fact that Kneissl danced at her wedding with President Vladimir Putin and then curtsied to him was mocked internationally. The chancellor's close contacts with Putin (three visits to Russia in 2018 alone) and with Hungarian Prime Minister Viktor Orbán, as well as distancing himself from German Chancellor Angela Merkel's foreign policy in appearances on German television, at Christlich-Soziale Union events and in interviews, have also caused alienation in the EU. Kneissl became a supervisory board member of the Russian oil company Rosneft in mid-2021 with a high salary of $500,000. She and the FPÖ were listed by the European Parliament as examples of Russian influence within the EU. Threatened by sanctions of the EU, after one year Kneissl gave up the position but continued to work as commentator for the Russian state broadcaster Russia Today.[21]

Kurz was Chancellor of a coalition government with the FPÖ for only 17 months. The transitional government he proposed and the federal president appointed without the FPÖ were voted out of office 5 days later by the first successful motion of no confidence in the Second Republic with the votes of the SPÖ, FPÖ and now defunct small party Jetzt.

A "transitional government of civil servants" led by former President of the Constitutional Court Brigitte Bierlein, Austria's first female chancellor, was sworn in on 3 June 2019. The government of civil servants held office for 218 days, to everyone's satisfaction. The fact that with Vice-Chancellor and Minister of Justice Clemens Jabloner, former President of the Administrative Court, the federal government had a Jewish member for the first time since Bruno Kreisky was probably ignored by the media as a sign of normality. Manfred Matzka, the long-time head of the federal chancellery, gave the Bierlein cabinet a first-class report card: "The calm, unagitated administration, the renunciation of any media hullabaloo, law-abidingness, the effort to provide true factual information and an overall modest demeanour" had won within a short time a broad popular acceptance.[22]

In the ensuing election campaign, Kurz staged himself as a martyr of the motion of no confidence, which he presented as illegitimate. The ÖVP achieved, with Kurz as its top candidate, a clear election victory at the end of September 2019 with 37.5 per cent of the vote, an increase of six per cent. The SPÖ lost almost six per cent and suffered with 21.2 per cent, the biggest electoral defeat in its history. The FPÖ also fell by 10 per cent to 16 per cent. The other big winner were the Greens, who managed to re-enter parliament with 14 per cent of the vote and 26 mandates after their disastrous defeat in 2017. The role of the Greens will be analysed in the next chapter. The NEOS increased their share of the vote by 2 to 8 per cent.

After winning the election and relatively short negotiations with the Greens, an ÖVP–Green coalition government was formed for the first time, and Sebastian Kurz was re-inaugurated as Federal Chancellor on 7 January 2020. Kurz's second chancellorship lasted 21 months and was overshadowed by the effects of the coronavirus pandemic and, from May 2021, by the investigations of the Public Prosecutor's Office for Economic Affairs and Corruption (WKStA). Due to the allegations against him, Sebastian Kurz stepped down in two phases: on 9 October 2021, he gave in to the demand of the Greens and resigned as Federal Chancellor, but wanted to continue to determine the policies of the ÖVP as club chairman and party leader. After the lifting of his immunity and the continuation of investigations into false statements, corruption, manipulated polls and fraud, he left poli-

## FROM WOLFGANG SCHÜSSEL TO SEBASTIAN KURZ

tics altogether on 2 December 2021. Since March 2022, Kurz has been working as a "global strategist" for the controversial right-wing German-American billionaire Peter Thiel. He also set up a consulting firm, establishing business contacts with dubious figures in the United States and Israel.[23]

What was the secret of Sebastian Kurz? What is the record of the two Kurz governments? How could a youthful dazzler who "never said a sentence that didn't seem like it had been learned by heart",[24] subdue the largest party in Austria by far, rich in tradition with over half a million members?[25] Before we get to the political downfall, it is worth mentioning the description given of the Kurz system at the peak of success by probably one of the best-connected young journalists, Klaus Knittelfelder, who is almost the same age as Kurz.

> The ÖVP is completely organised "top down", everything is decided at the top, "and decisively by a small group of largely unknown people". In this system, ministers and M.P.s do not have the autonomy of earlier days". In the parliamentary club as well as in the ministries, there are now carefully selected outsiders hired who are absolutely loyal to the chancellor and "are not at the beck and call of anyone else. Almost all power is concentrated (...) in the conspiratorial and never publicly visible troop group Kurz.[26]

Knittelfelder is so impressed that he even believes that politicians in other countries also want to adopt this system, since it apparently leads to electoral success. Kurz's closest advisors are then portrayed, especially Cabinet Chief Bernhard Bonelli and the "head" of the team, Stefan Steiner. Kurz phoned both of them every morning; he had 6,127 numbers stored in his iPhone. For the Kurz people, the *Kronen Zeitung* and in Germany the *Bild* are "role models and leading media". After the announcement of the ÖVP-Green government, each major medium was given a 20-minute interview with only minimally differing answers: only for *Bild* and for the *Krone* did Kurz take a whole hour off. Incidentally, it was also symbolic that *Bild* and *Krone* also reported on the Chancellor's resignation even before the official announcement.

Among the revealing details about the notorious "message control" that Knittelfelder describes in his book is that Kurz liked to call the editors-in-chief himself, while press officer Johannes Frischmann made hundreds of phone calls every day to those journalists who wrote the newspaper articles. During the 2017 election campaign, he made 311 phone calls on a single day. The *Krone* was the leading medium. This is remarkable, the author states: "In contrast to predecessors like Wolfgang Schüssel, who preferred to read the *Neue Zürcher Zeitung* and was rather at odds with Austria's most important newspaper, Kurz likes *Krone* and *Ö3*, and not only for professional reasons: Kurz is also where the majority stands in the media". Kurz even visited the editorial office of the *Krone* on the occasion of its 60th anniversary, brought along a Wurlitzer from 1959 and praised the newspaper in a speech as a "mirror of the Austrian soul".

About Kurz's broad impact, we learn that in mid-April 2020, his page on Facebook had almost one million fans. In addition, there were 400,000 followers on Twitter and 330,000 subscribers on Instagram. The party's email newsletter went to 100,000 people.

The author's conclusions show Kurz's popularity at the height of his power: "Whether you like him or not (...), there is one thing you cannot deny Sebastian Kurz (....): He has created a new political system in Austria. And he is extremely successful with it". The magic word, according to Knittelfelder, is control. An "executive board" headed by Kurz is the centre of power and communication, to whose command everyone listens, in the government as well as in the parliamentary benches. The party and the government are run like a company, decisions are made at the top, and absolute unanimity is the motto for communication. "The system is supported by a small, highly professional and

# FROM WOLFGANG SCHÜSSEL TO SEBASTIAN KURZ

boundlessly loyal group of young conservatives who, together with Kurz, have advanced to the levers of power. At the end, with a reference to the then almost absolute ÖVP majority in the polls after the first coronavirus weeks, Knittelfelder asks the rhetorical, but in retrospect almost prophetic question: "What else could knock this system out?".[27]

*A case for the courts*

The answer was provided barely a year later by the mobile phone records of a Kurz confidant named Thomas Schmid, voted "Person of the Year 2021" by news magazine *Profil*. Approximately 300,000 chat messages on his data carrier were seized during a house search formed the basis of the investigations by the Public Prosecutor's Office for Economic Affairs and Corruption (WKStA) against the Federal Chancellor and his closest associates. On 6 October 2021, for the first time in post-war history, police searches took place in the federal chancellery, the ÖVP party headquarters, the ministry of finance, the editorial office of the tabloid Österreich and in some private residences. Documents, data carriers and mobile phones were seized. The WKStA press release on the searches expresses the suspicion that:

> between the years 2016 and at least 2018, budgetary funds of the Federal Ministry of Finance were used to finance exclusively party-politically motivated, sometimes manipulated surveys by an opinion research company in the interest of a political party and its top functionary(s). These survey results were published (without being declared as an advertisement) in the editorial section of an Austrian daily newspaper and in other media belonging to this group. In return, payments were made—according to the suspicion—on the part of the public officials involved to the media company within the framework of media and advertisement cooperations. The payments for these co-operations were—according to the suspicion—essen-

tially hidden quid pro quos for the possibilities of influencing the editorial reporting in this media company which were actually granted to the accused.[28]

The 104-page search warrant sets out in great detail how Sebastian Kurz, the "wunderkind", is alleged to have used dishonest methods to seize first the top position in the ÖVP and then the chancellorship. Thomas Schmid, as head of cabinet of the finance minister and later secretary-general of the ministry of finance, is said to have diverted money from the ministry of finance via bogus invoices in order to use it for doctored surveys and advertisements supporting the ÖVP published in the daily newspaper *Österreich* and its TV channel oe24.TV. Kurz was suspected of having commissioned this illegal procedure during his time as foreign minister, which he denies. A number of close associates, who saw themselves as "family" (according to former Finance Minister Gernot Blümel to Thomas Schmid) and "praetorians" (according to Thomas Schmid to Sebastian Kurz), allegedly had a hand in this.

Schmid's chats, characterised by vulgar language, spitefulness, megalomania and at the same time submissiveness, were also about the job he wanted as sole director general of the newly founded ÖBAG, the state holding company worth 27 billion euros. They show his closeness to politicians like Kurz or Blümel. For example, as Secretary General in the Ministry of Finance, Schmid was able to write himself the tender documents for the top position in ÖBAG and also choose the members of the supervisory board that later appointed him.

Before his appointment to the ÖBAG board, Schmid asked Chancellor Kurz not to make him "a board member without a mandate". Kurz's answer: "You get everything you want anyway". To which Schmid replied: "I love my chancellor", followed by several kissing emojis. Blümel to Schmid: "Schmid AG done". Schmid's joy was understandable in view of a gross annual salary of

# FROM WOLFGANG SCHÜSSEL TO SEBASTIAN KURZ

400,000 euros plus generous success bonuses. The question of whether Chancellor Kurz had only been informed, but not involved, in the appointment of Schmid as sole director of ÖBAG is occupying the Economic and Corruption Public Prosecutor's Office, which has also accused Kurz of making, on three occasions, false statements to the committee of enquiry into the Ibiza affair.

The presumption of innocence applies, but the startlingly vulgar news, classified by *Der Spiegel* as "almost homoerotic", weighs almost more heavily. Schmid in the chat to Kurz: "(...) Mitterlehner is a left-wing dilettante and a giant asshole!!!! I hate him, kissy, Thomas". Kurz to Schmid: "Thanks Thomas, it was great that Spindi moved out today. I'm sure that's what bothers his ass the most ...". Kurz's reaction when Schmid informed him about the popular plan of the SPÖ–ÖVP coalition leadership to promote afternoon care for children with additional funds showed how purposeful and ruthless he was. Since Kurz, then still foreign minister of the coalition government, wanted to portray it as completely impotent, he was alarmed. "Not good at all!!! How can you stop it?" asked Kurz back, adding, "Can I stir up a province?" He was pleased about the poor popularity ratings of the ÖVP, still led by Mitterlehner, in the doctored polls, which, according to the self-reporting of pollster Sabine Beinschab, were presumably paid for with money from the ministry of finance: "Good poll, good poll!"

The contempt for humanity and arrogance that emerged from these communications and many others exposed the "new style" promised by Kurz as a hollow phrase. They also caused such an uproar within the ÖVP, among the provincial governors, that in the end there was no option left for Kurz but to leave politics.

The power of the still functioning media apparatus of the Kurz group was proved by the 99.4 per cent vote for Kurz at the end of August 2021 at the ÖVP congress, re-electing him for the first time as party chairman. The Vienna correspondent of the *Frankfurter Allgemeinen* described it as "a barricade of waggons" that the party was setting up around Kurz and quoted the governor of Styria province Hermann Schützenhöfer: "We won't let our Sebastian be shot out of our ranks". After the publication of the text of the search warrants, and in view of the fact that only a fraction of the 300,000 chat messages seized on Schmid's data carrier were known, the "Wagenburg" proved to be a house of cards that collapsed in a flash. Just 5 weeks later, on 9 October 2021, the same correspondent soberly stated: "Kurz has a problem ...".[29]

A new phase was opened in the court case against Sebastian Kurz in the autumn of 2022 with the full confession by Thomas Schmid, who seeks to gain the status of a crown witness. A 454-page-long summary of his confessions[30] accuses Kurz and his associates of a series of crimes committed to the detriment of the republic. These allegations were flatly denied by Kurz.

*A summary*

It would be too much to analyse in detail the domestic political tremors, unparalleled in the Second Republic, forcing three changes at Ballhausplatz within a year. After Kurz, Foreign Minister Alexander Schallenberg held office only for 52 days, followed in December 2021 by former Interior Minister Karl Nehammer, who in May 2022 was also elected as ÖVP chairman.

More important and relevant are the lessons from the Sebastian Kurz case. He was undoubtedly the most skilful political communicator I have witnessed in Austria. As a grandiose political actor, he appeared flawless, well-mannered and almost always perfect in his appearance: a careerist determined to the extreme who, highly gifted and versatile, masterfully played the keyboard of social jealousies and xenophobic emotions of Austrian society. He presented himself as effortlessly and seemingly convincingly as the architect of an ÖVP–FPÖ right-of-centre coalition as he did

# FROM WOLFGANG SCHÜSSEL TO SEBASTIAN KURZ

after its fall as the inventor of the ÖVP–Grünen coalition as the "best of both worlds". Disturbed by no moral inhibitions, Kurz was able to state in front of the TV cameras (in the 2017 Austrian Broadcasting Corporation (ORF) Summer Talk), after a year of clandestine inner-party intrigues against his demoralised party leader and vice-chancellor, "the surprise was then great for me when Reinhold Mitterlehner resigned".

The Austrian writer Thomas Stangl characterised the young chancellor who had whipped the ÖVP into a frenzy: a "game with nothingness, a game with emptiness, that was his communication strategy".

> He became a politician not out of any particular commitment to a cause, out of idealism or out of righteous or unrighteous anger. But simply to be a politician, like another becomes businessman, chess player or actor (....) This almost-nothingness is perhaps the secret of this man, who in his government career so far and in the election campaign has been able to keep his outer form immaculate and untouchable and at the same time—often changing roles from sentence to sentence—appear changeable. In his appearances, he gave the pop star who does not shy away from reaching into the kitsch box in order to bind the audience to him, the conservative who is conscious of values and memoranda, the preacher-style counsellor, the vicious demagogue and the statesman, all with the same gentle persuasiveness.

> If one compares Sebastian Kurz with Austria's last disturbingly gifted and novel politician, Jörg Haider, the most striking difference is that nothing about Kurz invites one to want to psychoanalyse him. There seem to be no secret drives, no family entanglements, no ambivalences and ambiguities. He always shows as much emotion as seems necessary for the argument at hand; reproduces emotions, so to speak, without giving the impression that he—that is, the production—is guided or hindered by his own feelings.[31]

The final chapter of the Kurz era is being written by the courts. His absurd, self-exhilarating phrases, such as "The pandemic is mastered", "A cool time is coming" and "The pandemic is over for everyone who has been vaccinated" will soon be forgotten. The lessons of political corruption by manipulated or bought media, from Faymann to Kurz, the reasons for the sympathy of so many voters for the path to the authoritarian state and for the "strong man" at home and abroad should be a warning to Austrian society.

10

# THE "REAL" AUSTRIANS AND THE GREENS

On a sunny Thursday, on 12 September 2019 to be precise, the three of us—my wife Zsóka, our friend, the historian Waltraud Heindl and I—were on our way to the Hofburg for a lunch with Federal President Alexander Van der Bellen and his wife. He had invited me on the occasion of my significant round number birthday, which had taken place shortly before. What remained forever anchored in my memory was the following sentence in his speech: "We both became Austrian citizens in the same year, 1959". He tactfully did not mention the age difference—he was 15 and I was 30 in that fateful year for both of us.

*The Van der Bellens: an eventful family history*

It was only during the research for this book that I realised that Alexander Van der Bellen's life from the beginning to the present day has truly been an adventurous story, full of surprising twists and turns that have helped shape not only his personal biography but also political developments in Austria. His official curriculum vitae on the internet begins with the statement: "My home is

## AUSTRIA BEHIND THE MASK

Tyrol, Vienna, Austria and Europe". Then it briefly says: "Born on 18 January 1944 in Vienna. The mother was born in Estonia, the father was born in Russia with Dutch ancestors. After fleeing the Soviets several times, the family finally found a new home in Austria, first in Vienna, then in Tyrol". Behind these matter-of-fact messages lie the diverse and ultimately dramatic phases of the story of an unusual family.

A refugee child, his family history was only known to him in fragments as his parents had told him little about the past, and the rest he had found out through research. According to family legend, his ancestors came to Russia from the Netherlands at the end of the eighteenth century. His great-great-grandfather was a landowner near the city of Pskov and was ennobled. His grandfather was head of the local government in Pskov after the abdication of the Tsar and supported the Whites in the civil war after the October Revolution. After the victory of the Bolsheviks, the family fled to neighbouring Estonia. For his new stage of their lives, the refugees changed the "von" to "Van" as proof of their middle-class and Dutch origins. Since the beginning of the nineteenth century, all first-born male ancestors bore the first name Alexander, as was the father of the Federal President. He studied economics at the University of Tartu, became an Estonian citizen in 1934 and later managed the Tallinn branch of a British bank. Here, his father married his mother, who was born in Tsarist Russia yo Estonian parents. She moved with her parents to Tallinn in 1917, the capital of the new, independent Estonia, and became a trained singer and pianist. In 1940, the invasion of the Red Army into the capital of Estonia, which had been ascribed to the Soviet sphere of influence in the secret protocol of the Stalin–Hitler Pact, meant a new threat for the anti-communist Russian refugee family. In the spring of 1941, the Van der Bellen family managed to leave Tallinn, pretending to be ethnic Germans, by train and went to East Prussia from where after a

# THE "REAL" AUSTRIANS AND THE GREENS

stay in a camp near Würzburg, they made their way to Vienna. Here, Alexander's father was employed in a foreign trade company and in 1944 the future Federal President was born. Soon, however, the Van der Bellens had to flee again from the approaching the Red Army. They were justifiably afraid of being deported to the Soviet Union as Estonian citizens. Finally they found shelter in the customs house of Feichten in the Tyrol, a picturesquely situated village at an altitude of almost 1300 metres, which even today has under 600 inhabitants. Van der Bellen grew up here and studied in Innsbruck, the Tyrolean capital. His father founded a foreign trade company in 1948 to export products from the chemical industry. He still recounts how greatly his parents, who spoke Russian with each other at home, had feared the Russians:

> I was told as a child in Innsbruck that I should avoid the street past the Soviet consulate at all costs—it was too dangerous". Although Russian was his parents' first language, Van der Bellen never learned it. "My parents wanted me to avoid anything that indicated we were refugees".[1]

The Protestant immigrant child never felt any discrimination and was even class spokesman in the Innsbruck grammar school; he studied economics and made a career as a university professor of economics, first in Innsbruck and then in Vienna. According to his autobiography, "he could not imagine a more attractive profession as an academic". He was a member of the SPÖ for a while, from the mid-1970s to the end of the 1980s, and also a freemason for about 10 years.

*A factor of stability in turbulent times*

It was his former doctoral student Peter Pilz, then federal spokesman of the Greens, a parliamentary party since 1987, who was able to convince the 50-year-old university professor to stand as a candidate for the Greens in the 1994 election. Van der Bellen remained a member of parliament until 2012. His winning personality and his moderate-liberal, pro-European course made a decisive contribution to the electoral success of the Greens. Their share of voters rose from 4.8 per cent to 12.42 per cent and the number of MPs from 8 to 24.

Van der Bellen succeeded not only to end the inner-party disputes that were fought out in public and to improve the image of party in the mass media but also to moderate the often-fundamentalist ideological positions. Even if Van der Bellen's immensely important, democracy-stabilising role as federal president is to be appreciated first and foremost, his earlier, eminently important contribution to the survival of a left-liberal party in difficult times should not be forgotten either.

Only today, looking back at the period of turmoil between 2017 and 2021, from the Ibiza video to the chat scandals, from Strache's fall to Kurz's forced departure, can the fateful significance of Van der Bellen's victory in the run-off election for the office of federal president in 2016 be appreciated. It suffices to recall the events before and after the general elections in 2019; the domestic political turbulence that formed the background to the unprecedentedly high frequency of changes of governments and ministers in the history of the Second Republic: the swearing-in of some 60 members of government and of a federal chancellor six times. The international press also praised the federal president's style and his speeches, which avoided any sign of dramatisation and exerted a calming influence.

Already at his first inauguration, the new Federal President delivered a "modest and at the same time great speech", according to the *Süddeutsche Zeitung*.[2] Even the first words proclaimed the uniqueness of his personal destiny and identity as the head of the Republic: "Austria is a truly great country! I stand here today with a feeling of unreality! You see here a refugee child.

# THE "REAL" AUSTRIANS AND THE GREENS

Born in Vienna, fled with my parents to Kaunertal. And now I may stand before you as Federal President". His reference to Austria as "a country of unlimited possibilities" hit the mark, considering his complex family history. On his understanding of his office, he said, "I will do my utmost to be a non-partisan Federal President, a Federal President for all people living in Austria. I will speak out when fundamental questions of our community arise, or are at stake".[3]

Van der Bellen has repeatedly put this promise into practice in critical times. His hope that "after six years, as many people as possible should say: Yes, things have changed for the better", was, however, not fulfilled. Instead, we are experiencing a dramatic change of times, both in domestic politics and internationally, due to the covid epidemic and the Ukraine war, with enormous social and economic consequences.

These were, of course, also the topics of our long conversation almost on the eve of his decision to run again for Federal President.[4] First, we talked about his family. He had only recently learned from a relative that his mother was not born in Moscow, but in Pskov. His younger son, who works in tourism, lives in Tulcea in Romania. His wife, a Romanian, is employed there. The Federal President sees them and he grandchild only once or twice a year. Unfortunately, the three other grandchildren from his younger son's first marriage live in Australia. His older son runs a cattle farm in the German state of Baden-Württemberg. He is in his second marriage, since 2015, to his long-time partner Doris Schmidauer, who was the executive director of the Green parliamentary club for many years.

Then he answered my questions about political developments in our country thoughtfully and openly, but of course "off the record" (i.e. not for quotation). Nevertheless, his explanations helped me to better understand some critical situations and the role of certain personalities. I left the tradition-steeped office room, where I had often spoken with the predecessors (Rudolf Kirchschläger, Kurt Waldheim, Thomas Klestil and Heinz Fischer) over half a century, with thoughts of the good fortune that this extraordinary personality ultimately had in making the trend-setting decisions in the days that were so decisive for the Second Republic.

One should not overlook the fact that despite all the turbulence in domestic politics, his re-election in October 2022 as Federal President with almost 57 per cent of the votes in the first round and against six other candidates was an unmistakable sign of change. It recalls the times when people still hoped to win the 1970 National Council election with posters of Josef Klaus as "a real Austrian" against Bruno Kreisky, who was Jewish and therefore, of course, not a real Austrian.

### Alma Zadić: from refugee child to minister

In some respects, the career of the Federal Minister of Justice, Alma Zadić, is even more impressive personally and perhaps even more encouraging in socio-political terms.

She is the first female minister of justice and, moreover, the first member of the government who was not born in Austria. Who would have predicted it when she came to Vienna with her parents from the Bosnian town of Tuzla as a refugee in 1994 at the age of ten without any knowledge of German? Her curriculum vitae reflects a storybook career in the best sense of the word.[5] As an 8-year-old, she experienced the outbreak of the war in Bosnia, which was started by the Great Serb nationalists, and the ethnic cleansing that was instigated against people with Muslim names, in this city of 110,000 people, which is now predominantly inhabited by Bosniaks and is the third largest in the Federation of Bosnia and Herzegovina: "In May 1992, I was picked up from school by my father and we ran because we heard gunshots. Then we spent the next few months in the basement". Before the escape, her father had been a university professor for electrical engineering, and her mother worked as a building inspector for the municipality. The flight to Vienna was an incredible challenge. None of them knew German. Her father first made his way to Vienna alone and quickly got a job. Alma, her mother and her brother Armin, who was 4 years younger, were only able to leave the embattled city a year later with a UN aid convoy.

As a "Zuagraster" (i.e. not a native Viennese, with an indelible foreign accent to boot), I can probably judge her extraordinary personal achievement and meteoric rise better than most "real" Austrians. Her curriculum vitae states that she "attended a primary school and the Realgymnasium Ettenreichgasse in Vienna". Behind this dry statement lies the drama of a new beginning for a 10-year-old migrant child. What the beginning meant for a pupil with painful experiences who did not yet speak German can only be guessed at. She still remembers a tram ride where she asked the conductor, "Is this right to the sports centre?" He looked at her and said, "Tschuschen[6] have no business here". She adds, "Those were moments when I realised that I was not part of society, that I didn't belong".

She also had a similar experience in primary school, which was shattering for a child. When she asked a teacher to explain a maths problem to her, she replied dismissively, "What's the point, you can't do it anyway". At this first school, she was the only pupil who did not know German, and she almost broke down from lack of affection. After changing to another school with more migrant children and with extra lessons, Alma learned German very quickly; she became a preferred pupil and graduated with dazzling grades. She then studied law at the University of Vienna and spent a semester abroad in Milan. After graduating, she was an intern at the International Tribunal for War Crimes in the Former Yugoslavia in The Hague. She then completed her judicial year in

Vienna, followed by two years of LL.M. training at Columbia University in New York. In 2017, she received her Doctor of Laws degree from the University of Vienna. "If you don't try twice as hard, you won't make it here", is a sentence many children from migrant families like her grew up with, she says.

Natural talent, great determination and the support of her parents helped her to overcome the enormous challenges. In all her interviews, she convincingly addressed the dialectic between the search for identity and self-discovery. During her years in New York, Alma Zadić understood that one could have different identities and that she didn't have to decide whether she was Austrian or Bosnian: "The diversity of New York showed me that you can be Austrian, Bosnian and European at the same time".

She worked for 6 years in conflict resolution at an international business law firm. When I asked her how she found her way into politics, she answered by referring to a girl-friend and to her contacts with the well-known lawyer and author Alfred Noll, both later MPs on the Peter Pilz list. She accepted the invitation to join this list and was then elected to parliament. The lessons of the Yugoslav wars for international law and human rights, as well as the increased right-wing agitation, motivated her. She wanted to shape and contribute to the fight against the right-wing populists.

It was undoubtedly a huge leap from the secure existence of an international law firm into the ruthless world of politics. Her switch from the Pilz/Jetzt list to the Greens after the call for new elections in the wake of the Ibiza video was also a bold move. The Greens reached their best result ever in this election. Zadić, placed fifth on the Green federal list, was re-elected to parliament in September 2019. Subsequently, party chairman Werner Kogler nominated her to become a member of the exploratory team at the negotiations with the ÖVP, and then she was elected as one of the four Green members in the coalition government.

# THE "REAL" AUSTRIANS AND THE GREENS

A truly brilliant career for a refugee child. The fact that her name was in the headlines even before she was sworn in was the result of a massive hate campaign from the extreme right. The background: while still a member of the previous parliament, she put the photo of a right-wing demonstrator with a Hitler salute on Twitter. Underneath she wrote: "No tolerance for neo-Nazis, fascists and racists". The fraternity member declared that he had only waved to school friends among the demonstrators and sued her. Zadić was ordered to pay 700 euros by the Vienna Criminal Court. As it was a media law judgement, there was no entry in the criminal record. On social media, identitarians and FPÖ supporters started a xenophobic and misogynistic campaign against "a Muslim justice minister", although the Greens made it clear that Zadić had no religious affiliation. As there were also death threats, she received police protection. The FPÖ had even asked the head of state not to nominate her as minister because of the open court case. At the handover of office, her predecessor Clemens Jabloner spoke of an orgy of abuse and of a "perfidy" of those responsible for agitation against her.

*Werner Kogler: saviour of the Greens*

The fact that the Greens readily agreed to the nomination of a former MP of another party, who had joined them only a few months earlier, as a minister of justice was undoubtedly the result of the persuasive efforts of Vice-Chancellor Werner Kogler. No Green federal spokesperson has ever had such authority as Werner Kogler (born in 1961), who was active in the Green movement from the very beginning after graduating in economics from the University of Graz. A member of parliament between 1999 and 2017, Kogler immediately took over as interim chairman after the Greens failed to clear the 4 per cent hurdle in the 2017 parliamentary election and had to leave parliament. In his first statement he announced: "The election result is a setback for the Greens, a low blow, almost a precipitation. But don't worry, we will get up again and strive for new goals".[7] Over the next two years, with incredible energy and unwavering stamina, he led the Greens as the top candidate to their greatest success ever in the 2019 parliamentary elections, with a 13.9 per cent share of the vote and 26 MPs.

Participation in the Kurz II government was not only a decision with far-reaching consequences for the future of Austria. It was also, after more than three decades in opposition, a deeply personal about-turn for him. In the detailed history of the Greens,[8] one can read how Kogler, as a participant in the negotiations on the formation of a coalition with the ÖVP in 2003, expressed strong reservations from time to time on the economic and pension issues. Meeting him for the first time for an in-depth interview,[9] and discussing the failed negotiations with the ÖVP under Schüssel, he was still not sure whether Wolfgang Schüssel did not hold parallel talks with the Freedom Party from the very beginning.

Be that as it may, Werner Kogler's personal merit in setting two important courses in the political history of the Second Republic must be acknowledged without reservation. His contribution to the rebirth of the Greens was the basis for the first ÖVP–Green coalition government, which meant a positive turnaround after the recent disastrous government experiment with the FPÖ. The second merit for political stability was his role in the forced resignation of Sebastian Kurz as chancellor and in his involuntary departure from politics. As Vice-Chancellor and Federal Minister for the Arts, Culture, Public Service and Sport since January 2020, the politician, who comes from a Styrian farming and working-class family, has consistently acted as a responsible politician, displaying courage in critical situations.

The bon mot by the famous Austrian actor, Helmut Qualtinger, "Austria is a labyrinth in which everyone knows their way

# THE "REAL" AUSTRIANS AND THE GREENS

around", applies mutatis mutandis to the circumstances surrounding Kurz's fall in two phases as Federal Chancellor and two months later as ÖVP party leader. Although Kogler is known to have played a decisive role behind the scenes in both cases, he did not want to take credit for his role, either in public or even in background conversation with me. Modesty and a sense of proportion, so rare in Austrian domestic politics, seem to me to be defining traits in the Vice-Chancellor's personality. I was also impressed in our long and frank conversation that he unreservedly appreciated the abilities of Peter Pilz, who "jumped ship" in 2017, and admitted that the Greens had nominated the wrong person as minister of health during the pandemic in 2021.

As for his role in the Kurz case, the Vice-Chancellor also emphasised in private that his action had not been planned beforehand but was a reaction to the revelations in the chats found during the investigations. In response to a remark by the author of a report in the *Spiegel* (the German news magazine) that Chancellor Kurz, who had long been considered invincible, had failed because of Werner Kogler, the Vice-Chancellor replied: "It was not my intention to let anyone fail (....) Kurz and his closest circle failed because of themselves". The leader of the Greens stressed repeatedly that they had not stirred up the "whole quarrel" and that Kurz had finally buckled under strong internal party pressure from the heads of the ÖVP organisations in the provinces. The Greens had sought reliability and stability.

*Sigrid Maurer's key role in the coalition*

This attitude is by no means self-evident against the background of earlier Green policies and in view of the power struggles at that time still raging in the Green ranks in the Vienna branch. Kogler expressly praised the contribution of Sigrid Maurer, the Green Party's chairwoman. The Tyrolean, born in 1985, is the only member of the Green Club who was already an MP in 2013–17. In contrast to her earlier, rather inflammatory role as Green chairwoman of the Austrian Students' Union, she has been the architect of a functioning coalition axis together with the chief of the ÖVP parliamentary group, August Wöginger. Listening to her speeches in parliament defending government resolutions, it is difficult to imagine that 12 years ago the same person was banned from parliament for 18 months for throwing leaflets into the plenary hall from the visitors' gallery and chanting opposition slogans.

Coming from a family of teachers in Tyrol, the politician has become known primarily for her courageous public backlash against mass hate mail on social media. In one case, when Maurer posted obscene messages directed at her, the operator of the Facebook account she had named, the owner of a craft beer shop, sued her, claiming that he did not write the message himself; anyone who entered his shop could be considered the author. Courts dealt with the absurd story between 2018 and 2021, until the shop owner (later revealed as a murder suspect) finally withdrew the charges. On 7 April 2022, Maurer was physically assaulted; a man recognised her in a restaurant garden in Vienna's city centre, insulted her over the federal government's coronavirus measures and threw a glass in her face. She remained unharmed. The young attacker, who was apprehended by the police, later apologised for the incident. Maurer received hundreds of solidarity messages, but remarks in social media also hinted that she had somehow provoked this attack. Petra Stuiber, deputy editor, warned in the *Standard*: "The hatred towards women who express and expose themselves politically in public has a dimension that is unacceptable for a civilised society".[10] Asked about the physical attack only a few days later, the politician appeared calm, relaxed and almost philosophical in a personal conversation with me: "If you are in politics, you have to expect attacks".

# THE "REAL" AUSTRIANS AND THE GREENS

The key role of "Sigi" Maurer is also attributable to the fact that in contrast to earlier coalitions, there is no steering committee, but the heads of the two parliamentary groups prepare the topics for the cabinet meetings on a weekly basis. When assessing Maurer's role, one must also bear in mind that the majority of Green MPs (apart from Kogler and Maurer) have little to no parliamentary experience. It is remarkable that women form the majority of MPs, with 15 to 11, and that five MPs are migrants or come from immigrant families. The fact that Alexander Van der Bellen, Alma Zadić and many other MPs from immigrant families today shape Austria's destiny is undoubtedly a glimmer of hope for the future.

11

A DEPLORABLE MORAL PICTURE

Russia's war of aggression against the Ukraine not surprisingly triggered an immediate debate about Austria's neutral status.[1] The announcement by Finland and Sweden about their intention to apply for NATO membership gave a further impetus to the debate. No one talked any more about the Western military alliance being "obsolete" (Donald Trump) or "brain dead" (Emmanuel Macron).[2] It was the influential Austrian People's Party (ÖVP) senior politician, Andreas Khol, former President of Parliament, and his party's candidate at the 2016 presidential election who first spoke out publicly in favour of an entry into NATO.[3] His statement reminded observers of a similar initiative by the then Chancellor Wolfgang Schüssel 20 years ago comparing neutrality to Mozart Bonbons and to Lipizzaner horses, as likeable but basically insignificant myths.[4]

The new Federal Chancellor Karl Nehammer, only recently appointed, hastened to stop the debate before it had really begun with a controversial statement: "Austria was neutral; Austria is neutral; Austria will also remain neutral".[5] However, his inept attempt quickly failed, and soon afterwards a group of prominent public personalities demanded in an open letter to the president, the government and parliament a public debate about Austria's security. However, any hope of a meaningful debate has petered out for several reasons.

The most important factor is that neutrality has become a part of Austrian identity, with all opinion polls showing a huge majority in favour. Even after the Russian attack against the Ukraine and the decision of Finland and Sweden to join NATO, 70 per cent of Austrians spoke out in favour of neutral status, and 90 per cent regard it as a part of national identity.[6] Thus, any attempt to join NATO and to give up neutrality would be political suicide for any party or any government.

Nevertheless, 80 per cent felt that Austria was not secure enough in case of an attack. Austria's military spending, at 0.6 per cent of GDP, ranked after Ireland as the lowest in the European Union. Though the government proposed, and all parties represented in parliament approved, an increase in military expenditure, the debate reflected the lack of confidence in the ministry of defence. This was not surprising since an earlier project to reform the army proved to be a failure. The cabinet minister in charge since January 2020, Claudia Tanner, is a complete novice in matters of defence. Before her appointment she had dealt with agricultural policy for a more than a decade as a functionary of the Lower Austrian branch of the ÖVP. The media speculated that her surprising rise to prominence may have been due to the fact that she was the sister-in-law of the closest political adviser of Chancellor Kurz. No wonder that observers criticised the lack of the presence of independent defence experts before taking decisions about the allocation of the increased expenditure.

Of course, one must note the fact that in striking contrast to the geopolitical situation before the collapse of the Soviet bloc in 1989, Austria is now, except for Switzerland, surrounded on all

# A DEPLORABLE MORAL PICTURE

sides by member states of NATO. This is the underlying explanation for the easy-going approach to national security. Instead of the theoretical debates about the concept of neutrality, one should review past mistakes in foreign and security policy of neutral Austria.

*Kneissl's deep curtsey to Putin was not the beginning*

Although Russia's war against Ukraine has manifold direct consequences in Austria, such as the massive influx of refugees, energy problems and inflation, there has been a potentially much more direct danger to the country's independence posed by political actors on the domestic stage. In recent years, there have been alarming tendencies of unprofessional naivety and covert complicity, adorned with intellectual negligence and arrogance born of ignorance. The personal and business links of senior politicians, managers, entrepreneurs and journalists with the Kremlin and Russian state-owned companies have been politically extremely dangerous and also economically harmful.

Instead of a morally credible and politically impeccable attitude towards Putin's Russia, both the two government parties, the ÖVP and the Greens, as well as the opposition parties, the SPÖ and FPÖ, have so far failed to heed the right warnings from history. It is only the small liberal party, the NEOS, founded in 2012,[7] whose chairwoman, Beate Meinl-Reisinger, has consistently criticised the ambivalence and opportunism of the ÖVP Chancellors Kurz and Nehammer for their policy of restraint in dealing with the authoritarian regimes of Viktor Orbán and Aleksander Vucìc in Hungary and Serbia. NEOS spokeswoman in the subcommittee investigating the corruption scandal involving the ÖVP, Stephanie Krisper, did not mince her words when asked about Russia's deep penetration of this European Union member state: "Russian influence in Austria hast to be investigated thoroughly. For many years, connections to Moscow permeated our political system. Now, the economic and political dependence on Russia has finally become visible to everyone as a security threat".[8]

It should not be forgotten that Austria's policy towards Russia did not slide into a precarious position with Foreign Minister Karin Kneissl's deep curtsy after the waltz with Putin after her wedding nor with Chancellor Kurz's verbal gestures of submission. Years before, the former social democratic chancellor Alfred Gusenbauer[9] had already served as a fabulously paid lobbyist for authoritarian post-Soviet regimes as one of the Vice-Presidents of the Socialist International and as President of the Renner Institute, the SPÖ think tank in Vienna. Even more important was his role since 2016 as member of the supervisory board of the Russian sponsored think tank "Dialogue of Civilisations" headed by Vladimir Yakunin, Putin's confidant and former head of the Russian state railways. He was even awarded an "international prize" by the organisation. The ex-Chancellor gave lectures, time and again, at events staged by the organisation. He strongly criticised Western sanctions against Russia imposed after the annexation of Crimea: "They are not a way out of the crisis, but lead deeper into it".[10]

Following in his footsteps was the social democratic successor Christian Kern, who lost no time during his short chancellorship (May 2016 to December 2017) to speak out "for the gradual lifting of the EU sanctions" at the St. Petersburg Economic Forum, in an interview with the Russian propaganda channel *Sputnik*. His companions, Siegfried Wolf, ex-Magna boss and long-time manager in the group of Oleg Deripaska, the Russian oligarch, and Rainer Seele, director general of ÖMV, the Austrian oil concern, expressed similar views. Both men also received the "Order of Friendship" from Putin on this occasion.

At the event in St. Petersburg, Kern, the only EU head of government present, was treated, according to press reports,[11] as a "star guest" and was even addressed on first name terms by Putin during a joint photo opportunity and a press briefing. Kern again criticised the EU sanctions, as a result of which Austria's GDP lost 0.3 per cent. During Kern's chancellorship, the so-called Sochi Dialogue was also initiated. Due to the developments after the Russian attack against the Ukraine, the projects connected with the Sochi Dialogue have been put on hold until further notice.

Although Kern resigned from his position as a member of the supervisory board of the Russian state railways, which he had held since July 2019, following public criticism shortly after the Russian attack, he had spoken out just two days earlier against what he called "a rhetoric of a thundering fist": "Sanctions have at best a symbolic effect. They cannot bring about a regime or policy change". Moreover, not everything in the Russian argumentation was wrong".[12] In the Austrian TV programme *Im Zentrum*, he pleaded several times for understanding towards Russia and during the hour long debate did not utter one single word of criticism about Russia.[13] He even referred to "24 million Soviet citizens who sacrificed their lives ... and liberated us from the Hitler-regime". Such references, which also mentioned the "great historical links", can only be regarded under the present circumstances as absurd attempts by those who "understand" Putin to divert attention from the aggression and war crimes committed by the present Russian regime. Against the background of Kern's position as Chairman of the European China Business Council, his voluntary attempts to whitewash the destruction of democracy in Hongkong without even being asked about it, can be only regarded as peculiar.

*Massive dependence on Russian gas*

It was probably no coincidence that a year after Kern's mission Chancellor Sebastian Kurz had the same companions on his trip to St. Petersburg, namely Siegfried Wolf and Rainer Seele, this time supplemented by the billionaire René Benko, and a meeting with President Putin on the agenda. The fact that Austria is more dependent on Russian gas than any other EU country was the result of a deliberate policy. The architects of the closest possible cooperation with Russia's Gasprom were Rainer Seele as ÖMV's director general (2015–21) and the omnipresent Siegfried Wolf, who sat on the supervisory board of the state holding ÖBAG (between 2002 and 2015) and served from 2014 as board chairman.

Gerhard Roiss, Seele's predecessor as ÖMV boss, who was booted out 2015, revealed the background to the Russian deals in a conspicuous interview.[14] After the Russian attack against Ukraine, he decided that he "could no longer silently overlook the fact that Austria and the ÖMV were deliberately steered into a dependency on Russia by a group of people, all 'Putin-friends'. These people have put their own financial interests above any morals". He also pointed out that the representative of the federal state in charge of its share capital in the ÖMV between 2014 and 2017 was the ÖVP Finance Minister Hans Jörg Schelling, who only a few months after leaving office became an adviser to Gazprom on the Nordstream 2 pipeline project in which the ÖMV is also involved. "Already during his term in office, Schelling's joint visits to Russia with Seele and Wolf had caused a stir in the industry..." Roiss said, adding: "This shows a general problem that has become visible in the past five or six years—the close interlocking between politics and business. Now we no longer have only oligarchs from the East; we have for a long time had also small Austro-oligarchs".

The partly state-owned ÖMV and Russia's Gazprom extended their gas supply contract until 2040 (!) in June 2018 in Vienna. A photo, often displayed, shows the two company bosses, Rainer Seele and Alexei Miller in an almost intimate embrace, with Kurz and Putin, smiling jovially, standing behind them. A few weeks later, Putin attended Kneissl's wedding in southern Styria, and the photos of the Russian president dancing with the Austrian foreign minister caused worldwide critical and derisive comments. The fact that Sebastian Kurz paid an official visit to Moscow in October of the same year for the opening of an exhibition, thus meeting Putin for the fourth time within a year, astonished observers, not only in Austria.[15]

The role of Kneissl as foreign minister and the consequences of the ÖVP–FPÖ coalition era with all intelligence services controlled by the FPÖ-run interior and defence ministries have seriously damaged Austria's reputation as a reliable partner in the European Union.[16] Following the Russian attack against Ukraine, the EU parliament demanded that the European Union should take a stronger stance against the interference of Russia and China. The report explicitly named former Foreign Minister Karin Kneissl and the FPÖ as negative examples of the Kremlin's influence on the EU. It was well known that at the end of 2016 the top leadership of the FPÖ signed in Moscow "an agreement on cooperation and collaboration" with the Kremlin party "United Russia", valid for 5 years. The two parties agreed, among other things, to regularly discuss current issues concerning the situation in Russia and Austria and to exchange experiences in areas such as party organisation, youth policy and legislation. Cooperation in the economic and trade spheres was also envisaged. As the deal expired at the end of 2021 and had not been extended, FPÖ Chairman Herbet Kickl rejected the accusations. Nevertheless, the FPÖ called for an end to the sanctions against Russia during the Ukraine war several times with reference to "Austria's neutral status".[17]

*The explosive chat transcript*

The publication of chat transcripts from the cell phones of key figures in Austrian politics and business have confirmed that the manager and entrepreneur Siegfried Wolf, mentioned already in this chapter, may have played a key role in tying the threads between Moscow and Vienna. The 65-year-old multi-millionaire was a top manager at the Magna car company and, until 2019, co-owner of a vehicle and engineering factory, with the majority of the capital held by Oleg Deripaska, an oligarch close to Putin. Between 2012 and 2022, Wolf was also the chairman of the supervisory board of the European branch of Sberbank, one of the largest Russian banks. Ex-Chancellor Kurz had held Wolf in high esteem and wanted to propose him again as chairman of the supervisory board of ÖBAG, the restructured state holding.

The chats, which were made public in March 2022,[18] reveal how Wolf repeatedly asked Kurz to help to mitigate the US sanctions against the Russian oligarch Deripaska. Wolf wrote on 6 November 2018: "Sebastian, good morning. If you talk to the US officials today than they should tell us please, what else the US wants from us?" A month later he even asked Kurz to call the then US treasury secretary Steven Mnuchin or secretary of state Mike Pompeo: "I need your help again in my case".

On 21 February 2019, during Kurz's trip to the US, Wolf wrote to him again about the US sanctions against Deripaska's car factory, GAZ, in which Wolf also had a stake: "Dear Sebastian—good morning. Tell me, did you manage to achieve something? Please, inform me. Thanks—Sigi". The answer from Kurz: "Dear Sigi! It was very, very good. Please let us talk directly as soon as I am back in Vienna". What "very, very good" meant in practice is not known. However, Deripaska is still on the US sanctions list. Wolf tried again later, in January 2020, that is, already during the ÖVP–Greens coalition and asked Kurz "to call the White House ... again, please".

For a normal citizen, it must seem like an excerpt from a Netflix thriller series to have an Austrian businessman ask his own prime minister to intervene with two US cabinet ministers

# A DEPLORABLE MORAL PICTURE

in favour of one of the richest Russian oligarchs. What could have been a major scandal in other democratic countries was however overshadowed by the juicy details of Wolf's own tax problems.

In December 2021, it became known that the Austrian Public Prosecutor's Office for Economic Affairs and Corruption had already been investigating Thomas Schmid, the former secretary general in the ministry of finance and other unnamed persons for bribery since July 2021. In this context, Wolf is said to have been illegally relieved of 629,941 euros in tax debts. A tax official is said to have been promoted for her cooperation in the case. As always, the presumption of innocence applies. According to newspaper reports, the flat and the office of the official was searched and Wolf's tax files were found in the private residence of the official.[19]

However, it was a taped chat between Thomas Schmid, the highest ranking official in the ministry of finance and a clerk in the cabinet of the finance minister about the tax problems of Wolf that provided stuff for cabaret jokes and satirical columns: on 6 January 2017 "Sigi" (Siegfried Wolf) wrote to "Thomas" (Schmid) with the request to support him in contesting a tax assessment.

Schmid to the clerk in the minister's cabinet office: "Please meet his tax adviser on Monday. The boss (i.e. Finance Minister Hans Jörg Schelling) had promised him that".

The clerk replied: "Sounds like fun—ok".

Schmid: "Best Programme to start a successful season! Don't forget—you are chopping in an ÖVP cabinet!! You are the whore for the rich!"

The clerk: "Thank you for allowing us to discuss this so frankly".

Schmid's spiteful comment about public servants as "whores for the rich" immediately became an often quoted remark, as the bon mot (made in Austria) of the year.[20]

# AUSTRIA BEHIND THE MASK

*Putin's friends in Austria*

The characterisation of Wolf's relationship with Russia would not be complete without recalling his frequent praise of Vladimir Putin. For example, after the annexation of Crimea, he declared in a speech in Graz that he knew Russian President Putin very well; he had "very personal conversations" with him regularly. Putin reacts to criticism "in a positive, cool way, and he is a very, very correct man". Putin displays "leadership", which he misses "to a great extent" in the EU: "I would like to see there a bit more Russian *democratur*, that people decide and stand by their decisions. When I look at the EU, I see that it needs clear leadership, which Putin has, even I don't always agree with him", Wolf said. He added that "one has no idea here of his approval ratings. He is regarded as someone who doesn't put up with anything".[21] Wolf has defended the annexation of the Crimea and praised Putin's leadership qualities in several interviews: "I can report only positive things that I have experienced with Mr. Putin. Such a country needs strong leadership".[22]

Thus, it is not an exaggeration to consider Siegfried Wolf as the front man of the visible faction of Putin's influential friends in Vienna. He is not alone in view of the substantial economic relations between the two countries. Russia is the country's number-two foreign investor after Germany, with 23 billion euros worth of assets in Austria. Raiffeisen Bank International, the country's second biggest bank, made half of its profits, 1.4 billion euros in 2021, in Russia, where it has more than 9,000 employees.

The Russian oligarch and Wolf's business partner, Oleg Deripaska, also had a 27.8 per cent holding in Strabag, the Austrian construction and engineering concern with an annual turnover of 16 billion euros and 75,000 employees worldwide. After the Russian attack against Ukraine, the EU put Deripaska on the sanction list. Strabag stopped paying him dividends, and his representative was eliminated from the supervisory board, which is incidentally headed by the former SPÖ chancellor, Alfred Gusenbauer.

Deripaska's connections with Wolf, who was at that time director general of the Magna car factory and member of the supervisory board of Strabag, provided the background to the lightning fast naturalisation of the daughter of former Russian President Boris Yeltsin and her family as Austrian citizens in 2009. As Austria has one of the most rigid naturalisation laws, the case was later reported with lurid details in a cover story by a news magazine.[23] She was not the only one to profit from the close ties between Russian oligarchs and their influential Austrian friends. Numerous luxury hotels in Tyrol and other centres of Austrian tourism have been bought up by Russian investors. The penetration of the Austrian intelligence services by Russia became particularly evident when Jan Marsalek, an Austrian-born manager who was, as the key figure, involved in the biggest post-war financial scandal in Germany (the collapse of the Wirecard giant financial service company) fled to Russia with the help of Austrian intelligence officers. Marsalek is reported to have formed close ties with Russian security services. It is no wonder that following the take-over of key portfolios (the ministries of interior, defence and foreign affairs) by the FPÖ with close links to Russia between 2017 and 2019, and in view of the Marsalek scandal, Austria was described as "Russia's tunnel into the heart of Europe".[24]

*Flirting with authoritarian neighbours*

However, one should not focus exclusively on Russia when looking at the seduction of recent Austrian governments by regimes of "strong men" in the neighbourhood. The ÖVP–FPÖ government under Chancellor Kurz had no compunction about cultivating close ties with the governments of Viktor Orbán in Hungary and Aleksandar Vucic in Serbia. Although Kurz even attended a meeting of the four so-called Visegrád states (Hungary, Poland, Slovakia and the Czech Republic) in Budapest in June 2018, claiming to act as a "bridge builder", Orbán's true sympathy belonged to the extreme right, to the FPÖ. He effusively welcomed the FPÖ Vice-Chancellor HC Strache in Budapest in May 2019, proclaiming in an interview: "Europe should adopt the Austrian model. The centre right works together with the right. Seen from Budapest this appears to be successful".[25] Two weeks later the government fell after the "Ibiza video" showed Strache seeming to accept money from a woman pretending to be the niece of a Russian oligarch in order to buy the *Kronen Zeitung*, the daily with the largest circulation in Austria. Strache boasted: "We want a media landscape similar to Budapest. Orbán's media man, Heinrich Pecina[26] could help to take over the Krone". The Austrian banker's media company played a key role in eliminating *Népszabadság*, the liberal opposition daily, and assisting Orbán taking over all regional dailies in Hungary.

Even after the collapse of the coalition with the far-right Freedomites, Kurz stuck to his line criticising "Western arrogance" and calling for "fairness for Hungary and Poland" in Brussels, when the two countries came under attack for dismantling independent justice and corruption practices.[27] He also intensified relations with the right-wing populist Slovenian Premier Janez Janša; he went mountain climbing with him and even wished him good luck for the next parliamentary elections. It did not help; Janša lost these by a landslide in April 2022.

Kurz also paid his respects to the authoritarian, nationalistic Serbian President, Aleksandar Vučić in Belgrade. On this occasion, the Chancellor was even awarded "Ribbon of the Order of the Republic of Serbia" for his "services in promoting relations with Serbia and with the entire region of Western Balkans".[28]

# A DEPLORABLE MORAL PICTURE

All this made critical observers wonder about the roots of this fraternizing with strong-man rulers: merely a mixture of abysmal ignorance, vanity and naivety, or something more? Is it rather, as the *Standard* columnist, Hans Rauscher thinks, that Kurz considers the East European authoritarian rulers as role models?[29] Or is the left-liberal commentator Armin Thurnher right in his "farewell editorial":

> Kurz has failed twice in European and in national policy. He has steered Austria into an east-central European position. Instead helping states as Hungary, Poland or Slovenia with the democratisation and the solution of legal-system problems, he took the side of the far right state leaders and on top of it, discredited the justice system at home .... Kurz was not a political talent, but a political showman with a switched-off internal moral warning system.[30]

Or did the two grand old men of the ÖVP, Wolfgang Schüssel and Andreas Khol, whom he explicitly thanked for their advice in his farewell speech, help to shape his view of the world? We will never know, but the fact that he was hired by bizarre extremist US-German billionaire and political activist, Peter Thiel, as a kind of "Europa ambassador" seems more likely to confirm the gloomy version.

*Exorbitantly expensive "message control"*

The enormously large structure in the federal chancellery is a proof of how important the control of the media was for the Kurz government. The chancellor's cabinet office alone had 38 employees. In addition, there was a special unit "Think Austria" with a staff of six. Furthermore, there were 59 people dealing only with media matters. In all, 109 employees were counted in Kurz's chancellery. A former top civil servant reckoned in his book that 64 officials were working directly for the chancellor, synchronising government communication ("message control").[31]

Between 2005 and 2018, expenditure for public relations and communication jumped from 30 million to 45 million euros. He estimated that the federal government, the regional administrations and state-owned enterprises spent two billion euros on advertising and consultancy since the year 2000.

In a study of the political influence exerted on the media, the political scientist Oliver Rathkolb calculated that the Austrian government spent 117.2 million euros of taxpayers' money on advertisements, above all in tabloid media, between 2013 and mid-2020. The federal government in Berlin spent slightly more (129.8 million euros) in the same period. Calculated per capita, however, this expenditure totalled 1.82 euros in Austria in 2013 against 10 cents in Germany.[32]

Another Austrian specialty is advertising with photos of various ministers. A peculiar case is the banker, Franz Gasselsberger, the director general of the Oberbank, which is a large regional bank. His photo regularly appears in advertisements for the bank; he is always dressed differently, pronouncing a short message. He might be saving his shareholders some money by not using external photos, but I know of no other bank boss who appears regularly and exclusively in advertisements. Another well-known banker, Andreas Treichl, until recently head of Erste Bank, never did anything like that. He came into the public spotlight in May 2011. Although he had been purser of the ÖVP between 1991 and 1997, Treichl attacked the politicians as being "cowardly", "stupid" and "clueless". In a witty rejoinder, the political scientist Anton Pelinka conceded that there might be dilettantes in high offices, but at the same time he emphasised: "The degree of stupidity that one might detect in politics is clearly more democratically legitimised than the analogous degree of stupidity among bankers or managers. A state is governed by 'stupid' politicians when they have been delegated to office by the voters. Can the same be said about 'stupid' bankers?" The bank director was also

# A DEPLORABLE MORAL PICTURE

annoyed, Pelinka added, that many politicians did not understand "why it should be necessary to double the compensation for the members of the supervisory board of the Erste Bank when the financial institution had just been saved with tax revenues".[33] However, it seems to me that Treichl's initiative in 2015 to give the Hungarian state, by then fully controlled by the Orbán government, a 15 per cent stake in the Hungarian subsidiary of the Erste bank, at the same time as for the EBRD, the London-based bank, was politically more damaging.[34] Since then, the Orbán-regime has thoroughly reorganised the Hungarian banking sector in the interest of the kleptocracy Orbán commands. Erste bank serves him as a useful decoration. In contrast to the Creditanstalt director general, Heinrich Treichl (1970–81, not to be confused with his son Andreas!), and to the boss of the Raiffeisen Zentralbank, Walter Rothensteiner (1995–2017), there are hardly any humanistically minded philanthropes among Austrian bankers and industrialists these days. Frierich Heer's saying about the Viennese heart being made of Krupp steel is still valid for most politicians and businessmen.

Although the dimension and the intensity of "message control" by the Kurz government was unprecedented, this disreputable instrument of manipulation of the media was first used on large scale, as already mentioned, by the former SPÖ Chancellor Werner Faymann, above all in the tabloid *Kronen Zeitung*. The case of Hungary in particular proves the tremendous importance of the freedom of the media for the defence of liberal democracy. Two lucky events, the famous "Ibiza video" about the attempt of a far-right Austrian party to buy newspapers and the confiscation of the cell phone of a high-ranking civil servant with 344,000 chat messages, have contributed to saving press freedom in Austria. The key role has been played by the Economic and Corruption Prosecution Office, but the broad impact was also due to the coverage by Austrian Broadcasting Corporation (ORF), the public TV network and the independent press.[35]

The rule of law, separation of powers and an independent judiciary are the crucial conditions for the existence of free media. The first head of the Economic and Corruption Prosecutor's Office, Walter Geyer (2009–13), rightly stressed "the soft start, the creeping transition from the permissible to the questionable ad to getting used to it" with regard to the veiled corruption through advertisements.[36]

But despite all the repulsive facts that have come to light in the chats and the subsequent 454-page long confessions of Tomas Schmid (who in his bid for the status of crown witness is the key figure in the case against ex-Chancellor Sebastian Kurz and his associates), I see no reason to doubt the achievements of the Second Republic. Compared with the failed First Republic, and taking into account the entire period since the Second World War in Central and Eastern Europe, both the economic successes and the maintenance of social peace mean that on the whole it can be considered a happy epoch. The literary critic Hans Weigel once castigated "the tendency towards negative generalisation, the Austrian self-distrust, the negative patriotism of the Austrians.... The essence of Austrian achievements is namely they nevertheless take place. Mostly not noticed by the public. The side effects are provincial, the achievements are not".[37]

*Quo vadis, Austria?*

Since the ongoing war in Ukraine, Austria is also faced with incalculable dangers. History demonstrates all too vividly that unchecked tensions can lead to extremism and social conflict. The latest opinion polls show that many citizens have lost faith in the ability of the ÖVP–Greens coalition government to cope with the consequences of inflation, climate crisis, energy shortage and social tensions. What is more ominous is that many lost faith in liberal democracy. Due to the signs of the decadence of

## A DEPLORABLE MORAL PICTURE

the country's traditional hierarchy of power, the government lost much of its moral authority.

Austria has recently been under "observation"[38] by the international community and foreign media only in two short periods, between 2017 and 2019 during the ÖVP–FPÖ coalition government and then between 2019 and 2020 at the time of turbulence before Sebastian Kurz's resignation as Chancellor and ÖVP Chairman. In view of the persistently low popularity ratings of the first ÖVP–Greens coalition in the opinion polls, an early election before 2024 hardly appears to be a realistic alternative.

The "Austrian Democracy Monitor", launched by the SORA Institute, presented the results of representative surveys on attitudes about the political system in Austria for the fifth time at the end of 2022[39] and found that 64 per cent of participants were convinced that the political system functioned unsatisfactorily or not at all, a rise of 30 per cent since 2018! Nevertheless, nine out of ten people still viewed democracy as the best form of government. The proportion of those who were in favour of "a strong leader who does not have to worry about parliament and elections" rose in the same period from 18 per cent to 26 per cent, and at the same time the share of those who firmly rejected authoritarian tendencies declined from 56 per cent to 46 per cent. At the same time, confidence in the government dropped from 43 per cent to 33 per cent and in parliament from 48 per cent to 38 per cent. Particularly worrying are the figures for the third of the population with the lowest income: 73 per cent feel they are treated as "second-class people", and 68 per cent do not see themselves represented in parliament.

The great Swiss historian Jacob Burckhardt pointed out that moments of crisis are sometimes moments of opportunity; there are successful and failed crises. The chances for a "successful crisis" in the foreseeable future in Austria are doubtful. The Western model of liberalism, parliamentary democracy, rule of law, market economy and social security, pluralism and individualism, is threatened by the authoritarian challenge from China and Russia, but also from the right-wing and left-wing populist movements in the European societies.

The Russian invasion of the Ukraine, a breach of international law and the biggest humanitarian catastrophe since World War II in Europe, shattered the erstwhile optimism regarding the final victory of the Western model of progress. In Austria, the revelations about the moral wreckage of the ÖVP–FPÖ era under the Chancellorship of Sebastian Kurz have contributed to the discrediting of the political class itself. Never before have there been so many, so severe, so unpredictable crises as in the year of the Ukraine war. Unfortunately, the quality of the top political personnel in Austria, with few exceptions, is insufficient to meet the people's need for credible and decisive leadership. With a timely warning to his own party (the ÖVP), Claus Raidl, the respected former president of the National Bank, spoke out against the tendency of "covering everything up".[40] Although the conservative governing party and its supporting organisations are in the centre of the corruption scandal, Raidl's call for action petered out without any reaction from the top of the party.

Nevertheless, it would be misleading to forget the mendacity of how the other traditional governing party, namely the SPÖ, dealt with the burden of the various bribery scandals. The major historian of the social democracy, Norbert Leser (1933–2014), noted more than two decades ago "a frightening lack of personalities at the federal and regional level which can be traced back to a wrong selection procedure". The present party leader, Pamela Rendi-Wagner, would be well advised to heed this warning from Leser: "It would be disastrous if the SPÖ believed that it could only profit from the mistakes of the ÖVP government's policy and count on a more or less automatic swing of the pendulum in the other direction".[41] It is a reflection of the sad state

# A DEPLORABLE MORAL PICTURE

of the Austrian social democracy that the former SPÖ Vice-Chancellor and Finance Minister of the "golden Kreisky era", Hannes Androsch, today a successful industrialist, basically repeated Leser's old indictment, accusing his party of having forgotten how to address existing fears and to commit to a cosmopolitan internationalism.[42]

A key factor behind the current economic and social difficulties is also the jungle of competences and responsibilities that are the consequences of the federalism and an inhibiting bureaucracy. All attempts to reform the frozen federal structure based on the power of the nine provinces have failed. Twenty years ago, seventy experts worked on a reform for two years in vain, producing almost a thousand pages of evidence and proposals. The conference of the nine provincial governors,[43] meeting twice-yearly, with a rotating chairmanship, is not mentioned in the constitution at all, but is regarded as being in fact more powerful than the governments. Stability at the top plays a decisive role. The ÖVP, for example, has provided the governor in Lower Austria, Tyrol and Vorarlberg for 77 years, and the SPÖ has provided the governor in Vienna for 77 years and in Burgenland for 58 years!

In view of these frozen structures with real or supposed personal privileges, talented young men and women are increasingly choosing better paid management positions, both in the provinces and in Vienna, instead of engaging in political functions where they are inevitably under the magnifying glass of press attention.

The personal and political stability at regional level has recently been in stark contrast to the upheavals at the federal government level. At the time of this writing, the ÖVP–Greens government is headed by the third federal chancellor, after seven government reshuffles. The re-election of Federal President Alexander Van der Bellen provides an important factor of stability for the next 6 years.

# AUSTRIA BEHIND THE MASK

In this book, I have tried to draw a critical balance between the leading politicians and the major political parties, not only on the basis of documents and autobiographical statements, but also by collecting personal impressions in background discussions with former and still active political figures, managers and commentators. I sought to summarise my memories and experiences without feelings of prejudice or sympathy. In view of the crimes I witnessed and partly experienced first-hand under the brown and red dictatorships in Hungary, I always felt consciously or subconsciously the obligation to bear witness to the lurking danger threatening Austria at any given time. This is why I am concerned about the decline of the major centre-left and centre-right parties, the SPÖ and the ÖVP, as well as the dramatic resurgence of the extreme right. The two small parties, the Greens and the liberal NEOS have so far failed to fill the void in the centre. But in striking contrast to neighbouring Hungary, Austria is still a country with an independent judiciary, a free and vocal media, and a strong civil society.

Despite the shadows of the past and the real dangers of the present, I am infinitely grateful to this country and its people who offered me a new home in dark times. But the love for Austria must be and must remain a critical one.

# NOTES

## 1. THE BURDEN OF THE PAST

1. For my adventures in Hungary and the road to freedom see Paul Lendvai, *Blacklisted*, London 1999, and Paul Lendvai, *Inside Austria*, London 2010.
2. Friedrich Heer, *Der Kampf um die österreichische Identität*, Wien 1981.
3. Friedrich Heer, *Europäische Rundschau*, Wien 2/1977.
4. Ernst Bruckmüller, *Nation Österreich*, Wien 1996.
5. Derogatory expression for Germans in Austrian slang.
6. Gordon Brook-Shepherd, *The Austrians*, London 1996, p. 366.
7. For a summary of the debate see Katrin Hammerstein in *Deutschland Archiv*, 4.5.2017.
8. Quoted by Harald Weinrich, *Lethe, Kunst und Kritik des Vergessens*, München 1967, pp. 230–2.
9. Ibid. pp. 163–6.
10. Moritz Csáky, *Das Gedächtnis Zentraleuropas*, Wien 2019.
11. *Profil*, 3.9.2013.
12. Quoted by Csáky, op. cit. p. 141.
13. *Die Presse*, 15.6.1991.
14. All figures from Daten, Zahlen und Fakten zu Migration und Integration 2021 des Österreichischen Integrationsfonds (ÖIF), Wien 2021.
15. *Die Presse*, 28.9.2021.
16. Bertolt Brecht, *Flüchtlingsgespräche*, Frankfurt 1961; translation by the author.

17. Ilija Trojanow, *Nach der Flucht*, Frankfurt, 2017, pp. 11–12.
18. Trojanow, op. cit. p. 102.

2. MYTH AND REALITY: THE LEGACY OF THE HABSBURGS

1. *Wiener Zeitung*, 2.11.1999.
2. *Die Presse*, 9.12.1998.
3. Rathkolb, op. cit, p. 423.
4. Princeton, 2018, pp. 328–9.
5. *Trend*, 27/2011.
6. From an interview on 10.1.2000 for a TV documentary on Bruno Kreisky.
7. Barbara Toth, *Karl von Schwarzenberg, Die Biografie*, Wien 2017.
8. Johannes E. Schwarzenberg, *Erinnerungen und Gedanken eines Diplomaten im Zeitwandel*, Wien 2013.
9. Barbara Toth, *Karl von Schwarzenberg, Die Biografie*, Wien 2017, p. 185.
10. Toth, op.cit., p. 145.
11. Friedrich Torberg (1908–79) was an Austrian Jew, writer and essayist, who lived after the "Anschluss" in the United States, returning to Austria in 1951. The text of the speech was printed in Europäische Rundschau, 2.2015.
12. A. Huber/L. Erker/K. Taschwer, *Der Deutsche Klub-Austro-Nazis in der Hofburg*, Wien 2021.
13. Op. cit., p. 230–1.
14. Albert Rohan, *Diplomat am Rande der Weltpolitik*, Wien, 2002. pp. 9–21.
15. German text from Weinrich, op. cit. p. 17 (translated by the author).

3. HITLER'S SHADOW, YESTERDAY AND TODAY

1. Manfred Rauchensteiner, *Unter Beobachtung, Österreich seit 1918*, Wien, 2nd revised edition, 2021.
2. Rauchensteiner, op. cit., pp. 75–8.
3. Rauchensteiner, op. cit. p. 10.
4. *Frankfurter Allgemeine Zeitung*, 30.1.2018.
5. Peter Longerich, *Hitler, Biographie*, München, 2015, pp. 996–7.
6. Brigitte Hamann, *Hitlers Wien*, München, 1998, p. 576.
7. Friedrich Heer, *Der Kampf um die österreichische Identität*, p. 433.

8. Johan Prossliner, *Lexikon der Nietzsche-Zitaten*, München, 1999, p. 370.
9. Carl Zuckmayer, *Als wär's ein Stück von mir*, Frankfurt 1966, pp. 70–8.
10. Gertrude Enderle-Burcel/Ilse Reiter-Zatloukal (Hg.), *Antisemitismus in Österreich 1933–1938*, Göttingen, 2018, p. 19.
11. Kurt Yakov Tutter confirmed to me in a long telephone conversation the following details, also reported in *Der Standard*, 8.11.2021 and *APA*, 9.11.2021.
12. *Der Standard*, 4.10.2021.
13. *Der Standard*, 8.11.2021.
14. Lendvai, *Mein Österreich (Inside Austria)*, pp. 268–9.
15. Stuart E. Eisenstat, *Unwillkommene Gerechtigkeit*, München 2003, pp. 352–69.
16. Harald Weinrich, *Lethe, Kunst und Kritik des Vergessens*, p. 14.
17. *APA*, 2.9,2021.

4. THE ROLLERCOASTER RIDE OF THE FPÖ: FROM FRIEDRICH PETER TO JÖRG HAIDER

1. *Kreisky Reden*, Band II, Wien 1981, p. 547.
2. Heinz Fischer, *Die Kreisky Jahre*, Wien, 1993; Hein Fischer, *Reflexionen*, Wien, 1998; Lendvai, *Mein Österreich (Inside Austria)*.
3. Friedrich Weissensteiner, *Der Wegbereiter Friedrich Peter*, *Wiener Zeitung*, 5.5.2004.
4. Paul Lendvai in *Frankfurter Allgemeine Zeitung*, 7.2.2000.
5. Anton Pelinka, *Nach der Windstille, Eine politische Autobiografie*, 2009, pp. 114–19.
6. Paul Lendvai, *Inside Austria*.
7. Werner A. Perger in *Die Zeit*, 14.10.2008.

5. SCHÜSSEL'S DANGEROUS EXPERIMENT

1. In an interview with the author on 7.2.2007.
2. *Die Furche*, 16.12 2021.
3. He was sentenced by a Vienna court in a not-final judgment on 4.12.2020 of various corruption charges to 8 years prison. According to the indictment, the total damage caused by his actions amounted to 10 million euros.

4. Rauchensteiner, *Unter Beobachtung*, p. 542.
5. The text reprinted in the *Europäische Rundschau*, 3/2013.
6. The German papers, *Süddeutsche.de* and *Spiegel Online*, published on 7.5.2019 showed excerpts from a video, secretly taped, about a meeting between Strache and the head of the FPÖ parliamentary group, Johann Gudenus with the alleged niece of a Russian oligarch in a villa on the island of Ibiza back in July 2017. The two politicians were willing to engage in corruption practices, in illegal party finance and the "Orbanisation" of the media landscape. Both resigned.
7. Franz Schuh, *Lachen und Sterben*, Wien, 2021, p. 66.
8. *orf.at*, 26.6.2021.
9. *Die Presse*, 30.4.2019.
10. Quoted in Manfred Wagner, *Im Brennpunkt:ein Österreich*, Wien, 1976, pp. 66–7.
11. Heer, op.cit., p. 334.
12. *Der Standard and Kronen Zeitung*, 9.2.2023.
13. Bernhard Weidinger, *Im nationalen Abwehrkampf der Grenzlanddeutschen-Akademische Burschenschaften und Politik in Österreich nach 1945*, Wien, 2015. Interview with the author 10.12.2021.
14. Hans-Henning Scharsach, *Stille Machtergreifung—Hofer, Strache und die Burschenschaften*, Wien 2017, pp. 9–15.
15. *Der Standard*, 5.5.2018.

6. KARL RENNER AND BRUNO KREISKY: TWO GREAT PERSONALITIES OF SOCIAL DEMOCRACY

1. Jacques Hannak, *Karl Renner und seine Zeit. Versuch einer Biographie*, Wien, 1965.
2. His personality is described in Chapter 1.
3. Bruno Kreisky, *Zwischen den Zeiten*, Wien 1986, p. 46.
4. Cited by Hannak op. cit., p. 671, referring only to 1949 as the year of publication.
5. Ernst Lothar, *Das Wunder des Überlebens*, 2nd edition, Wien, 2020.
6. Robert Knight, *Ich bin dafür, die Sache in die Länge zu ziehen*, 2nd edition, Wien, 2000.
7. Herbert Lackner, *Rückkehr in die fremde Heimat*, Wien, 2021.
8. See for the "brown" stains of the Socialists, Lendvai, op. cit. pp. 101–9.

9. Herlinde Koelbl, *Jüdische Portraits*, Frankfurt 1989; interview with Kreisky, pp. 195–208.
10. https://www.marxists.or/deutsch/archiv/plechanow/1898/rolle/rolle2htm#t6.
11. Paul Lendvai/Karl-Heinz Ritschel, *Kreisky-Porträt eines Staatsmannes*, Wien, 1972, p. 142.

7. GREED INSTEAD OF PRINCIPLES: THE DECLINE OF SOCIAL DEMOCRACY

1. Ralf Dahrendorf, *The Sozialdemokratie ist am Ende ihrer Kunst*, Die Zeit, 237.3.1992.
2. Oliver Nachtwey, *Die Abstiegsgesellschaft*, Berlin, 2016.
3. Franz Walter, *Vorwärts oder Abwärts–Zur Transformation der Sozialdemokratie*, Berlin, new edition, 2021.
4. Theodor W. Adorno, *Vorträge 1949–1968*, Berlin, 2019, pp. 440–1. The quote is from a speech at a meeting of the socialist student federation in Vienna on 6.4.1967.
5. *New York Review of Books*, 17.12.2007.
6. Norbert Leser, *Der Sturz des Adlers*, Vienna, 2008, p. 189.
7. From an interview with the author in 2007.
8. Michael Häupl (with Herbert Lackner), *Freundschaft*, Wien, 2022, pp. 106–7.
9. For details see *Profil*, 6.3.2018; *Der Standard*, 27.7.2018, 21.9.2018, 7.11.2019, 3.9.2021.
10. Häupl, op. cit. pp. 142–50 and p. 163.
11. The quotes are from interviews with the author and from Ratkolb, op. cit. pp. 226–8.
12. Häupl, op. cit. p. 162.

8. THE ÖVP, THE MOST UNUSUAL CONSERVATIVE PARTY IN EUROPE

1. Ernst Trost, *Figl von Österreich*, Wien, 1972.
2. *Salzburger Nachrichten*, 24.5.1989.
3. *Profil*, Wien, 10.8.1995.
4. *Der Standard*, 16.8.1995.

5. Martin Eichtinger/Helmut Wohnout: *Alois Mock: Ein Politiker schreibt Geschichte*, Wien, 2008 pp. 159–259.
6. David Wise, *The Felix Bloch Affair*, 13.5.1990.
7. Kriechbaumer/Schausberger, *Volkspartei—Anspruch und Realität, Zur Geschichte der ÖVP seit 1945*, p. 75.
8. Friedrich Nietzsche, *Menschliches, Allzumenschliches*, 2nd edn, München, 1986, p. 270.
9. Paul Lendvai, *Hungary-Between Democracy And Authoritarianism*, London, 2012.
10. For the texts see Paul Lendvai, *Leben eines Grenzgängers*, Wien, 2013, p. 246.

9. FROM WOLFGANG SCHÜSSEL TO SEBASTIAN KURZ: FROM TRIUMPH TO CRASH

1. See Chapter 5, fn. 13.
2. Lendvai, *Inside Austria*, pp. 149–71.
3. My interview with Rudolf Burger, 14.5.2007.
4. Lendvai, op. cit. pp. 149–52.
5. Rathkolb op. cit. p. 204.
6. My interview with Wolfgang Schüssel, 9.3.2021 and 15.2.2022.
7. Wolfgang Schüssel (with Alexander Purger), *Offen gelegt*, Salzburg, 2009, pp. 273–7.
8. Hans Rauscher, *Der Standard*, 28.8.2012.
9. *Profil*, 19.8.2013.
10. *Tagesanzeiger*, Zürich, 14.3.2014.
11. *Süddeutsche Zeitung*, München, 18.9.2015.
12. Interview with the author, 25.5.2021.
13. *Die Presse*, Wien, 3.12.2021.
14. Robert Misik, *Herrschaft der Niedertracht*, Wien, 2019, pp. 45–7.
15. Klaus Knittelfelder, *Inside Türkis: Die neuen Netzwerke der Macht*, Wien, 2020, pp. 21–33.
16. Interview with the author, 26.5.2021.
17. *Der Spiegel*, 36, 2014.
18. *Die Zeit*, Berlin, 6.10.2017.

19. Michael Gehler, *Tiroler Tageszeitung*, Innsbruck, 8.8.2021 and *International*, Wien, 1/2020.
20. *Falter*, Wien, 19.9.2017, see also Peter Pilz, *Kurz, ein Regime*, Wien, 2021.
21. *Der Standard*, 4.2.2021 and 22.5.2022.
22. Manfred Matzka, *Hofräte, Einflüsterer, Spin-Doktoren—300 Jahre graue Eminenzen am Ballhausplatz*, Wien 2020, pp. 242–6.
23. *Der Standard*, 4.10.2022.
24. Misik, *Herrschaft der Niedertracht*, p. 33.
25. *Statista*, 13.2.2019. The SPÖ had 180,000, the FPÖ 60,000, the Greens 7,300 and the Neos 2,500 members.
26. Knittelfelder, op. cit. pp. 15–16.
27. Knittelfelder, op. cit. pp. 109–10 and 221–4.
28. Text in *News Special*, Wien, *Die Akte Kurz*, 12.10.2021.
29. *FAZ*, 9.10 2021.
30. *Profil*, Wien, 23.10.2.
31. *Die Zeit*, Hamburg, 26.10.2017.

10. THE "REAL" AUSTRIANS AND THE GREENS

1. Biographical details in Alexander Van der Bellen, *Die Kunst der Freiheit*, Wien, 2015; Herwig C. Höller, *Alexander Van der Bellen: Ein Flüchtlingskind*, *Die Zeit*, Hamburg, 23.3.2016; Christian Neuwirth, *Alexander Van der Bellen, Ansichten und Absichten*, Wien, 2001; interview with the author, 27.4.2022.
2. Cathrin Kahlweit, 26.1.2017.
3. *Parlamentskorrespondenz* Nr. 60, 26.1.2017.
4. Interview with the author, 27.4.2022.
5. Details from *Die Zeit*, Hamburg, 16.1.2020; *Der Standard*, 20.1.2020, *News* 4/2020 and from interview with the author, 20.11.2021.
6. The Austrian equivalent for "wogs" in English, an insulting term for people with a foreign accent.
7. *Vorarlberger Tageszeitung*, 21.10.2017.
8. Robert Kriechbaumer, *Nur ein Zwischenspiel(?)—Die Geschichte der Grünen in Österreich*, Wien, 2018.
9. Interview with the author, 5.4.2022.
10. 8.4.2022.

## 11. A DEPLORABLE MORAL PICTURE

1. The Austrian parliament approved on 26.10.1955 the law regarding the country's permanent neutrality: Austria will not join any military alliance nor allow foreign military bases on its territory. It was a sequel to the Austrian State Treaty signed on 15.5.1955 by the four occupation powers—Britain, France, the Soviet Union and the United States, followed by the evacuation of all foreign troops from Austrian territory.
2. Donald Trump as US President-elect, 15.1.2017, *Reuters*; in *The Economist*, 7.11.2019.; French President Emmanuel Macron interview in *The Econom*ist, 7.11.2019.
3. *Kleine Zeitung*, Graz, 6.3.2022.
4. Peter Pelinka, *Wolfgang Schüssel, Eine politische Biografie*, Wien, 2003, p. 158.
5. He was sworn in on 6.12.2021. For the statement see *Kurier*, Wien, 8.3.2022.
6. Gallup poll, *Heute* Wien, 32.6.2022.
7. NEOS entered parliament in 2013; at the last general elections in 2019, it received 8 per cent of the votes and won 15 seats.
8. *Washington Post*, After the invasion of Ukraine, a reckoning on Russian influence in Austria, 5.7.2022.
9. See Chapter 7.
10. *Kurier*, Wien, 28.9.2014.
11. *Kurier*, Wien, 2.6.2017.
12. *Salzburger Nachrichten*, 22.2.2022.
13. *ORF* Im Zentrum 22.2.2022; all quotes from *the APA* transcript of the broadcast.
14. *Profil*, Wien, 5.3.2022.
15. *Trend*, Wien, 2.10.2018.
16. *The Washington Post*, op.cit.
17. According to the text of the agreement, it remains in force for another 5 years if it has not been terminated before the expiration date. Nevertheless, the FPÖ and also a spokesman of the Russian party confirmed that even without a formal notice the agreement has become a dead letter. *APA* and *Kurier*, Wien, 9. and 10.3.2022.
18. All details from *Der Standard*, Wien, 24 and 26 3.2022 and *Die Presse*, Wien, 23.3.2022.

19. *Falter*, Wien, 20.12.2021; *NEWS*, 20.12.2021, *Profil* 22.12.2022.
20. Full text in *Profil*, Wien, 22.12.2021.
21. *Der Standard*, Wien, 19.6.2014.
22. *Trend*, Wien, 6.2.2014.
23. *News*, Wien, 2013/7.
24. *New Statesman and Nation*, London, 11.4.2022. See also *The Economist*, London, 12.4.2022 and the *Washington Post*, op. cit.
25. *Kleine Zeitung*, Graz, 5.5.2019.
26. Heinrich Pecina was the founder and senior partner of the Vienna Capital Partners. He was found guilty of fraud in a corruption trial connected with the Hypo bank, sentenced to a suspended sentence of 22 months in jail and a fine of 288,000 euros; *Wiener Zeitung*, 22.11.2017.
27. *Frankfurter Allgemeine Zeitung*, 11.10.2021; *Kurier*, Wien, 8.11.2019.
28. *Der Standard*, Wien, 5.9.2021.
29. *Der Standard*, 11.12.2021.
30. *Falter* 49/2021.
31. Manfred Matzka, *Hofräte, Einflüsterer. Spin-Doktoren—300 Jahre graue Eminenzen am Ballhausplatz*, Wien, 2020.
32. *Frankfurter Allgemeine*, 20.12.2021.
33. *Die Zeit*, Hamburg, 26.5.2011.
35. *Salzburger Nachrichten*, 7.11.2022. The chief editors of *Die Presse*, the quality daily and of the *ORF TV* news service resigned after compromising chats revealed their contacts with ÖVP and FPÖ politicians, respectively.
36. *Falter*, 22/2017.
37. *Europäische Rundschau*, Wien, 1977/2.
38. See Chapter 5, Austria always under "observation".
39. Sora News, 28.11.2022.
40. *Kurier*, 1.6.2022.
41. Norbert Leser, "*auf halben Wegen und und zu halber Tat*", Wien, 2000. pp. 148–9.
42. Hannes Androsch (in Zusammenarbeit mit Bernhard Ecker), *Was jetzt zu tun ist*, Wien, 2022, pp. 96–7.
43. Vienna, Lower and Upper Austria, Salzburg, Styria, Vorarlberg, Tyrol, Carinthia and Burgenland.

# SELECT BIBLIOGRAPHY

Adorno, Theodor W: *Vorträge 1949–1968*, Berlin 2019.
Albrecht, Thomas W: *Die Rhetorik des Sebastian Kurz*, Berlin 2019.
Andics, Hellmut: *Der Staat, den keiner wollte*, Wien 1968.
——— *Die Insel der Seligen*, Wien 1968.
Androsch, Hannes: *Warum Österreich so ist, wie es ist*, Wien 2003.
——— *Was jetzt zu tun ist*, Wien 2020.
——— (in co-operation with Bernhard Ecker): *Was jetzt zu tun ist*, Wien 2022.
Androsch, Hannes/Fischer, Heinz/Maderthaner, Wolfgang (eds): *Österreichische Sozialdemokratie seit 1889*, Wien 2020.
Androsch, Hannes/Pelinka, Peter (eds): *Zukunft—Perspektiven einer neuen Welt*, Wien 2018.
Bacher, Gerd/Schwarzenberg, Karl/Taus, Josef (eds): *Standort Österreich*, Graz 1990.
Barea, Ilsa: *Vienna*, London 1966.
Becher, Peter (eds): *Kakanische Kontexte*, Salzburg 2014.
Bischof, Günter/Pelinka, Anton (eds): *The Kreisky Era in Austria*, London 1994.
Bollmann, Ralph: *Angela Merkel*, München 2021.
Brandstaller, Trautl/Busek, Erhard: *Republik im Umbruch*, Wien 2016.
Brandstätter, Helmut: *Kurz & Kickl*, Wien 2019.
——— *Letzter Weckruf für Europa*, Wien 2020.
Brecht, Bertolt: "Flüchtlingsgespräche" in *Große kommentierte Berliner und Frankfurter Ausgabe*, 18:3, Verlag 1995.

# SELECT BIBLIOGRAPHY

Bronsen, David: *Joseph Roth, Eine Biographie*, Köln 1974.
Brook-Shepherd, Gordon: *The Austrians*, London 1996.
Brousek, Karl M: *Wien und seine Tschechen*, München 1980.
Bruckmüller, Ernst: *Nation Österreich*, Wien 1996.
Bruckmüller, Ernst/Diem, Peter: *Das Österreichische Nationalbewusstsein*, Wien 2020.
Brusatti, Alois/Heindl, Gottfried (eds): *Julius Raab*, Wien 1986.
Burger, Rudolf: *Ptolemäische Vermutungen*, Lüneburg 2001.
——— *Re-Theologisierung der Politik?*, Lüneburg 2005.
Busek, Erhard/Bećirović, Muamer: *Heimat*, Wien 2020.
Charim, Isolde/Rabinovici, Doron (eds): *Österreich—Berichte aus Quarantanien*, Frankfurt 2000.
Csáky, Moritz: *Das Gedächtnis Zentraleuropas*, Wien 2019.
Czernin, Hubertus (eds): *Wofür ich mich meinetwegen entschuldige—Haider, beim Wort genommen*, Wien 2000.
Eichtinger, Martin/Wohnout, Helmut: *Alois Mock—Ein Politiker schreibt Geschichte*, Wien 2008.
Eizenstat, Stuart E.: *Unvollkommene Gerechtigkeit*, München 2003.
Enderle-Burcel, Gertrude/Reiter-Zatloukal, Ilse (eds): *Antisemitismus in Österreich 1933–1938*, Wien 2018.
Fischer, Heinz: *Die Kreisky-Jahre 1967–1983*, Wien 1993.
——— *Reflexionen*, Wien 1998.
——— *Wende-Zeiten*, Wien 2003.
——— *Überzeugungen*, Wien 2006.
——— *Eine Wortmeldung*, Salzburg 2016.
——— (ed.): *100 Jahre Republik*, Wien 2018.
——— *Spaziergang durch die Jahrzehnte*, Salzburg 2018.
Fleischhacker, Michael: *Politiker-Beschimpfung*, Salzburg 2008.
Föderl-Schmid, Alexandra: *Journalisten müssen supersauber sein*, Wien 2013.
Friedländer, Otto: *Letzter Glanz der Märchenstadt*, Wien 1975.
Gräser, Marcus/Rupnow, Dirk (eds): *Österreichische Zeitgeschichte*, Wien 2021.
Grohmann, Judith: *Sebastian Kurz*, München 2019.
Hackl, Erich (ed.): *Wien, Wien allein*, Darmstadt 1987.

# SELECT BIBLIOGRAPHY

Hamann, Brigitte: *Hitlers Wien*, München 1996.

—— *Österreich*, München 2009.

Hannak, Jacques: *Karl Renner und seine Zeit. Versuch einer Biografie*, Wien 1965.

Hannis, Ernst: *Der lange Schatten des Staates*, Wien 1994.

Hartmann, Michael: *Die Abgehobenen, Wie die Eliten die Demokratie gefährden*, Frankfurt 2018.

Haslinger, Josef: *Politik der Gefühle*, Darmstadt 1987.

Häupl, Michael, (in co-operation with Herbert Lackner): *Freundschaft*, Wien 2022.

Heer, Friedrich: *Der Glaube des Adolf Hitler*, München 1968.

—— *Der Kampf um die österreichische Identität*, Wien 1981.

Heindl, Waltraud: *Josephinische Mandarine*, Wien 2013.

Hinteregger, Gerald: *Im Auftrag Österreichs*, Wien 2008.

Hofer, Thomas/Tóth, Barbara: *Wahl 2019*, Salzburg 2019.

Horaczek, Nina/Tóth Barbara: *Sebastian Kurz*, Salzburg 2017.

Huber, Andreas/Erker, Linda/Taschwer, Klaus: *Der Deutsche Klub—Austro-Nazis in der Hofburg*, Wien 2021.

Johnston, William M: *The Austrian Mind–An Intellectual and Social History*, Oakland 1972.

Judt, Tony: *Geschichte Europas von 1945 bis zur Gegenwart*, München 2006.

Jung, Jochen (ed.): *Glückliches Österreich*, Salzburg 1978.

—— (ed.): *Vom Reich zu Österreich*, Salzburg 1983.

Kirchschläger, Rudolf: *Ins Heute gesprochen*, Wien 2015.

Klaus, Josef: *Macht und Ohnmacht in Österreich*, Wien 1971.

Knapp, Edwin/Braunsteiner, Herbert: *Ein erfülltes Leben als leidenschaftlicher Österreicher, großer Arzt, Wissenschaftler und Klinikvorstand*, Innsbruck 2014.

Knaus, Gerald: *Welche Grenzen brauchen wir?*, München 2020.

Knight, Robert (ed.): *»Ich bin dafür, die Sache in die Länge zu ziehen«*, Frankfurt 1988.

Knittelfelder, Klaus: *Inside Türkis*, Wien 2020.

Koelbl, Herlinde: *Jüdische Portraits*, Frankfurt 1989.

Kopeinig, Margaretha: *Franz Vranitzky*, Wien 2021.

Korom, Philipp: *Die Wirtschaftseliten Österreichs*, Konstanz 2013.

# SELECT BIBLIOGRAPHY

Krawagna-Pfeifer, Katharina/Thurnher, Armin: *Die Wege entstehen im Gehen*, Wien 2008.

Kreisky, Bruno: *Der Mensch im Mittelpunkt*, Wien 1996.

―――― *Reden*, Band I und II, Wien 1981.

―――― *Zwischen den Zeiten*, Wien 1986.

―――― *Im Strom der Politik*, Wien 1988.

―――― *Seine Zeit und mehr*, Wien 1998.

Kriechbaumer, Robert: *Nur ein Zwischenspiel (?)*, Wien 2018.

Kriechbaumer, Robert/Schausberger, Franz (Hg.): *Volkspartei—Anspruch und Realität, Zur Geschichte der ÖVP seit 1945*, Wien 1995.

Kropiunigg, Rafael: *Eine österreichische Affäre*, Wien 2015.

Kunz, Johannes: *Erinnerungen*, 3 Bände, Wien 1989, 1994.

Lackner, Herbert: *Rückkehr in die fremde Heimat*, Wien 2021.

Lappin-Eppel, Eleonore: *Ungarisch-Jüdische Zwangsarbeiter und Zwangsarbeiterinnen in Österreich 1944/45*, Wien 2010.

Lendvai, Paul: *Blacklisted: A Journalist's Life in Central Europe*, London 1998.

―――― *1956, One Day that Shook the World*, Princeton 2008.

―――― *Inside Austria: New Challenges, Old Demons*, London 2010.

―――― *Mein verspieltes Land—Ungarn im Umbruch*, Salzburg 2010.

―――― *Die verspielte Welt, Begegnungen und Erinnerungen*, Salzburg 2019.

Lendvai, Paul/Ritschel, Karl Heinz: *Kreisky—Porträt eines Staatsmannes*, Wien 1972.

Leser, Norbert: *Salz der Gesellschaft*, Wien 1988.

―――― *auf halben Wegen und zu halber Tat*, Wien 2000.

―――― *Der Sturz des Adlers*, Wien 2008.

―――― *Skurrile Begegnungen*, Wien 2011.

Levitsky, Steven/Ziblatt, Daniel: *Wie Demokratien sterben*, München 2018.

Longerich, Peter: *Hitler, Biographie*, München 2015.

Lothar, Ernst: *Das Wunder des Überlebens*, 2 edn, Wien 2020.

Maier, Ferry/Ortner, Julia: *Willkommen in Österreich*, Innsbruck 2017.

Malinowski, Stephan: *Die Hohenzollern und die Nazis, Geschichte einer Kollaboration*, Berlin 2021.

Matzka, Manfred: *Hofräte, Einflüsterer, Spin-Doktoren*, Wien 2020.

Menasse, Peter/Wagner, Wolfgang (eds): *Vom Kommen und Gehen: Burgenland*, Wien 2021.

# SELECT BIBLIOGRAPHY

Menasse, Robert: *Das Land ohne Eigenschaften*, Wien 1992.

——— *Dummheit ist machbar*, Wien 1999.

Mesner, Maria (ed.): *Entnazifizierung zwischen politischem Anspruch, Parteienkonkurrenz und Kaltem Krieg*, München 2005.

Mielke, Gerd/Ruhose, Fedor: *Zwischen Selbstaufgabe und Selbstfindung*, Bonn 2021.

Misik, Robert: *Christian Kern*, Salzburg 2017.

——— *Die falschen Freunde der einfachen Leute*, Berlin 2019.

——— *Herrschaft der Niedertracht*, Wien 2019.

Mitchell, A Wess: *The Grand Strategy of the Habsburg Empire*, New Jersey 2018.

Mitterlehner, Reinhold: *Haltung*, Salzburg 2019.

Mock, Alois: *Visionen im Spiegel der Zeit*, St. Pölten 2014.

Müller, Jan-Werner: *Freiheit, Gleichheit, Ungewissheit*, Berlin 2021.

Nachtwey, Oliver: *Die Abstiegsgesellschaft*, Berlin 2016.

Nasko, Siegfried: *Karl Renner*, Wien/Salzburg 2016.

Neugebauer, Wolfgang/Schwarz, Peter: *Der Wille zum aufrechten Gang*, Wien 2005.

Neuwirth, Christian: *Alexander Van der Bellen*, Wien 2001.

Nietzsche, Friedrich: *Menschliches, Allzumenschliches*, München 1994.

Oberreuter, Heinrich: *Parteien zwischen Nestwärme und Funktionskälte*, Zürich 1973.

Pelinka, Anton: *Nach der Windstille*, Wien 2009.

Pelinka, Anton/Weinzierl, Erika (eds): *Das große Tabu*, Wien 1987.

Pelinka, Peter: *Österreichs Kanzler*, Wien 2000.

——— *Wolfgang Schüssel*, Wien 2003.

Petritsch, Wolfgang: *Bruno Kreisky*, Salzburg 2010.

Pfabigan, Alfred (ed.): *Vision und Wirklichkeit*, Wien 1989.

Pick, Hella: *Und welche Rolle spielt Österreich?*, Wien 1999.

Pieper, Dietmar/Saltzwedel, Johannes (eds): *Die Welt der Habsburger*, München 2020.

Pilz, Peter: *Kurz, ein Regime*, Wien 2021.

Pisa, Karl: *1945—Geburt der Zukunft*, Wien 2005.

Portisch, Hugo: *Aufregend war es immer*, Salzburg 2017.

——— *Österreich an der Schwelle zum 21 Jahrhundert*, Wien 2000.

# SELECT BIBLIOGRAPHY

———— *Österreich II*, Wien 1985.

———— *Was jetzt*, Salzburg 2011.

Rady, Martyn: *Die Habsburger*, Berlin 2021.

Rathkolb, Oliver: *Die paradoxe Republik*, Wien 2015.

Rauchensteiner, Manfried: *Unter Beobachtung*, Wien 2017/2021.

Rauscher, Hans: *Vranitzky—eine Chance*, Wien 1987.

———— (ed.): *Das Buch Österreich*, Wien 2005.

———— *Was gesagt werden muss*, Salzburg 2017.

Reimann, Viktor: *Die Dritte Kraft*, Wien 1980.

———— *Fünf ungewöhnliche Gespräche*, Wien 1991.

Reiter, Margit: *Die Ehemaligen, Der Nationalsozialismus und die Anfänge der FPÖ*, Göttingen 2019.

Riedl, Joachim: *Das Geniale, Das Gemeine*, München 1992.

Rohan, Albert: *Diplomat am Rande der Weltpolitik*, Wien 2002.

Rohrer, Anneliese: *Charakterfehler—Die Österreicher und ihre Politiker*, Wien 2005.

———— *Ende des Gehorsams*, Wien 2011.

Ronzheimer, Paul: *Sebastian Kurz*, Freiburg 2018.

Rosecker, Michael: *Karl Renner*, Wien 2020.

———— (ed.): *Geschichten aus der Geschichte Österreichs 1945–1983*, Darmstadt 1984.

Scharsach, Hans-Henning: *Stille Machtergreifung*, Wien 2017.

Scheuba, Florian: *Wenn das in die Hose geht, sind wir hin*, Wien 2022.

Schneider, Katharina: *1001 Gründe Österreich zu lieben*, Wien 2013.

Scholl, Susanne: *Schäm dich, Europa!*, Wien 2021.

Schuh, Franz: *Lachen und Sterben*, Wien 2021.

Schulmeister, Otto (ed.): *Spectrum Austriae—Österreich in Geschichte und Gegenwart*, Wien 1980.

Schüssel, Wolfgang: *Offengelegt*, Salzburg 2009.

———— *Was. Mut. Macht.*, Salzburg 2020.

Schwarzenberg, Johannes E: *Erinnerungen und Gedanken eines Diplomaten im Zeitenwandel 1903–1978*, Wien 2013.

Seidel, Hans: *Österreichs Wirtschaft und Wirtschaftspolitik nach dem Zweiten Weltkrieg*, Wien 2005.

Serloth, Barbara: *Nach der Shoah*, Wien 2019.

# SELECT BIBLIOGRAPHY

Siebenhaar, Hans-Peter: *Österreich, Die zerrissene Republik*, Zürich 2017.

Sieder, Reinhard/Steiner, Heinz/Tálos, Emmerich (eds): *Österreich 1945–1995*, Wien 2005.

Sporrer, Maria/Steiner, Herbert (eds): *Rosa Jochmann—Zeitzeugin*, Wien 1983.

Stadler, Kurt R: *Adolf Schärf*, Wien 1982.

Stanek, Eduard: *Verfolgt Verjagt Vertrieben*, Wien 1985.

Stiefel, Dieter: *Entnazifizierung in Österreich*, Wien 1981.

Stiegnitz, Peter: *Österreich aus der Nähe*, Wien 2006.

Stourzh, Gerald: *Vom Reich zur Republik*, Wien 1990.

——— *1945 und 1955: Schlüsseljahre der Zweiten Republik*, Innsbruck 2005.

Strauß, Martin/Ströhle, Karl-Heinz (eds): *Sanktionen*, Innsbruck 2010.

Strelka, Joseph (ed): *Der Weg war schon das Ziel*, München 1978.

Thalberg, Hans J: *Von der Kunst, Österreicher zu sein*, Wien 1984.

Thurnher, Armin: *Das Trauma, ein Leben*, Wien 1999.

——— *Republik ohne Würde*, Wien 2013.

——— *Ach, Österreich*, Wien 2016.

Tóth, Barbara: *»Unterschätzen Sie nicht meine Boshaftigkeit«*, Salzburg 2011.

——— *Karl von Schwarzenberg*, Wien 2017.

Trojanow, Ilija: *Nach der Flucht*, Frankfurt 2017.

Trost, Ernst: *Figl von Österreich*, Wien 1972.

——— *Das tausendjährige Österreich*, Wien 1994.

Ulram, A Peter/Tributsch, Svila: *Kleine Nation mit Eigenschaften*, Wien 2004.

Ultsch, Christian/Prior, Thomas/Nowak, Rainer: *Flucht*, Wien 2017.

Unterreiner, Katrin: *Habsburgs verschollene Schätze*, Wien 2020.

Urschitz, Josef: *Stillstand*, Wien 2017.

Van der Bellen, Alexander: *Die Kunst der Freiheit*, Wien 2015.

Vranitzky, Franz: *Politische Erinnerungen*, Wien 2004.

Wagner, Manfred (ed.): *Im Brennpunkt: ein Österreich*, Wien 1976.

Walter, Franz: *Vorwärts oder abwärts?*, Berlin 2010, Neuaufl. 2021.

Wassermann, P. Heinz: *Naziland Österreich!?*, Innsbruck 2002.

Weidinger, Bernhard: *»Im nationalen Abwehrkampf der Grenzlanddeutschen«*, Wien 2015.

# SELECT BIBLIOGRAPHY

Weigel, Hans: *Flucht vor der Größe*, Graz 1978.

Weinrich, Harald: *Lethe, Kunst und Kritik des Vergessens*, München 1997.

Weinzierl, Erika/Skalnik, Kurt (eds): *Die Zweite Republik*, 2 Bände, Graz 1972.

Weinzierl, Ulrich (ed.): *Lächelnd über seine Bestatter: Österreich*, München 1989.

——— (ed.): *Österreichs Fall*, Wien 1987.

Weinzierl, Ulrich: *Hofmannsthal*, Wien 2005.

Wetz, Andreas: *Näher als erlaubt*, Wien 2021.

Wiesenthal, Simon: *Recht, nicht Rache*, Berlin 1988.

Zöchling, Christa: *Haider—Licht und Schatten einer Karriere*, Wien 1999.

Zöllner, Erich: *Der Österreichbegriff*, Wien 1988.

Zuckmayer, Carl: *Als wär's ein Stück von mir*, Frankfurt 1966.

# INDEX OF NAMES

Adenauer, Konrad, 43
Adler, Viktor, 89, 111
Adorno, Theodor, 102
Aliyev, Ilham, 110
Andics, Hellmut, 4
Androsch, Hannes, 97, 98, 103, 105, 130, 209
Avineri, Shlomo, 34

Babler, Andreas, 123
Bartoszewszki, Władysław, 16–17
Bauer, Otto, 4, 39, 54, 87
van Beethoven, Ludwig, 43
Beinschab, Sabine, 173
Benko, René, 111, 114, 196
Bielka, Erich, 30
Bierlein, Brigitte, 167–8
Blair, Tony, 101, 107
Bloch, Andrea, 137
Bloch, Felix, 135–7
Bloch, Kathleen, 137
Bloch, Lucille 'Lou', 135, 137
Blümel, Gernot, 154, 156, 162, 172
Bonelli, Bernhard, 162, 169

Braunsteiner, Herbert, 125–6
Brecht, Bertolt, 2, 20–21, 52
Bretschneider, Rudolf, 20
Brook-Shepherd, Gordon, 5
Büchner, Georg, 111
Bukharin, Nikolai, 54
Burckhardt, Jacob, 96, 207
Bures, Doris, 116, 122
Burger, Rudolf, 7, 61, 134, 146, 147
Busek, Erhard, 94, 130, 137, 138–40
Busek, Helga, 138
Bush, George Herbert Walker, 137

Carlyle, Thomas, 96
Charles I, Austrian Emperor, 23
Chiari, Eva, 30
Chirac, Jacques, 148
Churchill, Winston, 144
Claudius, Matthias, 36
Csáky, Moritz, 14

Dahrendorf, Ralf, 101

# INDEX OF NAMES

von Damm, Helene, 135
Deripaska, Oleg, 194, 198, 200
Dichand, Hans, 112, 113–14, 149
Đilas, Milovan, 139
Dollfuß, Engelbert, 39, 84
Dörfler, Gerhard, 66
Doskozil, Hans-Peter, 123

Ederer, Brigitte, 116
Eichtinger, Martin, 136
Eizenstat, Stuart, 50
Erdmann, Karl Dietrich, 7
Erdoğan, Recep Tayyip, 164
Eyskens, Mark, 40

Faßmann, Heinz, 18, 20
Faymann, Werner, 71, 105, 108, 111–18, 149, 151–2, 156, 205
Figl, Leopold, 86, 90, 125, 126–7, 129
Firtasch, Dmytro, 155
Fischer, Heinz, 28, 42, 55, 112, 130, 135, 182
Fischler, Franz, 163
Fleischmann, Gerald, 162
Freud, Sigmund, 3
Frischmann, Johannes, 162, 170

Gasselsberger, Franz, 204
Gehler, Michael, 41, 165
Gerstenbrand, Franz, 11
Geyer, Walter, 206
Gikman, Reino, 136
Gleißner, Heinrich, 92
Göncz, Árpád, 139

Gorbach, Alfons, 27, 128, 130
Grasser, Karl-Heinz, 64, 65, 71, 148, 150
Gratz, Leopold, 99
Griss, Irmgard, 71
Gudenus, Johann, 15, 167
Gusenbauer, Alfred, 66, 105, 107–11, 120, 148, 151, 163, 194, 201

Habsburg, Georg, 25
Habsburg, Karl, 23–5
Habsburg, Otto, 23, 24, 26–9, 128
Haider, Jörg, 7, 15, 43, 56, 60–67, 69, 73, 104, 138, 145
Hamann, Brigitte, 44
Handler, Mike, 1
Hannak, Jacques, 84
Haslauer, Wilfried, 130
Häupl, Michael, 108, 112, 115, 117, 120
Havel, Václav, 32
Heer, Friedrich, 2–3, 5, 6, 12, 44
Heindl, Waltraud, 177
Helmer, Oskar, 86, 89, 90, 91, 128
Himmler, Heinrich, 34
Hitler, Adolf, 4–5, 43, 45
Hofer, Norbert, 71–2, 73, 81
Home, Alexander Douglas-Home, Baron, 31
Hoor, Ernst, 5
Hussein, Saddam, 64

Innitzer, Theodor, 125–6

Jabloner, Clemens, 167, 185

# INDEX OF NAMES

Jäger, Bertram, 137
Jankowitsch, Peter, 58
Janša, Janez, 17, 202
Jonas, Franz, 14
Jospin, Lionel, 101
Judt, Tony, 103
Juncker, Jean-Claude, 135

Kaiser, Peter, 119
Kamitz, Reinhard, 127
Kann, Robert, 10
Kapellari, Egon, 66
Kern, Christian, 105, 118–21, 156, 166, 194–5
Khol, Andreas, 191, 203
Kickl, Herbert, 7, 56, 78, 81, 197
Kirchschläger, Rudolf, 30, 182
Klaus, Josef, 58, 93, 118, 128, 130, 149
Klaus, Václav, 33
Klestil, Thomas, 62, 104, 129, 130, 140, 146, 182
Klima, Viktor, 105, 106–7, 108, 145
Kneissl, Karin, 167, 194, 197
Knight, Robert, 86
Knittelfelder, Klaus, 162, 169, 170, 171
Kogler, Werner, 184, 185–7
Köhlmeier, Michael, 80
Kołakowski, Leszek, 139
Körner, Theodor, 92
Köstinger, Elisabeth, 162
Kouchner, Bernard, 155
Krainer, Josef, 129, 130

Kraus, Herbert, 56
Kreisky, Bruno, 2, 8, 11, 28, 29, 31, 85, 91–7, 130, 131, 168
Krisper, Stephanie, 193
Krones, Wolfgang, 24
Kühnert, Kevin, 154
Kurz, Sebastian, 30–31, 33, 48, 70, 72–3, 120, 157–76

Lacina, Ferdinand, 104
Lackner, Herbert, 90
Landbauer, Udo, 76–9
Lauder, Ronald, 48, 135, 136
Launsky-Tieffenthal, Peter, 158
Le Goff, Jacques, 13
Lenin, Vladimir, 84–5, 95
Leser, Norbert, 97, 105, 208
Lewis, Flora, 134, 135
Lingens, Peter Michael, 134
Longerich, Peter, 44
Löschnak, Franz, 136
Lothar, Ernst, 89
Lunacek, Ulrike, 154
Lütgendorf, Karl, 30

Macron, Emmanuel, 191
Maderthaner, Philipp, 162
Mahrer, Harald, 157
Marchetti, Nico, 154
Marsalek, Jan, 201
Martin, Wolf, 113
Matzka, Manfred, 168
Maurer, Sigrid, 187–9
Mayer-Gunthof, Franz Josef, 1
Meinl-Reisinger, Beate, 193

# INDEX OF NAMES

Melchior, Axel, 162
Merkel, Angela, 148, 164, 165, 167
Mikl-Leitner, Johanna, 18, 77
Miller, Alexei, 196
Misik, Robert, 161
Mitchell, Aaron Wess, 25
Mitterlehner, Reinhold, 72, 117, 119, 120, 156, 158, 165–6, 173, 175
Mnuchin, Steven, 198
Mock, Alois, 129–37, 140
Mock, Edith, 136, 137
Molotov, Vyacheslav, 126
Molterer, Wilhelm, 113, 148, 151–2
Mozart, Wolfgang Amadeus, *53*
Münz, Rainer, 18, 20

Nazarbayev, Nursultan, 110
Nehammer, Karl, 174, 191
Neisser, Heinrich, 129
Nietzsche, Friedrich, 13, 45, 138
Nödl, Frieda, 91
Noll, Alfred, 184
Nonnenmacher, Günther, 150

Orbán, Viktor, 17, 25, 81, 139, 150–51, 167, 193, 202
Ostermayer, Josef, 114, 117

Pecina, Heinrich, 202
Pelinka, Anton, 14, 61, 204–5
Perger, Werner, 66–7, 94
Peter, Friedrich, 54–5, 56, 57–60, 94

Pifﬂ-Perčević, Theodor, 149
Pilz, Peter, 179, 184, 187
Plassnik, Ursula, 148, 153
Plekhanov, Georgi, 95–6, 97–8
Pollak, Oscar, 87
Pompeo, Michael, 198
Prodi, Romano, 101
Putin, Vladimir, 107, 167, 193–8, 200

Qualtinger, Helmut, 186

Raab, Julius, 106, 125, 126, 129, 151
Rabinovici, Doron, 50
Rady, Martyn, 26
Raidl, Claus, 208
Rathkolb, Oliver, 8–9, 88, 97, 116, 147, 204
Rauchensteiner, Manfried, 37–8, 40–41
Rauscher, Hans, 203
Reimann, Viktor, 56–7
Reinthaller, Anton, 56, 57
Rendi-Wagner, Pamela, 119, 121–3, 208
Renner, Karl, 4, 27, 40, 83–8, 91, 126
Rességuier, Olivier, 30
Riegler, Josef, 130, 137
Riess-Passer, Susanne, 62, 63, 64, 65
Rilke, Rainer Maria, 17
Ritschel, Karl Heinz, 57
Rohan, Albert, 30, 35–6

# INDEX OF NAMES

Rohan, Karl Anton, 35–6
Rohrer, Anneliese, 24, 106
Roiss, Gerhard, 196
Roth, Joseph, vii, 44
Rothensteiner, Walter, 205
Rudas, Andreas, 106
Rusinow, Dennison, 10

Sarkozy, Nicolas, 148
Schallenberg, Alexander, 30–31, 174
Schallenberg, Wolfgang, 30
Schärf, Adolf, 4, 86, 89, 91
Scharsach, Hans-Henning, 80
Scheibenreif, Alois, 93
Schelling, Hans Jörg, 196, 199
Schenk, Otto, 159
Scheuch, Uwe, 66
Schiller, Friedrich, 50
Schmid, Thomas, 154, 156, 171–4, 199, 206
Schmidauer, Doris, 181
Schmidt, Heide, 62
Schmitz, Wolfgang, 129
Scholz, Roman, 57
Schröder, Gerhard, 101, 107
Schuh, Franz, 77
Schulmeister, Otto, 29
Schuschnigg, Kurt, 26
Schüssel, Wolfgang, 50, 60–62, 64–5, 70–71, 106, 130, 137, 140–51
Schützenhöfer, Hermann, 174
Schwarzenberg, Adolph, 34
Schwarzenberg, Johannes, 31, 34
Schwarzenberg, Karel, 31–4, 35, 74

Schwarzenberg, Therese, 35
Seele, Rainer, 194, 196
Seipel, Ignaz, 38
Seitz, Karl, 89
Silberstein, Tal, 120
Sinowatz, Fred, 43, 60, 98–9, 132
Smetana, Bedřich, 53
Sobotka, Wolfgang, 49, 162, 166
Spahn, Jens, 154
Spannocchi, Emil, 30
Spindelegger, Michael, 117, 153–6, 173
Stalin, Joseph, 84–5, 88
Stangl, Thomas, 175
Steger, Norbert, 60, 69
Steinbrück, Peer, 155
Steiner, Stefan, 162, 164, 166, 169
Steiner, Thomas, 166
Stourzh, Gerald, 7
Strache, Heinz-Christian, 15, 50, 56, 65, 71, 74–81, 143–4
Stuiber, Petra, 188

Tanner, Klaudia, 166, 192
Taus, Josef, 118, 129, 130, 131, 146
Thiel, Peter, 169, 203
Thurnher, Armin, 97, 203
Treichl, Andreas, 204–5
Treichl, Heinrich, 205
Trojanow, Ilija, 22
Trost, Ernst, 127
Truman, Harry, 27
Trump, Donald, 191
Tuđman, Franjo, 139

# INDEX OF NAMES

Tutter, Kurt Yakov, 47–8, 50
Twain, Mark, 138

Umlauft, Friedrich, 4
Urzidil, Johannes, 26

Van der Bellen, Alexander, 49, 71–2, 81, 157, 177–82, 189, 209
Van Rompuy, Hermann, 150–51
Van Tonningen, Meinoud Rost, 39
Vernet, Daniel, 135
Vorhofer, Kurt, 12, 84, 97, 127, 129, 131, 132, 134
Vranitzky, Franz, 52, 61, 95, 99, 103–6, 114, 130, 132, 138, 140, 145–6
Vučić, Aleksandar, 15, 193, 202

Waldheim, Kurt, 13, 14, 41–3, 47, 73, 99, 104, 132, 182
Walter, Franz, 101–2
Wandruszka, Adam, 10–11
Weigel, Hans, 206
Weinberger, Lois, 125

Weinrich, Harald, 51
Weissensteiner, Friedrich, 59
Westenthaler, Peter, 15, 64
Westerwelle, Guido, 154
Wiesel, Elie, 13
Wiesenthal, Simon, 42–3, 54–5, 59, 93
Withalm, Hermann, 58, 128, 129
Wöginger, August, 188
Wolf, Siegfried, 194, 196, 197–201
Wowereit, Klaus, 154

Yad Vashem, Jerusalem, 48, 74, 75
Yakunin, Vladimir, 194
Yanukovych, Viktor, 110
Yeltsin, Boris, 201

Zadić, Alma, 182–5, 189
Zeiler, Gerhard, 118, 120
Zimmerman, Alfred Rudolph, 38
Zita, Empress consort of Austria, 28
Zuckmayer, Carl, 45
Zweig, Stefan, 4

# INDEX

*Addendum*, 109–10
Adenauer, Konrad, 43
Adler, Viktor, 89, 111
Adorno, Theodor, 102
Afghan people, 19
Agency for the Modernisation of Ukraine, 155
Albanian people, 16, 17, 133
Aliyev, Ilham, 110
Alliance for the Future of Austria, 64
Allied occupation (1945–55), 5, 27, 40, 56, 83–92, 125–6
Alpine and Danube Provinces, 40
Alternative für Deutschland (AfD), 44, 68
Andics, Hellmut, 4
Androsch, Hannes, 97, 98, 103, 105, 130, 209
annexation, prohibition of, 4, 38, 39, 40
Anschluss (1938), 4, 5, 7, 10, 26, 34, 39, 40, 45, 86

anti-Semitism, 3, 5, 11, 16–17, 34, 37, 50, 51–2, 92
Anschluss pogroms (1938), 45–6
FPÖ and, 50, 54, 57, 62, 73, 74–81
expropriation of property, 5, 12–13, 46–7, 86, 90
Holocaust (1941–5), *see* Holocaust
Kreisky and, 92–5, 182
Kurz and, 158
November pogroms (1938), 48
ÖVP and, 139
songbook scandal (2018), 76–9
SPÖ and, 89–91, 92–5
*Antisemitism in Austria*, 46
*Arbeiter Zeitung*, 84, 87
Argentina, 107
aristocracy, 29–36
Armenian genocide (1915–17), 42
artificial intelligence, 101
'Aryanisation', 5, 12–13, 46–7, 86

235

# INDEX

Asfinag, 114
*Aula, Die*, 35
Auschwitz concentration camp, 16, 47, 49, 54, 95
Austria
    Allied occupation (1945–55), 5, 27, 40, 56, 83–92, 125–6
    Dual Monarchy (1867–1918), 1, 3–4, 8, 9, 25–6, 29, 38
    First Republic (1919–1938), 4, 5, 6, 9, 38
    Nazi period (1938–45), *see* Third Reich
    Second Republic (1945–), *see* Second Republic
Austrian Automobile Club, 158
Austrian Broadcasting Corporation, 2, 43, 66, 72, 98, 133, 154, 205
Austrian Democracy Monitor, 207
Austrian Integration Fund, 19, 20, 162
Austrian Mineral Oil Administration Stock Company, 106
Austrian National Bank, 39, 73, 105, 106, 127, 157, 166, 208
Austrian People's Party, *see* ÖVP
Austrian Society for International Politics, 149
Austrian Students' Union, 188
'Austrosolipsism', 9
authoritarianism, 111, 176, 193, 201–3, 207
Avineri, Shlomo, 34

Azerbaijan, 111

Babler, Andreas, 123
Baden-Württemberg, Germany, 181
Ballhausplatz, Vienna, 92
Bangkok, Thailand, 163
Bartoszewszki, Władysław, 16–17
Bauer, Otto, 4, 39, 54, 87
Bauernbund, 160
van Beethoven, Ludwig, 43
Beinschab, Sabine, 173
Belgium, 47, 150–51
Belgrade, Serbia, 15
Belvedere Palace, Vienna, 127
Benedictine Order, 29, 134
*Benko, René, 111, 114, 196*
Bertelsmann Foundation, 147, 150
Bielka, Erich, 30
Bierlein, Brigitte, 167–8
*Bild*, 169–70
Blair, Tony, 101, 107
Bloch, Andrea, 137
Bloch, Felix, 135–7
Bloch, Kathleen, 137
Bloch, Lucille 'Lou', 135, 137
Blümel, Gernot, 154, 156, 162, 172
Bohemia, 14
Bologna Centre, 135
Bonelli, Bernhard, 162, 169
Bosnia and Herzegovina, 15, 16, 17, 19, 65, 182
Braunsteiner, Herbert, 125–6
Brecht, Bertolt, 2, 20–21, 52

# INDEX

Bretschneider, Rudolf, 20
Brook-Shepherd, Gordon, 5
Buchenwald concentration camp, 34
Büchner, Georg, 111
Budapest, Hungary, 11, 28, 34, 45, 46, 202
budget (1971), 59
Bukharin, Nikolai, 54
Burckhardt, Jacob, 96, 207
Bures, Doris, 116, 122
Burgenland, 55, 74, 98, 122, 123
Burger, Rudolf, 7, 61, 134, 146, 147
Burschenschaften, 13, 51, 61, 75, 76–80
Busek, Erhard, 94, 130, 137, 138–40
Busek, Helga, 138
Bush, George Herbert Walker, 137
Business Confederation, 125, 126
Buwog, 148
BZÖ (Bündnis Zukunft Österreich), 64

Canada, 110
Caribbean, 110
Carinthia, 62, 65–6, 119, 148, 152
Carlyle, Thomas, 96
Cartellverband, 29, 129
Catholicism, 12, 16, 29, 57, 130
  Cartellverband, 29, 129
Chamber of Labour, 109
Chapel Hill, North Carolina, 137
Charles I, Austrian Emperor, 23

Charter 77 movement (1976–92), 53
chat transcripts scandal (2022), 171–4, 180, 193, 197–9, 205, 206
Chiari, Eva, 30
China, 121, 195, 197, 208
Chirac, Jacques, 148
Christian Democrats, vii
Christian Social Conservatives, 4
Christlich-Soziale Union, 24, 165, 167
Christlichsoziale Partei, 38
Churchill, Winston, 144
Claudius, Matthias, 36
climate change, 22, 101, 206
College of World Trade, 105
Cologne, Germany, 10
Columbia University, 184
Communist Party of Austria, 85, 88
Compromise (1867), 9
Concordia camp, Kansas, 10
*Confession Book of Austrian Poets*, 35
Constitutional Court, 25, 72
corruption scandals
  advertisements, 204–5
  chat transcripts scandal (2022), 171–4, 180, 193, 197–9, 205, 206
  Gusenbauer, 109–11, 194
  Ibiza affair (2019), 15, 75, 143–4, 158, 166–7, 180, 202, 205

237

# INDEX

Public Prosecutor's Office, 168, 171, 199, 205–6
Schüssel, 148
Covid-19 pandemic (2019–23), 20, 22, 51, 101, 156, 175–6, 181, 187, 188
Creditanstalt, 205
Crimea, 194, 200
Croatia, 16–17, 19, 98, 133, 139
Csáky, Moritz, 14
customs revenues, 38
Cyprus, 110
Czech people, 14
Czech Republic, 33
Czechoslovakia, 12, 14, 32–3, 38, 53, 87, 133

Dachau concentration camp, 127, 128
Dahrendorf, Ralf, 101
von Damm, Helene, 135
Declaration of Independence (1945), 85
denazification (1945–7), 56
Deripaska, Oleg, 194, 198, 200
Dialogue of Civilisations, 194
Dichand, Hans, 112, 113–14, 149
digitalization, 101
Đilas, Milovan, 139
Dollfuß, Engelbert, 39, 84
Dörfler, Gerhard, 66
Doskozil, Hans-Peter, 123
Dual Monarchy (1867–1918), 1, 3–4, 8, 9, 25–6, 29, 38, 73

East Germany (1949–90), 7, 28, 149

EBRD, 205
Economic and Corruption Prosecution Office, 168, 171, 199, 205–6
Ederer, Brigitte, 116
Eichtinger, Martin, 136
Eizenstat, Stuart, 50
elections
**1945** parliamentary elections, 85, 126
**1949** parliamentary elections, 56
**1951** presidential election, 92
**1966** parliamentary elections, 92–3, 128–9
**1970** parliamentary elections, 58, 93, 118, 182
**1971** parliamentary elections, 59, 96
**1979** parliamentary elections, 102, 132
**1983** parliamentary elections, 60, 97
**1986** parliamentary elections, 13, 41, 47, 73, 61, 99, 130, 132; presidential election, 41
**1990** parliamentary elections, 138
**1992** presidential election, 41, 62
**1994** parliamentary elections, 61, 79, 140, 145, 180
**1996** European Parliament delegation, 24
**1999** parliamentary elections,

# INDEX

61, 62, 79, 102, 145; European Parliament delegation, 24
2002 parliamentary elections, 63, 146, 147, 186
2006 parliamentary elections, 108, 111, 151
2008 parliamentary elections, 64, 151–2
2010 presidential election, 71; Vienna city councils, 161
2013 parliamentary elections, 71
2015 Vienna city councils, 15
2016 presidential election, 71, 74, 116, 117, 157, 180, 191
2017 parliamentary elections, 72, 102, 120–21, 165–6, 170, 185
2018 Lower Austrian elections, 76
2019 European elections, 119; parliamentary elections, 122, 168, 180, 184, 186
2023 regional elections, 81
*Emperor's Tomb, The* (Roth), vii
energy crisis (2022–), 193, 206
Enns River, 125
Erdmann, Karl Dietrich, 7
Erdoğan, Recep Tayyip, 164
Erste Bank, 204–5
Estonia, 178
Europa Forum Wachau, 134–5, 149, 157
*Europäische Rundschau*, 3, 139, 158

'Europe's End and Europe's Departure' (Lendvai), 75
European China Business Council, 121, 195
European Economic Community (EEC), 1, 40
European Investment Bank, 152
European Jewish Congress, 48, 158
European Liberal Forum, 62
European People's Party, 150
European Union (EU), 9, 18–19, 27, 33, 74
   anti-Semitism in, 37
   Austrian accession (1995), 40, 104, 111, 112, 131, 133
   Faymann letter (2008), 112–13, 149
   FPÖ, sanctions against (2000), 43, 147, 148
   Habsburg family and, 24, 27, 33
   Kurz government, relations with, 167
   Parliament, 24, 33
   Russia, relations with, 33, 81, 194, 195, 197, 200
   Schüssel, relations with, 148
'Evening Song' (Claudius), 36
extreme right, 51, 68, 74, 76, 185, 202
   fraternities, 76–80, 185
   neo-Nazis, 51, 74, 185
Eyskens, Mark, 40

*Falter*, 76, 165

# INDEX

Farmers' Confederation, 125
Faßmann, Heinz, 18, 20
Faymann, Werner, 71, 105, 108, 111–18, 149, 151–2, 156, 205
Federal Bureau of Investigation (FBI), 136, 137
Federal Railway Administration, 114
Federal Republic of Germany (1949–), 7, 44, 85
    Alternative für Deutschland (AfD), 44, 68
    Kurz government, relations with, 167
    refugees in, 69, 164, 165
    reunification (1989–90), 28, 85
    Schüssel, relations with, 148
Feichten, Austria, 179
Fidesz, 150
Figl, Leopold, 86, 90, 125, 126–7, 129
financial crisis (2008–9), 116
*Financial Times*, 1, 30, 31, 43, 103, 128
Finland, 191
First Republic (1919–1938), 4, 5, 6, 9, 38–40
    Anschluss (1938), 4, 5, 7, 10, 26, 34, 39, 40, 45, 86–7
    Dollfuß regime (1932–4), 39, 84
    hyperinflation (1922–3), 38
    League of Nations loans, 38–9
    Renner government (1919–20), 84
    Schuschnigg regime (1935–8), 26

Firtasch, Dmytro, 155
Fischer, Heinz, 28, 42, 55, 112, 130, 135, 182
Fischler, Franz, 163
Fleischmann, Gerald, 162
Flossenbürg concentration camp, 128
FPÖ (Freiheitliche Partei Österreichs), 7, 9–10, 13, 15, 44, 51, 53–67, 69–81, 102
    anti-foreigner petition (1993), 62
    anti-Semitism in, 50, 54, 57, 62, 73, 74–81
    budget (1971), 59
    BZÖ split (2005), 64
    compensation package (2000–1), 50, 71
    elections, *see* elections
    electorate, percentage of, 102, 105, 145, 168
    EU, relations with, 73
    founding of (1956), 56
    governments, *see* Government of Austria
    Habsburg crisis (1961–3), 27
    Haider's accession (1986), 69, 104, 105, 130
    Ibiza affair (2019), 15, 75, 143–4, 158, 166–7, 180, 202, 205
    Iraq, relations with, 64
    National Socialism and, 56–7, 59, 60, 61, 62, 65, 73–4, 75, 77
    Russia, relations with, 81, 167, 197

# INDEX

Shoah Wall of Names construction (2018–21), 48, 50, 158
songbook scandal (2018), 13, 76–9
Theresienstadt visit (1976), 54–5
Washington Agreement (2001), 50
xenophobia, 15, 61, 62, 73, 74, 76–7, 81, 116, 185
Zadić and, 185
France, 26, 38, 74, 85, 148
*Frankfurter Allgemeine*, 134, 173
fraternities
  Burschenschaften, 13, 51, 61, 75, 76–80, 185
  Cartellverband, 29, 129
freemasonry, 179
Freud, Sigmund, 3
Frischmann, Johannes, 162, 170
Funke Group, 114

Gasprom, 196
Gasselsberger, Franz, 204
Gehler, Michael, 41, 165
German Club, 34, 35
German Historical Museum, West Berlin, 7
German language, 4, 9, 14, 21
German people, 4, 9
Germany
  Democratic Republic (1949–90), 7, 28, 149
  Federal Republic (1949–), *see* Federal Republic of Germany

Nazi period (1933–45), *see* Third Reich
reunification (1989–90), 28, 85
Weimar Republic (1918–33), 44
Gerstenbrand, Franz, 11
Geyer, Walter, 206
Ghent, Belgium, 47
Gikman, Reino, 136
Gleißner, Heinrich, 92
Gloggnitz am Semmering, Austria, 83–4
Göncz, Árpád, 139
Gorbach, Alfons, 27, 128, 130
Göttweig Abbey, Austria, 134, 149, 157
Government of Austria
  **1945–1945** Renner (ÖVP-SPÖ-KPÖ), 4, 27, 83–8
  **1945–1949** Figl I (ÖVP-SPÖ-KPÖ), 86, 90, 126
  **1949–1952** Figl II (ÖVP-SPÖ), 86, 126
  **1952–1953** Figl III (ÖVP-SPÖ), 86, 126
  **1953–1956** Raab I (ÖVP-SPÖ), 1, 5, 7, 8, 40, 43, 47, 73, 126–7, 151
  **1956–1959** Raab II (ÖVP-SPÖ), 126–7, 151
  **1959–1960** Raab III (ÖVP-SPÖ), 126–7, 151
  **1960–1961** Raab IV (ÖVP-SPÖ), 126–7, 151
  **1961–1963** Gorbach I (ÖVP-SPÖ), 128, 149

241

# INDEX

**1963–1964** Gorbach II (ÖVP-SPÖ), 128
**1964–1966** Klaus I (ÖVP-SPÖ), 128, 145
**1966–1970** Klaus II (ÖVP), 128–9, 131, 145, 149
**1970–1971** Kreisky I (SPÖ), 58–9, 69, 94
**1971–1975** Kreisky II (SPÖ), 97, 103
**1975–1979** Kreisky III (SPÖ), 102, 132
**1983–1986** Sinowatz (SPÖ-FPÖ), 60, 61, 69, 70, 98–9, 132
**1986–1987** Vranitzky I (SPÖ-FPÖ), 103, 104, 105, 130
**1987–1990** Vranitzky II (SPÖ-ÖVP), 103, 130, 135–8
**1990–1994** Vranitzky III (SPÖ-ÖVP), 103, 133–4, 138–40, 145
**1994–1996** Vranitzky IV (SPÖ-ÖVP), 103, 135, 140–41, 145
**1996–1997** Vranitzky V (SPÖ-ÖVP), 103
**1997–2000** Klima (SPÖ-ÖVP), 105, 106, 145
**2000–2003** Schüssel I (ÖVP-FPÖ), 13, 43, 50, 60–66, 70–71, 73, 74, 106, 146–8
**2003–2007** Schüssel II (ÖVP-FPÖ-BZÖ), 64, 70, 148, 151, 186
**2007–2008** Gusenbauer (SPÖ-ÖVP), 108–9, 112–13, 148, 151–2
**2008–2013** Faymann I (SPÖ-ÖVP), 71, 112–16, 149, 152–3, 154, 162
**2013–2016** Faymann II (SPÖ-ÖVP), 71, 115, 117–18, 151, 153, 156–8, 163–5, 173
**2016–2017** Kern (SPÖ-ÖVP), 119, 156, 158, 165–6, 194
**2017–2019** Kurz I (ÖVP-FPÖ), *see* Turkish-Blue coalition
**2019–2020** Bierlein (transitional), 167–8, 184
**2020–2021** Kurz II (ÖVP-Green), 168, 169–70, 175, 184, 186, 188, 198
**2021–2021** Schallenberg (ÖVP-Green), 174, 188
**2021–2023** Nehammer (ÖVP-Green), 174, 188, 191, 206, 209

Grasser, Karl-Heinz, 64, 65, 71, 148, 150
Gratz, Leopold, 99
Graz, Austria, 200
great silence, 10–13
Greece, 42
Green Party (Austria), vii, 71, 99, 140, 147, 168, 179–89
Green Party (Czech Republic), 33
Griss, Irmgard, 71
Gudenus, Johann, 15, 167
Gunskirchen, Austria, 45

# INDEX

Gusenbauer, Alfred, 66, 105, 107–11, 120, 148, 151, 163, 194, 201

Habsburg monarchy (1282–1918), 4, 8, 25–6
Habsburg, Georg, 25
Habsburg, Karl, 23–5
Habsburg, Otto, 23, 24, 26–9, 128
*Habsburgs, The* (Rady), 26
Hague, The, 183
Haider, Jörg, 7, 15, 43, 56, 60–67, 69, 73, 104, 138, 145
  BZÖ foundation (2005), 64
  death (2008), 66–7
  FPÖ chair accession (1986), 69, 104, 105, 130
  Hypo Alpe Adria and, 66
  Iraq visit (2002), 64
  ÖVP, coalition with (2000–2003), 13, 43, 50, 60–66, 70–71, 73, 74, 106, 146–8
  Vranitzky, relationship with, 104
Hainburg, Austria, 99
Hamann, Brigitte, 44
Handler, Mike, 1
Hannak, Jacques, 84
Hapsburg Group, 110
Haslauer, Wilfried, 130
Häupl, Michael, 108, 112, 115, 117, 120
Havel, Václav, 32
Heer, Friedrich, 2–3, 5, 6, 12, 44
Heindl, Waltraud, 177
Heldenplatz, Vienna, 4, 45, 62, 127

Helmer, Oskar, 86, 89, 90, 91, 128
Helsinki Federation, 32
*Heti Válasz*, 150
*Heute*, 114
Himmler, Heinrich, 34
Hitler, Adolf, 4–5, 43, 45
Hofburg, Vienna, 28, 35, 80, 144, 146, 177
Hofer, Norbert, 71–2, 73, 81
Hohenems, Austria, 23
Holocaust (1941–5), 11, 12–13, 16, 24, 26, 34, 37, 42, 45–52
  in Austria, 45, 47–52, 71, 74, 86, 158
  in Belgium, 47
  in Czechia, 54
  Figl and, 127
  in Greece, 42
  in Hungary, 11, 12, 34, 45, 46, 143
  Kreisky and, 94, 95
Home, Alexander Douglas-Home, Baron, 31
homosexuality, 154, 156, 173
Hong Kong, 121, 195
Hoor, Ernst, 5
Hugo Boss, 163
Hungarian people, vii, 9, 19
Hungary, vii, 9, 11, 139, 202
  Dual Monarchy (1867–1918), 1, 3–4, 8, 9, 25–6, 29, 38, 73
  emigration, 19, 73
  Erste Bank and, 204
  FPÖ, relations with, 81, 202
  Habsburg and, 28

# INDEX

Holocaust in (1944–5), 11, 12, 34, 45, 46
Orbán government (2010–), 25, 81, 139, 150, 167, 193, 202–3
ÖVP, relations with, 150–51, 167, 193, 202
Revolution (1989), 38, 133
Uprising (1956–7), 22, 73
Visegrád summit (2018), 202
Hussein, Saddam, 64
hyperinflation (1922–3), 38
Hypo Alpe Adria, 66, 152
Ibiza affair (2019), 15, 75, 143–4, 158, 166–7, 180, 202, 205

identity, 2–22, 118
  'Austrosolipsism', 9
  Dual Monarchy and, 3–4, 8
  FPÖ and, 7, 9–10
  immigration and, 13–22
  Nazism and, 3, 4–6, 7, 10
  polling on, 6, 7–8, 9–10
  silence and, 10–13
*Im Zentrum*, 195
immigration, 13–22, 73, 74, 81, 164–5, 177–9, 182–5, 189
  Afghans, 19, 73
  Bosnians, 15, 16, 19, 182–5
  Czechs, 14
  Croats, 16, 19, 98
  Germans, 9, 18–19
  Hungarians, 19, 73
  Iraqis, 19
  Kosovo Albanians, 16
  names and, 14–15, 16

Poles, 19
polling on, 19–22
Romanians, 19
Serbs, 19
Somalis, 19
statistics, 9, 17–22
Syrians, 19, 73
Turks, 15, 19
Ukrainians, 22, 193
Westbahnhof arrivals, 164
*see also* xenophobia
*Imperfect Justice* (Eizenstat), 50
India, 155
inflation, 38, 81, 193, 206
Innitzer, Theodor, 125–6
Innsbruck, Austria, 28, 126, 179
*Inside Austria* (Lendvai), vii
Institute for the Danube region, 139
International Centre for Migration Policy Development, 155
International Criminal Tribunal for the former Yugoslavia, 183
International Press Institute, 42
Iraq, 64
Iraqi people, 19
Ireland, 192
Islam, 15, 51
Israel, 34, 50, 74, 94–5, 104, 120, 158, 169
Italy, 38, 58, 74

Jabloner, Clemens, 167, 185
Jäger, Bertram, 137
Jankowitsch, Peter, 58

# INDEX

Janša, Janez, 17, 202
Jerusalem, 50, 74
Jetzt, 167, 184
Jewish Documentation Centre, 54
Jewish people, vii, 3, 5, 11, 16–17, 28, 167–8
   Anschluss pogroms (1938), 45–6
   compensation package (2000–1), 50, 71
   expropriation of property, 5, 12–13, 46–7, 86, 90
   FPÖ, relations with, 74, 76
   Holocaust (1941–5), *see* Holocaust
   Marietta and Friedrich Torberg Medal, 34
   neo-Nazis and, 51
   November pogroms (1938), 48, 90
   returnees, 19, 89–91
'Jews in Austria' (Reimann), 57
Johns Hopkins University, 135
Jonas, Franz, 14
Jospin, Lionel, 101
Judt, Tony, 103
Juncker, Jean-Claude, 135

Kaiser, Peter, 119
Kamitz, Reinhard, 127
Kann, Robert, 10
Kapellari, Egon, 66
Kaunertal, Austria, 181
Kazakhstan, 110
Kern, Christian, 105, 118–21, 156, 166, 194–5
KGB, 136
Khol, Andreas, 191, 203
Kickl, Herbert, 7, 56, 78, 81, 197
Kirchschläger, Rudolf, 30, 182
Klagenfurt, Austria, 65–6
Klaus, Josef, 58, 93, 118, 128, 130, 149
Klaus, Václav, 33
*Kleine Zeitung*, 113
Klestil, Thomas, 62, 104, 129, 130, 140, 146, 182
Klima, Viktor, 105, 106–7, 108, 145
Kneissl, Karin, 167, 194, 197
Knight, Robert, 86
Knittelfeld, Austria, 64
Knittelfelder, Klaus, 162, 169, 170, 171
Kogler, Werner, 184, 185–7
Köhlmeier, Michael, 80
Kołakowski, Leszek, 139
Konrad Adenauer Foundation, 150
Körner, Theodor, 92
Kosovo, 15, 65, 133
Köstinger, Elisabeth, 162
Kouchner, Bernard, 155
KPÖ (Kommunistische Partei Österreichs), 85, 88
Krainer, Josef, 129, 130
Kraus, Herbert, 56
Kreisky, Bruno, 2, 8, 11, 28, 29, 31, 85, 91–7, 130, 131, 168
   1979–1983 (SPÖ), 97, 132
   anti-Semitism against, 92–5, 182

# INDEX

budget (1971), 59
Czechoslovakia visit (1976), 53–5
Dichand, relationship with, 114
FPÖ, relations with, 58–9, 69, 60, 70, 93
Gusenbauer, relationship with, 107
Israel, relations with, 94–5
parliamentary elections (1970), 58–9, 93
Reimann, relationship with, 57
South Tyrol policy, 58, 92
Theresienstadt visit (1976), 54–5
Krisper, Stephanie, 193
Kristallnacht (1938), 48, 90
*Kronen Zeitung*, 56, 57, 106, 112–15, 117–18, 146, 149, 169–70, 202, 205
Krones, Wolfgang, 24
Krupp, 205
KSJ (Katholische Studierende Jugend), 130
Kühnert, Kevin, 154
*Kurier*, 113
Kurz, Sebastian, 30–31, 33, 48, 70, 72–3, 120, 157–76
   1st government (2017–19), *see* Turkish-Blue coalition
   2nd government (2020–21), 168, 169–70, 175, 184, 186, 198
   authoritarianism and, 167, 193, 201–3
   chat transcripts scandal (2022), 171–4, 180, 193, 197–9, 205, 206
   Covid-19 pandemic (2019–23), 175–6
   EU, relations with, 167
   Foreign Minister (2013–17), 157–8, 163–5, 173
   Germany, relations with, 167
   Hungary, relations with, 167, 202
   immigration, views on, 164–5
   media, relations with, 169–70, 203–5
   no confidence motion (2019), 167, 168
   Project Ballhausplatz (2016), 165–6
   Remembrance Day speech (2019), 75
   resignation (2021), 168–71, 180, 186–7, 207
   Russia, relations with, 167, 193, 194–9
   Schüssel, relationship with, 203
   Shoah Wall of Names construction (2018–21), 50, 158
   Spindelegger, relationship with, 154, 156, 162
   Vienna elections (2010), 161

Lacina, Ferdinand, 104
Lackner, Herbert, 90
Landbauer, Udo, 76–9
Länderbank, 103

# INDEX

Landsmannschaften, 61
Lauder, Ronald, 48, 135, 136
Launsky-Tieffenthal, Peter, 158
Le Goff, Jacques, 13
League of Nations, 38, 39
Leipnik-Lundenburger, 152
Lenin, Vladimir, 84–5, 95
Leser, Norbert, 97, 105, 208
Lewis, Flora, 134, 135
liberal democracy, 38, 93, 105, 205, 206–9
Liberal Forum, 140
Liberal International, 69
liberalism, 56, 69, 96–7, 140, 152, 156, 180, 193, 206–9
Lingens, Peter Michael, 134
Linz, Austria, 140
London Hambros Bank, 1
Longerich, Peter, 44
Löschnak, Franz, 136
Lothar, Ernst, 89
Lower Austria, 55, 76, 122, 209
Lunacek, Ulrike, 154
Lütgendorf, Karl, 30

Macron, Emmanuel, 191
Maderthaner, Philipp, 162
Magna, 194, 198, 201
Mahrer, Harald, 157
Malta, 110
Marchetti, Nico, 154
Marietta and Friedrich Torberg Medal, 34
Marsalek, Jan, 201
Martin, Wolf, 113

Matzka, Manfred, 168
Maurer, Sigrid, 187–9
Mauthausen Committee, 76
Mauthausen concentration camp, 34
Mayer-Gunthof, Franz Josef, 1
Meinl-Reisinger, Beate, 193
Melchior, Axel, 162
Merkel, Angela, 148, 164, 165, 167
Mikl-Leitner, Johanna, 18, 77
Miller, Alexei, 196
Misik, Robert, 161
Mitchell, Aaron Wess, 25
Mitterlehner, Reinhold, 72, 117, 119, 120, 156, 158, 165–6, 173, 175
Mnuchin, Steven, 198
Mock, Alois, 129–37, 140
Mock, Edith, 136, 137
Molotov, Vyacheslav, 126
Molotov–Ribbentrop Pact (1939), 178
Molterer, Wilhelm, 113, 148, 151–2
*Monde, Le*, 134, 135, 143
Montenegro, 139
Moravia, 12, 14
*Mozart*, Wolfgang Amadeus, 53
MTI, 139
MTS, 150
Münz, Rainer, 18, 20

National Bank, 39, 73, 105, 106, 127, 157, 166, 208

# INDEX

National Socialism, 3, 5, 7, 34–5, 44, 50
  FPÖ and, 56–7, 59, 60, 61, 62, 65, 73–4, 75, 77
  ÖVP and, 128
  SPÖ and, 94
'National Strategy against Anti-Semitism' (2021), 52
NATO (North Atlantic Treaty Organization), 191–3
Nazarbayev, Nursultan, 110
Nazi Germany (1933–45), *see* Third Reich
Nehammer, Karl, 174, 191
Neisser, Heinrich, 129
neo-Nazism, 51, 74
NEOS (New Austria and Liberal Forum), 168, 193
*Népszabadság*, 202
Netherlands, 8, 74, 178
*Neue Ordnung*, 35
*Neues Wiener Tagblatt*, 86
*Neue Zürcher Zeitung*, 134, 170
Neutrality Act (1955), 7
neutrality, 191–3, 197
*New York Times*, 1, 134, 136
Nietzsche, Friedrich, 13, 45, 138
Nödl, Frieda, 91
Noll, Alfred, 184
Nonnenmacher, Günther, 150
Nordstream 2 pipeline, 196
Norica, 129, 153
November pogroms (1938), 48, 90
Novia, 110
Novomatic, 111

*Ö3*, 168
ÖAAB (Österreichischer Arbeiter und Angestellten Bund), 131, 160
*ÖBAG* (Österreichische Beteiligungs), 172–3, 196, 198
ÖBB (Österreichische Bundesbahnen), 114
Oberbank, 204
*Oberösterreichische Nachrichten*, 113
*Observer*, 88
oe24.TV, 172
OECD, 135
ÖIAG (Österreichische Beteiligungs), 129
ÖIF (Österreichische Integrationsfonds), 19, 20, 162
Olah, Franz, 126, 129
ÖMV (Österreichische Mineralölverwaltung Aktiengesellschaft), 194, 196
*On the Grand Strategy of the Habsburg Empire* (Mitchell), 25
*On the Role of Personality* (Plekhanov), 95–6
Orbán, Viktor, 17, 25, 81, 139, 150–51, 167, 193, 202
ORF (Österreichischer Rundfunk), 2, 43, 66, 72, 98, 133, 154, 175, 205
Organised Crime and Corruption Reports Project, 110
OSCE, 165
Ostarrichipark, Vienna, 45

# INDEX

Ostermayer, Josef, 114, 117
*Österreich*, 114, 171–2
Ostpolitik, 149
ÖVP (Österreichische Volkspartei), 56, 125–41
  authoritarianism and, 167, 193, 201–3
  Bloch case (1989), 135–7
  chat transcripts scandal (2022), 171–4, 180, 193, 197–9, 205, 206
  compensation package (2000–1), 50, 71
  elections, *see* elections
  electorate, percentage of, 140, 145, 168
  foundation (1945), 125
  governments, *see* Government of Austria
  Habsburg crisis (1961–3), 27, 128
  homosexuality and, 154
  Hungary, relations with, 150–51, 167, 193, 202
  Russia, relations with, 167, 193–201
  Shoah Wall of Names construction (2018–21), 50, 158
  structure of, 131–2, 137, 144, 153, 157, 160
  Theresienstadt visit (1976), 54
  Waldheim affair (1985–6), 13, 41, 47, 73, 99, 132
  Washington Agreement (2001), 50
  World Vision scandal (1998), 24

Pan-European Movement, 28
Pan-European Picnic (1989), 28
pan-German nationalism, 4–10, 14–15, 57, 58
  fraternities, 61, 79
  Nazism and, 3, 4–6, 7, 10, 15
  Renner and, 87
Paneuropa, 24
Pannonhalma Abbey, Hungary, 29
*Paradoxical Republic, The* (Rathkolb), 8–9, 88, 97, 116
passports, 2, 18, 20–21
Pecina, Heinrich, 202
Pelinka, Anton, 14, 61, 204–5
Perger, Werner, 66–7, 94
Peter Principle, 153
Peter, Friedrich, 54–5, 56, 57–60, 94
Piffl-Perčević, Theodor, 149
Pilz, Peter, 179, 184, 187
Plassnik, Ursula, 148, 153
Plekhanov, Georgi, 95–6, 97–8
Pöcking, Bavaria, 27
Poland, 16, 202
Polish people, 19
*Politika*, 15
Pollak, Oscar, 87
Pompeo, Michael, 198
Prague, Czechia, 17, 28
*Presse, Die*, 10, 29, 113, 139, 159
Prodi, Romano, 101

249

# INDEX

*Profil*, 111, 171
Project Ballhausplatz (2016), 165–6
Pröll, Erwin, 117, 130, 134, 149
proportional representation, 59, 61, 63
Pskov, Russia, 178, 181
Public Prosecutor's Office, 168, 171, 199, 205–6
Putin, Vladimir, 107, 167, 193–8, 200

Qualtinger, Helmut, 186

Raab, Julius, 106, 125, 126, 129, 151
Rabinovici, Doron, 50
Radio Austria International, 2
Rady, Martyn, 26
Raidl, Claus, 208
Raiffeisen Bank International, 200
Raiffeisen Zentralbank, 205
Rathkolb, Oliver, 8–9, 88, 97, 116, 147, 204
Rauchensteiner, Manfried, 37–8, 40–41
Rauscher, Hans, 203
Realgymnasium Ettenreichgasse, Vienna, 183
Rechnitz, Austria, 45
refugees, 17, 19, 20, 21, 69, 73, 74, 164–5
 Hungarian uprising, 22, 73
 Syrian war, 19
 Ukraine war, 22, 193

Westbahnhof arrivals, 164
 Yugoslav wars, 19, 182–5
Reimann, Viktor, 56–7
Reinthaller, Anton, 56, 57
Rendi-Wagner, Pamela, 119, 121–3, 208
Renner Institute, 110
Renner Institute, 194
Renner, Karl, 4, 27, 40, 83–8, 91, 126
renunciation, declarations of, 27
Republika Srpska, 15
resist the beginning, 37
Rességuier, Olivier, 30
Restitution Act
Riegler, Josef, 130, 137
Riess-Passer, Susanne, 62, 63, 64, 65
right-wing radicalism, 102–3
Rilke, Rainer Maria, 17
Ritschel, Karl Heinz, 57
Rohan, Albert, 30, 35–6
Rohan, Karl Anton, 35–6
Rohrer, Anneliese, 24, 106
Roiss, Gerhard, 196
Roma people, 50, 86
Romania, 45, 110, 120, 181
Romanian people, 19
Rosneft, 167
Roth, Joseph, vii, 44
Rothensteiner, Walter, 205
Rudas, Andreas, 106
rule of law, 37, 206, 207
Rusinow, Dennison, 10
Russia Today, 167

# INDEX

Russian Civil War (1917–23), 178
Russian Federation, 22, 81, 121, 150, 167, 191–201, 208
    Crimea annexation (2014), 194, 200
    EU, relations with, 33, 81, 194, 195, 197
    FPÖ, relations with, 81, 167, 197
    gas industry, 155, 194, 195–7
    Gusenbauer, relations with, 194
    Kern, relations with, 121
    Kneissl, relations with, 167, 197
    Kurz, relations with, 167, 193, 194–9
    ÖVP, relations with, 167, 193–201
    Schüssel, relations with, 150
    Ukraine War (2022–), 22, 79, 81, 121, 155, 181, 191–7, 200, 206–8
    Yanukovych, relations with, 110
Russian State Railways, 121
RWE, 150

Salonika, Greece, 42
Salzburg, 56
*Salzburger Nachrichten*, 56, 57, 113
Sarkozy, Nicolas, 148
Sberbank, 198
Schallenberg, Alexander, 30–31, 174
Schallenberg, Wolfgang, 30
Schärf, Adolf, 4, 86, 89, 91
Scharsach, Hans-Henning, 80
Scheibenreif, Alois, 93
Schelling, Hans Jörg, 196, 199
Schenk, Otto, 159
Scheuch, Uwe, 66
Schiller, Friedrich, 50
schilling, 39
Schmid, Thomas, 154, 156, 171–4, 199, 206
Schmidauer, Doris, 181
Schmidt, Heide, 62
Schmitz, Wolfgang, 129
Scholz, Roman, 57
Schönau transit camp, 13
Schröder, Gerhard, 101, 107
Schuh, Franz, 77
Schulmeister, Otto, 29
Schuschnigg, Kurt, 26
Schüssel, Wolfgang, 50, 60–62, 64–5, 70–71, 106, 130, 137, 140–51
    1st government (2000–2003), 13, 43, 50, 60, 61, 62–6, 70–71, 73, 74, 106, 146–8
    2nd government (2003–2007), 64, 70, 108, 148, 186
    compensation package (2000–1), 50, 71
    corruption scandals, 148
    Dichand, relationship with, 114
    EU, relations with, 43, 147, 148
    Grasser, relationship with, 150, 151
    neutrality, views on, 191
    Orbán, relationship with, 150–51
Schützenhöfer, Hermann, 174

# INDEX

Schwarzenberg, Adolph, 34
Schwarzenberg, Johannes, 31, 34
Schwarzenberg, Karel, 31–4, 35, 74
Schwarzenberg, Therese, 35
'sea of lights' demonstration (1993), 62
Second Republic (1945–), 1, 2, 9, 25, 55, 58, 126
   Allied occupation (1945–55), 5, 27, 40, 56, 83–92, 125–6
   aristocracy in, 29–36
   Bloch case (1989), 135–7
   Covid-19 pandemic (2020–23), 20, 22, 51, 101, 156, 175–6, 181, 187, 188
   Declaration of Independence (1945), 85
   denazification (1945–7), 56
   EEC/EU negotiations, 1, 40, 104, 111, 112, 131, 133, 140
   governments, *see* Government of Austria
   Habsburg crisis (1961–3), 27, 128
   Habsburg tiara affair (1996), 23
   Ibiza affair (2019), 15, 75, 143–4, 158, 166–7, 180, 202, 205
   neutrality, 191–3, 197
   Schönau ultimatum (1973), 13
   sea of lights demonstration (1993), 62
   Shoah Wall of Names construction (2018–21), 47–51
   songbook scandal (2018), 76–9

State Treaty (1955), 1, 5, 7, 8, 40, 43, 47, 73, 126–7
Ukraine War (2022–), 191–7, 200, 206–8
Waldheim affair (1985–6), 13, 41, 47, 73, 99, 132
World Vision scandal (1998), 24
Second World War (1939–45), *see* World War II
Seele, Rainer, 194, 196
Seipel, Ignaz, 38
Seitz, Karl, 89
Serbia, 15, 16, 19, 110–11, 193, 202
Shoah (1941–5), *see* Holocaust
Shoah Wall of Names, Vienna, 45, 47–51
Silberstein, Tal, 120
silence, 10–13
Sinowatz, Fred, 43, 60, 98–9, 132
Slavic names, 15
Slovakia, 14, 33, 45, 202
Slovenia, 17, 133, 202
*Smetana*, Bedřich, 53
Sobotka, Wolfgang, 49, 162, 166
Sochi Dialogue, 195
social democracy, 83–99, 101–23
   Anschluss (1938), 86–7
   decline of, 101–2, 105, 115
   Kreisky government (1970–83), 94–7
   Renner government (1945–50), 4, 27, 83–8
Social Democratic Academic Association, 122

# INDEX

Social Democratic Party, *see* SPÖ
Socialist International, 109, 194
Socialist Youth International, 107–8
Somali people, 19
songbook scandal (2018), 13, 76–9
Sopron, Hungary, 28
SORA Institute, 207
South Tyrol, 58, 92
Soviet Union (1922–91), 1, 40, 84, 88, 136, 178, 192
Spahn, Jens, 154
Spanish Riding School, 107
Spannocchi, Emil, 30
*Spiegel, Der*, 158, 163, 173, 187
Spindelegger, Michael, 117, 153–6, 173
SPÖ (Sozialdemokratische Partei Österreichs), vii, 4, 43, 56, 89, 101–23, 208–9
 anti-Semitism and, 89–95
 budget (1971), 59
 decline of, 101–2, 115
 elections, *see* elections
 electorate, percentage of, 102, 122, 145, 168
 governments, *see* Government of Austria
 Habsburgs and, 27, 28
 Olah, relations with, 129
 Theresienstadt visit (1976), 54–5
 Waldheim and, 43
*Sputnik*, 194

SS (Schutzstaffel), 54, 55, 59, 62, 94, 128
St Petersburg Economic Forum, 121
St. Stephen's Cathedral, Vienna, 29, 127
St. Stephen's Square, Vienna, 127
*Staatsnation*, 4
Stability Pact for South Eastern Europe, 139
Stalin–Hitler Pact (1939), 178
Stalin, Joseph, 84–5, 88
*Standard, Der*, 49, 188, 203
Stangl, Thomas, 175
Stars of David, 51
State Treaty (1955), 1, 5, 7, 8, 40, 43, 47, 73, 126–7
Steger, Norbert, 60, 69
Steinbrück, Peer, 155
Steiner, Stefan, 162, 164, 166, 169
Steiner, Thomas, 166
Stourzh, Gerald, 7
Strabag, 200, 201
Strache, Heinz-Christian, 15, 50, 56, 65, 71, 74–81, 143–4
 anti-Semitism and, 74–81
 Hungary, relations with, 202
 Ibiza affair (2019), 15, 75, 143–4, 158, 166–7, 180, 202, 205
 Israel, relations with, 50, 74, 79
 ÖVP, coalition with (2017–19), 51, 72–81
 Remembrance Day speech (2019), 75
 Serbia, relations with, 15

253

# INDEX

songbook scandal (2018), 79–80
'strong man' leadership, 17, 176, 201, 203, 207
*Struggle for Austrian Identity, The* (Heer), 5
Stuiber, Petra, 188
Sturmabteilung (SA), 11
Styria, 56, 130, 174, 186, 197
Sudeten Germans, 19, 87
Sweden, 91, 191
Switzerland, 8, 23, 192
Syria, 19, 79

Tallinn, Estonia, 178
Tanner, Klaudia, 166, 192
Taus, Josef, 118, 129, 130, 131, 146
Thailand, 163
Theresienstadt concentration camp, 54
Thiel, Peter, 169, 203
Think Austria, 203
Third Reich (1933–45), 1, 3, 4–6, 10–13, 26, 44–52
   Anschluss (1938), 4, 5, 7, 10, 26, 34, 39, 40, 45, 86–7
   aristocracy and, 34, 35
   'Aryanisation', 5, 12–13, 46–7, 86, 90
   Holocaust (1941–5), *see* Holocaust
   Molotov–Ribbentrop Pact (1939), 178
   Napola schools, 12
   November pogroms (1938), 48
   Slavs and, 15

third way, 101
Thurnher, Armin, 97, 203
titanium, 155
tobacco, 38
Together Austria, 162
TOP 09 group, 33
trade unions, 109, 116, 129
Traiskirchen, Vienna, 123
Transylvania, 45
Treichl, Andreas, 204–5
Treichl, Heinrich, 205
Trojanow, Ilija, 22
Trost, Ernst, 127
Truman, Harry, 27
Trump, Donald, 191
Tuđman, Franjo, 139
Tulcea, Romania, 181
Turkey, 42, 79, 164
Turkish people, 15, 19
Turkish Black-Blue coalition (2017–19), 51, 72–81, 143–4, 147, 157–9, 166–7, 174, 197, 207, 208
   authoritarianism and, 167, 193, 201–3
   EU, relations with, 167
   Hungary, relations with, 167, 202
   Ibiza affair (2019), 15, 75, 143–4, 158, 166–7, 180, 202, 205
   media, relations with, 169–70, 203–5
   no confidence motion (2019), 167, 168
   Russia, relations with, 167, 193, 194–9

# INDEX

Shoah Wall of Names construction (2018), 50, 158
Turnvereine, 61
Tutter, Kurt Yakov, 47–8, 50
Tuzla, Bosnia, 182
Twain, Mark, 138
Twitter, 164
Tyrol, 58, 92, 151, 179, 187, 201, 209

Ukraine, 22, 79, 81, 121, 155, 181, 191–7, 200, 206–8
Umlauft, Friedrich, 4
*Umvolkung*, 15
*Under Observation* (Rauchensteiner), 37–8
United Kingdom, 38, 85
United Nations (UN), 41
United States, 41, 85, 137, 169, 198
Université Libre de Bruxelles, 135
University of Cologne, 10
University of Graz, 185
University of Tartu, 178
University of Vienna, 3, 10, 11, 107
*Unstoppable Rise of Arturo Ui, The* (Brecht), 52
Upper Austria, 56, 58, 74
Urzidil, Johannes, 26
Ustasha (1929–45), 16

Van der Bellen, Alexander, 49, 71–2, 81, 157, 177–82, 189, 209
Van Rompuy, Hermann, 150–51

Van Tonningen, Meinoud Rost, 39
Vandalia, 74
Verband der Unabhängigen, 56, 57
Vernet, Daniel, 135
Vienna, Austria, 138
  Ballhausplatz, 92
  council elections (2015), 15
  Criminal Court, 185
  European Jewish Congress (2018), 158
  General Hospital, 99
  Heldenplatz, 4, 45, 62, 127
  Hitler in, 44
  Hofburg, 28, 35, 80, 144, 146
  immigration, 14, 15–16
  Jewish community, 74
  Ostarrichipark, 45
  Shoah Wall of Names, 45, 47–51
  St. Stephen's Cathedral, 29, 127
  University, 3, 10, 11, 107
  Westbahnhof, 164
Visegrád states, 202
Volkswagen, 107
von, use of, 25
Vorarlberg, Austria, 23, 137, 209
*Vorarlberger Nachrichten*, 113
Vorhofer, Kurt, 12, 84, 97, 127, 129, 131, 132, 134
Vranitzky, Franz, 52, 61, 95, 99, 103–6, 114, 130, 132, 138, 140, 145–6
Vučić, Aleksandar, 15, 193, 202

255

# INDEX

Wachau European Forum, 134–5, 149, 157
Waffen SS, 54, 55, 59, 62
Waldheim, Kurt, 13, 14, 41–3, 47, 73, 99, 104, 132, 182
Walter, Franz, 101–2
Wandruszka, Adam, 10–11
Washington Agreement (2001), 50
Washington, DC, United States, 42
Weigel, Hans, 206
Weimar Republic (1918–33), 44
Weinberger, Lois, 125
Weinrich, Harald, 51
Weissensteiner, Friedrich, 59
*Weltgeschichtliche Betrachtungen* (Burckhardt), 96
West Germany (1949–90), 7
Westbahnhof, Vienna, 164
Westenthaler, Peter, 15, 64
Westerwelle, Guido, 154
Wiesel, Elie, 13
Wiesenthal, Simon, 42–3, 54–5, 59, 93
Wiltshire, England, 42
Wirecard, 201
Wirtschaftsbund, 130, 160
Withalm, Hermann, 58, 128, 129
WKStA, 168, 171, 199
Wöginger, August, 188
Wolf, Siegfried, 194, 196, 197–201
Workers' and the Salaried Employees' Confederation, 125
World Jewish Congress, 43, 48

*World of Yesterday, The* (Zweig), 4
World Vision, 24
World War I (1914–18), 4, 38, 44
World War II (1939–45), 1, 4, 11, 35, 41, 178, 195
  Holocaust (1941–5), *see* Holocaust
Wowereit, Klaus, 154
Würzburg, Germany, 178

xenophobia, 7, 13–17, 19–20, 116, 139, 174
  FPÖ, 15, 61, 62, 73, 74, 76–7, 81, 116, 185

Yad Vashem, Jerusalem, 48, 74, 75
Yakunin, Vladimir, 194
Yanukovych, Viktor, 110
Yeltsin, Boris, 201
Yugoslav Wars (1991–2001), 16, 133, 140, 182, 183
Yugoslavia (1918–1992), 16–17, 19, 38

Zadić, Alma, 182–5, 189
Zeiler, Gerhard, 118, 120
*Zeit, Die*, 66–7, 116
Zeman, Miloš, 33
Zimmerman, Alfred Rudolph, 38
Zita, Empress consort of Austria, 28
Zuckmayer, Carl, 45
Zweig, Stefan, 4
Zyklon B, 51